# Standard Conditions of Sale:
# A Conveyancer's Guide

# Standard Conditions of Sale:
# A Conveyancer's Guide

*Seventh edition*

by Frances Silverman, LLM
Solicitor

Published by
Jordan Publishing Limited
21 St Thomas Street
Bristol BS1 6JS

**British Library Cataloguing-in-Publication Data**

A catalogue record for this book is available from the British Library.

ISBN 1 84661 008 7

Typeset by
Action Publishing Technology Ltd, Gloucester

Printed and bound in Great Britain by
Antony Rowe Ltd, Chippenham, Wilts

# Preface to seventh edition (2006)

It is with some feelings of guilt that I sit down to write this preface to the seventh edition. *Standard Conditions of Sale* was my first venture into published work and it therefore has a special place in my memories and my career. To have neglected the new edition for so long, albeit through pressures of other commitments somehow seems inexcusable. However, the time delay does have some compensations because this edition is able to deal not only with the fourth edition of the Standard Conditions, but also to include the second edition of the Standard Commercial Property Conditions and a newcomer to the market place, the Common Auction Conditions, the latter being published by the Royal Institution of Chartered Surveyors. I have also been able to include a new section on commonhold (although at the time of writing very few properties have as yet opted for this new type of title) and appropriate comments on the Home Information Pack which is due to be implemented in June 2007.

The Standard Conditions have now been in use, in their various editions, since 1999 and there are now very few instances of use of their predecessor conditions, the separately published Law Society's Conditions of Sale and the National Conditions of Sale. That being so, the sections in previous editions relating to these two individual sets of conditions have been removed from this edition. Full commentary on them is contained in earlier editions of this book should reference to them be required. Similarly, when this book was first published, there were very few 'general practitioner' books in publication dealing with conveyancing and therefore the book contained substantial commentary on background law and the practice of conveyancing. That situation no longer pertains and most practitioners will refer to such books as the Law Society's Conveyancing Handbook to resolve problems on law and practice. This edition therefore no longer contains long passages of background law but presumes to fulfil its primary purpose of providing practitioners with a clear and comprehensive commentary on the conditions of sale.

As always, I ask readers to assume that the use of the masculine pronoun in the text should read 'he or she' on the understanding that no disregard or disrespect is intended by this single sex form of address. To use both forms of address on every occasion where it occurs in the text would have lengthened the text immeasurably and thus have added unnecessary expense to the costs of the publication.

Similarly, and for the same reasons, I have not written 'licensed conveyancer or solicitor' on every occasion where such a phrase might have been desirable and I hope that licensed conveyancers will indeed use this book and find it relevant and helpful to the work which they do.

I acknowledge with thanks the permission of the Law Society and Solicitors Law Stationery Society plc to reproduce the text of the Standard Conditions in this book, and to the Law Society for their permission to reproduce the Standard Commercial Conditions. My thanks are also extended to the Royal Institution of Chartered Surveyors who have given their permission for the reproduction of the Common Auction Conditions.

I am also grateful to the staff at Jordans for their help and encouragement and without whose patience this edition would not have seen the light of day.

The law is stated as at 1 December 2005

Frances Silverman
Rowfold
West Sussex
1 December 2005

# Contents

*Contents*

*Contents*

# Table of Statutes

# Table of Statutory Instruments

# Table of European Legislation

# Table of Cases

# Chapter 1

# Tables and Checklists

## Introduction

**1.1**    The Standard Conditions of Sale are intended to form the basis of most contracts for the sale of land in England and Wales, both of domestic and commercial property. They were first published in March 1990 concurrently with the Protocol for domestic conveyancing promulgated by the Law Society; and the fourth edition, on which this text is based, came into operation on 13 October 2003. A checklist of the 4th edition of the Conditions and their time limits appears on page 2.

The Standard Conditions of Sale are drafted in modern English so that they can easily be understood by all those who use them, including clients. The order in which the conditions are presented reflects the order of events in a normal conveyancing transaction. The order in which the conditions are discussed in the following chapters also follows the order of events in a normal transaction, except that, for ease of reference, conditions which deal with particular circumstances, such as leasehold property and sales of part, have been grouped together in separate chapters towards the end of the book.

## The Standard Commercial Property Conditions

**1.2**    The *Standard Commercial Property Conditions* (first edition) were published jointly by the Law Society and Oyez in May 1999. For some time there had been concern in the solicitor's profession that the Standard Conditions of Sale were inappropriate to meet the demands of a commercial property transaction. The Standard Commercial Property Conditions are therefore designed to meet this need. They are based on the existing Standard Conditions, and follow the same broad numbering and order of those conditions, but have been adjusted and adapted to reflect the requirements of commercial transactions. In many cases the wording of the two sets of conditions is identical and users will therefore have little difficulty in familiarising themselves with the new conditions. In other cases the wording and numbering of sub-clauses in the Standard Commercial Property Conditions differs slightly from that which appears in the Standard Conditions. Care therefore needs to be exercised when dealing with amendments to the Standard Commercial Property Conditions to ensure that the correct sub-clause is deleted or amended in a

1

contract. The main differences between the Commercial Conditions and the Standard Conditions lie in the way in which insurance and compensation for late completion are dealt with. In both cases the Commercial Conditions have reverted to the conventional methods of handling these issues. In the case of insurance, risk passes to the buyer on exchange of contracts, and in relation to late completion, the concept of relative fault used in the Standard Conditions has been abandoned in favour of the traditional approach, namely, that only the buyer pays compensation for late completion. A comparative table of the Standard Commercial Property Conditions and the Standard Conditions appears at paragraph 1.11 below. Commentary on the Standard Commercial Property Conditions appears in each chapter under the relevant subject topic. The current edition of Commerical Conditions is the second edition which came into effect in June 2004.

## The Protocol

**1.3** The Protocol for domestic conveyancing was introduced by the Law Society in March 1990 with a view to simplifying and standardising the procedures involved in domestic conveyancing. Requirements of the Protocol are reflected in the drafting of the conditions.

### 1.4 Checklist of Standard Conditions of Sale (4th edition) and comparison with 3rd edition

| 4th ed | | 3rd ed | Main chapter reference |
|---|---|---|---|
| *1.* | *General* | 1 | |
| 1.1 | Definitions | 1.1 | 2 |
| 1.2 | Joint parties | 1.2 | 2 |
| 1.3 | Notices and documents | 1.3 | 4 |
| 1.4 | VAT | 1.4 | 3 |
| | | | |
| *2.* | *Formation* | 2 | |
| 2.1 | Date | 2.1 | 13 |
| 2.2 | Deposit | 2.2 | 11 |
| 2.3 | Auctions | 2.3 | 23 |
| | | | |
| *3.* | *Matters affecting the property* | 3 | |
| 3.1 | Freedom from incumbrances | 3.1 | 5 |
| 3.2 | Physical state | 3.2 | 20 |
| 3.3 | Leases | 3.3 | 21 |
| 3.4 | Retained land | 3.4 | |
| | | | |
| *4.* | *Title and transfer* | 4 | |
| 4.1 | Proof of title | 4.2 | 9 |
| 4.2 | Requisitions | 4.1 | 14 |
| 4.3 | Timetable | 4.1 | 13 |

## 1.5 Summary of changes made by the fourth edition of the Standard Conditions

The fourth edition of the Standard Conditions contains few major changes to its predecessor. The Conditions have been updated to reflect the coming in to force of the Land Registration Act 2002 and the provisions of the Commonhold and Leasehold Reform Act 2002.

Among the changes which should be noted are the abandonment of the confusing distinction between the use of the words 'agreement' and 'contract' ('contract' is the word used throughout the new edition), and the omission of a special condition on the front page of the printed form referring to the property being sold subject to the incumbrances specified in the contract. That special condition has now been incorporated in Condition 3.1.2 (a) – the overall position in this respect therefore remains unaltered in that incumbrances subject to which the property is sold must still be identified in a special condition.

References in the former edition of the conditions to 'solicitor' have been replaced with the generic word 'conveyancer' reflecting that fact that licensed conveyancers and others may now lawfully carry out conveyancing. The payment of the deposit by cheque is however restricted to payment from a solicitor's or licensed conveyancer's client account (Condition 2.2.3 and Condition 2.2.4) except on sales by auction.

The options of paying the deposit or completion moneys by banker's draft has been removed in recognition of the fact that most money is now transferred by direct credit.

A new provision appears in Condition 1.3.3 (b) enabling (subject to conditions) a document or notice to be served by email.

A general provision prohibiting the transfer by the buyer of the benefit of the contract has been reinstated as Condition 1.5 and removed from the leasehold conditions as being superfluous.

Condition 4.2 recognises that in practice title is normally deduced prior to exchange of contracts and so bars requisitions on title after exchange except in relation to matters not revealed before exchange.

A new condition relating to commonhold has been inserted as Condition 9 (chattels are now dealt with in Condition 10).

### 1.6    Standard Conditions of Sale – table of contents

*3rd edition to 4th edition*

| 3rd ed | | 4th ed |
|---|---|---|
| 1. | GENERAL | 1 |
| 1.1 | Definitions | 1.1 |
| 1.1.1 | | 1.1.1 |
| a | accrued interest | 1.1.1a |
| b | chattels price | b |
| c | bankers' draft | – |
| d | clearing bank | c |
| e | completion date | d |
| f | contract | – |
| g | contract rate | e |
| – | conveyancer | f |
| – | direct credit | g |
| h | lease | h |
| i | notice to complete | i |
| j | public requirement | j |
| k | requisition | k |
| l | solicitor | – |
| m | transfer | l |
| n | working day | m |

4

**1.7** Table of comparative conditions in the Standard Commercial Property conditions (Second Edition) and the Standard Conditions of Sale (Fourth Edition).

| STANDARD CONDITIONS OF SALE (FOURTH EDITION) | COMMERCIAL PROPERTY CONDITIONS (SECOND EDITION) |
|---|---|
| **1. GENERAL** | |
| 1.1.1 (f) 'contract' | DOES NOT APPEAR |
| 1.1.1 (e) contract rate | 1.1.1 (e) |
| 1.1.1 (h) lease | 1.1.1 (i) |
| 1.1.1 (i) notice to complete | 1.1.1 (v) |
| 1.1.1 (j) public requirement | 1.1.1 (l) |
| 1.1.1 (k) requisition | 1.1.1 (m) |
| 1.1.1 (l) transfer | 1.1.1 (m) |
| 1.1.1 (m) working day | 1.1.1 (o) |
| | |
| **2.2 DEPOSIT** The buyer is to pay or send a deposit of 10% of the total price no later than the date of the contract. Except on a sale by auction, payment is to be made by direct credit or cheque drawn on a solicitors' or licensed conveyancer's client account | 2.2.1 The buyer is to pay or send a deposit of 10% of the purchase price no later than the date of the contract. Payment by direct credit |
| 2.2.5 leapfrogging deposit | DOES NOT APPEAR |
| 2.2.6 stakeholder | 2.2.2 |
| 2.2.2 referred cheques | 2.3.7 (auctions only) |
| 3.1.2 (d) entries made before the date of the contract in any public register except those maintained by HM Land Registry or its Land Charges Department or by the Companies House | 3.1.2 (d) matters, other than monetary charges or incumbrances, disclosed or which would have been disclosed by the searches and enquiries which a prudent buyer would have made before entering into the contract |

| STANDARD CONDITIONS OF SALE (FOURTH EDITION) | COMMERCIAL PROPERTY CONDITIONS (SECOND EDITION) |
|---|---|
| 3.3.2(a)   copy lease supplied | 4.1.2 |
| 3.3.2(b)   seller to inform buyer if lease ends etc | 4.1.4 |
| 3.3.2(c)   seller not to agree change to lease | 4.1.3 (similar) |
| 3.3.2(e)   buyer to indemnify | 4.1.5 |
| 3.3.2(f)   rent lawfully recoverable | DOES NOT APPEAR |
| 3.3.2(g)   apportionment or rent | 4.1.6 |
| 3.3.2(b)   (part only) | 3.3.3 (a)–(d) |
| DOES NOT APPEAR | 3.3.5 |
| 3.3.2(b) | 3.3.6 |
| DOES NOT APPEAR | 4.2 Property management |
| DOES NOT APPEAR | 5 Rent reviews |
| 4.6.4 If after completion the seller will remain bound by any obligation affecting the property, but the law does not imply any covenant by the buyer to indemnify the seller against for future breaches of it | 6.6.4 If after completion the seller will remain bound by any obligation affecting the property and disclosed to the buyer before the contract is made, but the law does not imply any covenant by the buyer to indemnify the seller against liability for future breaches of it |

| STANDARD CONDITIONS OF SALE (FOURTH EDITION) | COMMERCIAL PROPERTY CONDITIONS (SECOND EDITION) |
|---|---|
| 5.1.1. The seller will transfer the property in the same physical state as it was at the date of the contract (except for fair wear and tear), which means the seller retains risk until completion | 7.1.4. Unless condition 7.1.2 or condition 8.1.3 applies:<br>(a) the seller is under no obligation to the buyer to insure the property;<br>(b) if payment under a policy effected by or for the buyer is reduced, because the property is covered against loss or damage by an insurance policy effected by an insurance policy affected by or for the seller, the purchase price is to be abated by the amount of that reduction |
| 5.1.2 If an any time before completion the physical sate of the property makes it unusable for its purpose at the date of the contract:<br>(a) the buyer may rescind the contract;<br>(b) the seller may rescind the contract where the property has become unusable for that purpose as a result of damage against which the seller could not reasonably have insured, or which it is not legally possible for the seller to make good | 7.1.2<br>(f) if before completion the property suffers loss or damage:<br>(i) pay to the buyer on completion the amount of policy moneys which the seller has received so far as not applied in repairing or reinstating the property; and |

| STANDARD CONDITIONS OF SALE (FOURTH EDITION) | COMMERCIAL PROPERTY CONDITIONS (SECOND EDITION) |
|---|---|
| | (ii) if no final payment has then been received, assign to the buyer, at the buyer's expense, all rights to claim under the policy in such form as the buyer reasonably requires, and pending execution of the assignment, hold any policy moneys received in trust for the buyer |
| 5.1.3 The seller is under no obligation to the buyer to insure the property | 7.1.1. Seller to insure if contract so provides or property subject to lease which obliges seller to insure. |
| 5.2 Possession before completion | |
| 6.3.1 Income and outgoings of the property are to be apportioned between the parties so far as the change of ownership on completion will affect entitlement to receive or liability to pay them | 8.3.1 Subject to condition 6.3.7 income and outgoings of the property are to be apportioned between the parties so far as the change of ownership on completion will affect entitlement to receive or liability to pay them |
| 6.3.2 If the whole property is sold with vacant possession or the seller exercises his option in condition 7.3.4, apportionment is to be made with effect from the date of actual completion; otherwise, it is to be made from completion date | 8.3.2 If the whole property is sold with vacant possession or the seller exercises its option in condition 7.3.4, apportionment is to be made with effect from the date of actual completion; otherwise it is to be made from completion date |

| STANDARD CONDITIONS OF SALE (FOURTH EDITION) | COMMERCIAL PROPERTY CONDITIONS (SECOND EDITION) |
|---|---|
| 6.3.3 In apportioning any sum, it is to be assumed the seller owns the property until the end of the day from which apportionment is made and that the sum accrues from day to day at the rate at which it is payable on that day<br>6.3.4 For the purpose of apportioning income and outgoings, it is to be assumed that they accrue at an equal daily rate throughout the year | 8.3.3 In apportioning any sum, it is to be assumed that the buyer owns the property from the beginning of the day on which the apportionment is to be made<br>8.3.4 A sum to be apportioned is to be treated as accruing:<br>(a) from day to day throughout the period for which it is payable or receivable by instalments, and at the rate from time to time applicable during the period for which the apportionment is made |
| DOES NOT APPEAR | 8.3.6 Property subject to service charge |
| DOES NOT APPEAR | 9.2 (c) the seller's duty to pay returned premium under condition 7.1.2 (e) (whenever received) is not affected |
| 7.3.1 If there is default by either or both of the parties in performing their obligations under the contract and completion is delayed, the party whose total period of default is the greater is to pay compensation to the other party<br>7.3.2 Compensation is calculated at the contract rate on the purchase price or (where the buyer is the paying party) the purchase price less any deposit paid, for the period by which the paying party's default exceeds that of the receiving party, or, if shorter, the period between completion date and actual completion | 9.3.1 If the buyer defaults in performing its obligations under the contract and completion is delayed, the buyer is to pay compensation to the seller<br>9.3.2 Compensation is calculated at the contract rate on the purchase price (less any deposit paid) for the period between completion date and actual completion, but ignoring any period during which the seller was in default<br>9.3.3 Any claim by the seller for loss resulting from delayed completion is to be reduced by any compensation paid under this contract |

| STANDARD CONDITIONS OF SALE (FOURTH EDITION) | COMMERCIAL PROPERTY CONDITIONS (SECOND EDITION) |
|---|---|
| 7.3.3  Any claim for loss resulting from delayed completion is to be reduced by any compensation paid under this contract<br>7.3.4  Where the buyer holds the property as tenant of the seller and completion is delayed the seller may give notice to the buyer, before the date of actual completion, that he intends to take the net income from the property until completion. If he does so he cannot claim the compensation under condition 7.3.1 as well | 9.3.4  Where the sale is not with vacant possession of the whole property and completion is delayed, the seller may give notice to the buyer, before the date of actual completion, that it will take the net income from the property until completion as well as compensation under condition 7.3.1 |
| 8.3.1  The following provisions apply if a consent to assign or sublet is required to complete the contract<br>8.3.2  (a)  The seller is to apply for the consent at his own expense, and to use all reasonable efforts to obtain it<br>(b)  The buyer is to provide all information and references reasonably required | 10.3 Consent to let, assign or sub-let required |
| DOES NOT APPEAR | 10.3.6 At any time after four months from the original completion date, either party may rescind the contract by notice to the other if:<br>(a)  consent has still not been given and<br>(b)  no declaration has been obtained from the court that consent has been unreasonably withheld |

| STANDARD CONDITIONS OF SALE (FOURTH EDITION) | COMMERCIAL PROPERTY CONDITIONS (SECOND EDITION) |
|---|---|
| 10.4 Ownership of the chattels passes to the buyer on actual completion | 12 Ownership of the chattels passes to the buyer on actual completion but they are at the buyer's risk from the contract date |
| DOES NOT APPEAR | PART II<br>A VAT |
| DOES NOT APPEAR | B CAPITAL ALLOWANCES |
| DOES NOT APPEAR | C REVERSIONARY INTERESTS IN FLATS |

## 1.8 Summary of changes made by the second edition Standard Commercial Property Conditions

The second edition of the Standard Commercial Property Conditions came into force in June 2004 and have undergone some major revisions which are summarised below.

The new edition takes account of the Land Registration Act 2002 and of the Commonhold and Leasehold Reform Act 2002.

As with the new edition of the Standard Conditions of Sale the word 'conveyancer' replaces previous references to 'solicitor'.

A new Condition 5 deals with Rent Reviews . Provisions relating to occupation by the buyer before completion have been removed. The provisions dealing with consent to a assignment have been substantially re-drafted.

The new conditions have been divided into two parts. Part I is of general application and Part II contains three optional conditions dealing with VAT, capital allowances and reversionary interests in leases.

## 1.9 The Common Auction Conditions

The Common Auction Conditions, now in their second edition, are published by the Royal Institute of Chartered Surveyors and are reproduced in Appendix 3. They are otherwise available from the RICS website. These conditions relate exclusively to sales by auction and commentary on them is contained in Chapter 23.

# Chapter 2

# Definitions

## Standard Condition 1.1

**2.1** The definitions section of the Standard Conditions of Sale explains the terminology used in the general conditions. The definitions contained in Condition 1.1 are as follows:

'1.1.1. In these conditions:
(a) "accrued interest" means:
  (i) if money has been placed on deposit or in a building society share account, the interest actually earned.
  (ii) otherwise, the interest which might reasonably have been earned by depositing the money at interest on seven days' notice of withdrawal with a clearing bank
  less, in either case, any proper charges for handling the money
(b) "chattel price" means any separate amount payable for chattels included in the contract
(c) "clearing bank" means a bank which is a shareholder in CHAPS Clearing Co Limited
(d) "completion date", has the meaning given in condition 6.1.1
(e) "contract rate", unless defined in the agreement, is the Law Society's interest rate from time to time in force
(f) "conveyance" means a solicitor, duly certificated notary public, licensed conveyancer or recognised body under sections 9 or 23 of the Administration of Justice Act 1985
(g) "direct credit" means s direct transfer of cleared funds to an account nominated by the seller's conveyancer and maintained by a clearing bank
(h) "lease" includes sub-lease, tenancy and agreement for a lease or sub-lease
(i) "notice to complete" means a notice requiring completion of the contract in accordance with condition 6
(j) "public requirement" means any notice, order or proposal given or made (whether before or after the date of the contract) by a body acting on statutory authority
(k) "requisition" includes objection
(l) "transfer" includes conveyance and assignment
(m) "working day" meant any day from Monday to Friday (inclusive) which is not Christmas Day, Good Friday or a statutory Bank Holiday.

1.1.2 When used in these conditions the terms "absolute title" and "office copies" have the special meanings given to them by the Land Registration Act 2002.

1.1.3 A party is ready, able and willing to complete:

(a)    if he could be, but for the default of the other party, and

(b)    in the case of the seller, even though the property remains subject to a mortgage, if the amount to be paid on completion enables the property to be transferred freed of all mortgages (except any to which the sale is expressly made subject).

1.1.4  These conditions apply except as varied or excluded by the contract.

1.2.   *Joint parties*
       If there is more than one seller or more than one buyer, the obligations which they undertake can be enforced against them all jointly or against each individually.'

# Accrued interest

**2.2**    Accrued interest may be payable by one party to the other in three circumstances:

(a) on the amount of a deposit held pending completion (Condition 8, see Chapter 11);

(b) on the return of a deposit following rescission of the contract (Condition 7.2, see Chapter 19);

(c) where one party has failed to comply with a notice to complete (Conditions 7.5 and 7.6, see Chapter 18).

The calculation of the amount of interest payable in these circumstances is prescribed by this definition, and is similar to the way in which interest is calculated under the Solicitors' Accounts Rules 1991.

Unless the amount of money to be deposited is very large, most practitioners will probably choose to place the money in a general clients' deposit account, in which case (b) of the definition will apply to the assessment of the interest and a calculation of the amount due will have to be made having regard to the particular bank's base rate prevailing while the money was on deposit.

# Clearing bank

**2.3**    This definition is relevant to the method of payment of the deposit (Condition 2.2.1, see Chapter 11), and to the methods of payment of money on completion (Condition 6.5, see Chapter 17) and are further discussed in the context of these matters. The condition as drafted defines a clearing bank as a bank which is a member of CHAPS.

The following is a list of banks which are members of CHAPS:

**CHAPS Sterling Members**

| | |
|---|---|
| Abbey | The Co-operative Bank plc |
| ABN AMRO NV | Deutsche Bank AG |
| Bank of England | HSBC Bank plc |
| Bank of Scotland (HBOS) | Lloyds TSB Bank plc |
| Barclays Bank plc | National Westminster Bank plc |

| | |
|---|---|
| Citibank NA | The Royal Bank of Scotland plc |
| Clydesdale Bank plc | Standard Chartered Bank |

**CHAPS Euro Members**

| | |
|---|---|
| Abbey | DnB Nor Bank ASA |
| ABN Amro Bank NV | HSBC Bank plc |
| Bank of America BA | JP Morgan AG |
| Bank of England | Lloyds TSB Bank plc |
| Bank of Scotland (HBOS) | National Australia Bank |
| Barclays Bank plc | National Westminster Bank plc |
| The Bank of Tokyo-Mitsubishi Ltd | The Royal Bank of Scotland plc |
| Citibank NA | Standard Chartered Bank |
| The Co-operative Bank plc | Wachovia Bank NA |
| Deutsche Bank AG | |

A cheque or draft drawn on any of the banks shown in the above list will thus be acceptable to the seller when tendered in payment of the deposit or completion money.

Since these lists of banks include the major banks operating within England and Wales it is unlikely that the seller would need to alter this definition. A buyer who intends to tender the deposit or completion money through a bank which is not included in the list should put the seller on notice of this fact at an early stage in the transaction and should seek to amend the draft contract to permit payment to be made through his chosen specified bank. From the seller's point of view, amendment of this definition may not be desirable. If, for instance, the buyer were to make payment through a foreign bank not included in the above list, some delay could be experienced in the clearance of funds, which might inconvenience a seller who needed to use the money quickly in a related transaction.

# Completion date

**2.4**    Unless there is contrary provision in the contract, completion date is defined in Condition 6.1.1 as being twenty working days after the date of the contract. Normally the parties will specify a completion date by special condition in the contract, and in residential conveyancing it is common to find that the specified date is shorter than twenty working days from the date of exchange of contracts. This definition is further discussed in Chapter 17.

# Contract rate

*Definition*

**2.5**    This definition is relevant to the payment of compensation for late completion (Condition 7.3, see Chapter 18) and to the licence fee payable by a buyer who takes possession of the property before completion (Condition 5.2, see Chapter 15). If the contract is silent, compensation (or the licence fee) is payable at the Law Society's interest rate on the balance then outstanding of the purchase price. The Law Society's interest rate is published at regular intervals in the *Gazette*. Normally the parties will specify a particular interest or contract rate by special condition in the contract. Such rate is frequently geared to the base rate of a named clearing bank, for example, 'the contract rate shall be x% above the base rate of Y bank plc from time to time in force'. A fixed interest rate is sometimes found in a contract, for example, 'the contract rate shall be 15% per annum', but is less popular than a rate which floats with bank base rate, since if base rates were to alter dramatically between the date of the contract and the date when compensation became payable one party might be severely disadvantaged by the fixed contract interest rate.

*Purpose of contract rate*

**2.6**      The object of the contract rate in the context of late completion is to compensate the innocent party for loss sustained by the other party's default. In theory, the seller's solicitor should have regard to the losses which his client is likely to sustain in the event of completion being delayed by the buyer and set the contract rate at an appropriate figure to cover such losses. However, the seller may himself be liable to pay compensation to the buyer if the reason for the delayed completion is the seller's default (Condition 7.3.1), and this fact acts as a deterrent to the seller against setting an unrealistically high contract rate. A very high contract rate may also be void as a penalty. In residential conveyancing an interest rate of 3–5% above a named bank's base rate is common. A higher interest rate may be acceptable in a commercial contract or where the circumstances of the transaction indicate a higher than normal risk of a delayed completion.

# Lease

**2.7**      This word is expressed to include tenancies, subleases, and agreements for leases and subleases.

# Notice to complete

**2.8**      A notice to complete may be served by one party on the other when completion has been delayed by the other party. The effect of the notice is to make time the essence of the contract. A notice to complete is defined in Condition 1.1.1(i) and is further discussed in Chapter 18.

# Public requirement

**2.9**      This definition, which is relevant to the seller's duty of disclosure, is discussed in Chapter 5.

## Conveyancer

**2.10**　The definition of this word includes a barrister. Employed barristers are permitted by the Bar Council's code of conduct to undertake conveyancing work, but they are not 'qualified persons' under section 22 of the Solicitors Act 1974, and so cannot draw a contract or transfer for the sale of land for fee or reward. Despite the inclusion of barristers within this definition there is some doubt whether a barrister has the authority to give a binding undertaking.

Licensed conveyancers are within this definition, and may generally be regarded in the same light as solicitors since they are bound by similar rules relating to conduct and the handling of clients' money as are solicitors. As drafted, the definition does not take into account 'authorised conveyancing practitioners' who will be entitled to undertake conveyancing services under the Courts and Legal Services Act 1990 if and when the relevant sections of that Act are brought into force.

The definition includes a 'recognised body', ie an incorporated practice.

## Working day

**2.11**　This definition is included to assist in the calculation of the procedural timetable between exchange of contracts and completion (Condition 4.3, see Chapter 13). It is also relevant to the calculation of compensation for late completion (see Chapter 18). Working days are Mondays to Fridays inclusive but not Christmas Day, Good Friday, or statutory bank holidays. The definition of a non-working day can be extended by special condition to include any days specified in that special condition. The most usual extensions of non-working days occur to cover the slack period between Christmas and New Year or non-Christian religious holidays.

## Land Registration Act definitions

**2.12**　'Absolute title' is defined by the Land Registration Act 2002.

'Office copies' as defined by the Land Registration Act 2002 means copies of the register entries which are issued by the Land Registry and which bear the Registry's official seal or mark. Office copies are admissible in court to the same extent as the original document.

## Joint parties

**2.13**　For the avoidance of doubt, Condition 1.2 states that where there is more than one seller or buyer, the liability of the parties is to be joint and several.

# Standard Commercial Property Conditions

**2.14**    Standard Commercial Property Condition 1 provides:

'1.    **GENERAL**

1.1.    **Definitions**

1.1.1 In these conditions
(a)    "accrued interest" means:
  (i)    if money has been placed on deposit or in a building society share account, the interest actually earned
  (ii)    otherwise, the interest which might reasonably have been earned by depositing the money at interest on seven days' notice of withdrawal with a clearing bank
    less, in either case, any proper charges for handling the money
(b)    "apportionment day" has the meaning given in condition 8.3.2.
(c)    "clearing bank" means a bank which is  a shareholder in CHAPS Clearing Co Limited
(d)    "completion date"has the meaning given in condition 6.1.1
(e)    "contract rate", is the Law Society's interest rate from time to time in force
(f)    "conveyancer" means a solicitor, includes barrister, certificated    notary public, licensed conveyancer or recognised body under sections 9 or 23 of the Administration of Justice Act 1985
(g)    "direct credit" means a direct transfer of cleared funds to an account nominated by the seller's solicitors and maintained by a clearing bank
(h)    "election to waive exemption" means an election made under paragraph 2 of Schedule 10 to the Value Added Tax Act 1994
(i)    "lease" includes sub-lease, tenancy and agreement for a lease or sub-lease
(j)    "notice to complete" means a notice requiring completion of the contract in accordance with condition 8
(k)    "post" includes a service provided by a person licensed under the Postal Services Act 2000
(l)    "public requirement" means any notice, order or proposal given or made (whether before or after the date of the contract) by a body acting on statutory authority
(m)    "requisition" includes objection
(n)    "transfer" includes conveyance and assignment
(o)    "working day" means any day from Monday to Friday (inclusive) which is not Christmas Day, Good Friday or a statutory Bank Holiday.

1.1.2 In these conditions the terms "absolute title" and "office copies" have the special given to them by the Land Registration Act 2002.

1.2    **Joint Parties**

If there is more than one seller or more than one buyer, the obligations which they undertake can be enforced against them all jointly or against each individually.'

**2.15**    The definitions set out above are almost identical to those set out in the Standard Conditions and which are discussed in the preceding paragraphs.

# Direct credit (SCPC 1.1.1(g))

**2.16**    With the exception of money paid on exchange of contracts where a property is sold by auction, all money to be paid under the terms of the SCPC is to be paid by direct credit into the seller's solicitor's account at a clearing bank. This will normally be done by a CHAPS payment but BACS could also be used. It should be noted that the definition of 'direct credit' embodies a requirement for cleared funds. If, for example, contracts were to be exchanged late in the afternoon of a working day, it would not be possible to comply with this requirement until the following working day, since banks will not transmit funds after a stated time (which varies) in the afternoon. This potentially means that the buyer's solicitor will not have complied with his obligations under the contract on exchange and leaves the buyer in a vulnerable position. Although this will not normally cause a problem, because the funds will be remitted early in the morning of the next working day, in order to avoid any difficulties it may be sensible to provide for this eventuality on the contract. A standard amendment to this condition may therefore be made to provide that if exchange of contracts takes place after (say) 2.30 pm the buyer will remit the deposit in accordance with Condition 1.1.1(g) as soon as possible on the next working day and that this payment shall be deemed to have been made in accordance with the provisions of the condition.

If it is desired to deal with money other than by direct credit, an appropriate amendment to the contract should be made. Similarly, if funds are to be remitted to or from a bank other than as defined in the definition of 'clearing bank' (eg to or from a foreign bank) an appropriate amendment will be needed.

# Implied rules of construction

**2.17**    In addition to the definitions given in the Conditions, the following additional rules of construction are implied by section 61 of the Law of Property Act 1925 unless the context otherwise requires:

'Person' includes corporation;

'Month' is a calendar month;

'Masculine' includes feminine and vice versa;

'Singular' includes plural and vice versa.

**2.18**    It should be noted that the SCPC use the pro-noun 'it' throughout when referring to the seller and the buyer. This is to reflect the fact that the parties to many commercial transactions will be corporate bodies and not private individuals. The pronoun 'he' is used throughout the Standard Conditions.

# Chapter 3

# The Standard Form of Contract

## Introduction

**3.1**    The front page of the contract forms are designed to set out the main details of the transaction including the parties' names, the property and price. Incumbrances to which the property is subject are also intended to be dealt with on the front page, but so little space is allowed for their inclusion that it seems inevitable that the only reference which will be made here will be to a special condition on the reverse of the form which will give full details of the incumbrances. Although the parties are free to agree a different 'contract rate', the Law Society encourages solicitors to insert 'the Law Society's contract rate' in the space provided for this matter on the form, thus introducing uniformity throughout the profession. Deduction of title is also to be dealt with on the front of the Standard Conditions contract form, and not by special condition. The nature of the seller's title guarantee (full or limited) must also be shown on the front page of the contract form. Where the covenants implied by the Law of Property (Miscellaneous Provisions) Act 1994 are modified or varied by the seller it is suggested that details of the modification are set out in a special condition on the back page of the form. The buyer's attention should be drawn to the modification by use of words on the face of the contract such as 'the seller sells with [limited] title guarantee as modified by special condition X'. A full discussion of title guarantees is contained below.

Title guarantee is not mentioned on the front of the SCPC form of contract.

## Special conditions

**3.2**    Where there is conflict between the general and special conditions, the special conditions prevail.

Very few special conditions are printed on the contract form. Special Condition 1 of the Standard Conditions form states that the Standard Conditions (Fourth Edition) are incorporated into the contract. The definitions within the general conditions are extended so as to apply also to words used in the special conditions. Special Condition 1 in the SCPC is similar in effect.

Special Condition 2 (SCS) refers to the title guarantee given by the seller and is further discussed in 3.5 below. No equivalent Special condition appears in the SCPC and it is suggested that for the sake of clarity a special condition dealing with title guarantee should always be added to the contract.

Special Condition 3 (SCS) states that chattels which are itemised in a schedule to the contract are deemed to be included in the sale. Under the Protocol, the Fixtures, Fittings and Contents form should be completed and attached to the contract (see Chapter 10). Chattels are dealt with by SCPC Special Condition 3 which refers to chattels itemised on an attached list, the Fixtures Fittings and Contents form being irrelevant to a commercial sale.

Special Condition 4 (SCS) and Special Condition 2 (SCPC) are printed in the alternative, either allowing a sale with vacant possession, or making the sale subject to leases or tenancies which must be listed in the special condition. Where the sale is subject to a long list of tenancies, it may be preferable to list them in a schedule to the contract and make reference in Special Condition 4 (SCS) or Condition 2 (SCPC) to that schedule.

## Particulars of sale

*Purpose of particulars*

**3.3**     The purpose of the particulars of sale is to give an accurate physical description of the land being sold, together with information as to which type of estate in that land is being sold. The particulars will usually commence with the words 'The freehold (*or leasehold as appropriate*) land ...', followed by a brief physical description of the land being sold. Care must be exercised in the drafting of the particulars since an inaccuracy may give rise to a liability in misdescription (see Chapter 7). In the case of registered land, the description of the land in the property register should be checked to see how the property is currently described and whether any alteration of that description is necessary to meet the requirements of the present contract. In unregistered land, the conveyance to the present seller should be checked for this purpose. In many cases the requirements of the particulars will be met simply by reciting the postal address of the property, but if only part of the seller's present land is being sold, or if the boundaries are not clearly defined, a fuller description will be necessary, and it should preferably be accompanied by an accurate plan.

*Implied obligation*

**3.4**     Unless the contract states to the contrary, it will be implied that the seller is selling a freehold estate free from incumbrances. The onus is on the seller to show otherwise. Therefore, if land is leasehold, the particulars should give details of the term of the lease, its rent and commencement date, and it should be stated either in the particulars or by special condition, that the sale to the buyer is subject to the terms and conditions of the lease. A copy of the lease (if already in existence) or draft lease (if the contract is for the grant of a new lease) must be sent to the buyer with the draft contract (see Chapter 22).

*Incumbrances and easements*

**3.5**    If freehold land is to be sold subject either to incumbrances or to rights being retained by the seller, this fact should be stated, but the detail of such matters is dealt with by special condition. In the same way, rights, the benefit of which will pass with the land, should be mentioned here, the detail again being reserved to a special condition.

See further Chapters 5, 6, 7, 8, 20, 21, 22, 24.

## Agreement for sale

**3.6**    This recites the agreement for the sale and purchase as outlined in the particulars and special conditions and subject to the general conditions as varied (if at all) by the special conditions. The contract is normally drawn up in two identical parts, each part being signed by one party and dated on exchange. Condition 2.1 (see Chapter 13) deals with cases in which no date has been inserted. The contract must be signed personally by the parties or their properly authorised agents. A solicitor does not have implied authority to sign on behalf of his client (*Suleman v Shahsavari* (1989)).

## Title guarantee

*Seller's capacity*

**3.7**    It is not necessary to indicate the seller's capacity in the contract or purchase deed because it has no legal effect to include it. Implied covenants for title, previously given to the buyer by virtue of section 76 of the Law of Property Act 1925 (as modified by section 24 of the Land Registration Act 1925 in registered land), the extent of which was dependent on the nature of the seller's capacity, are now governed by the Law of Property (Miscellaneous Provisions) Act 1994 which came into force on 1 July 1995. (The provisions of this Act are explained below. Section numbers contained in this Chapter are references to the 1994 Act unless otherwise stated.)

This does not mean, however, that capacity is now irrelevant to the transaction. The buyer will only obtain a good title if he buys from an estate owner who owns the estate purported to be sold. The onus is on the buyer to check (preferably at the pre-contract stage) that the seller, as shown on the contract, does have full capacity to sell the land. In particular it is necessary to ensure that where land is held on trust for sale (eg by co-owners) that the sale is conducted by at least two trustees, in order to obtain a valid receipt for capital monies arising under the transaction (Law of Property Act 1925, s 27(2)) and that all proving PR's are shown as parties to and sign the contract for sale (Law of Property (Miscellaneous Provisions) Act 1994, s 16).

The Law of Property (Miscellaneous Provisions) Act 1994 repealed section 76 of the Law of Property Act 1925 and associated legislation relating to covenants for title and replaced them with 'statutory guarantees' which are implied in a transfer document by the use of the key words 'with full guarantee' or 'with limited guarantee' (or their Welsh equivalents). An indication of whether full or limited guarantee is being given to the buyer (or no guarantee) must be included in the contract. Standard Condition 4.6.2 and SCPC Condition 6.6.2 both provide that the seller will sell with full title guarantee and will therefore need to be amended by special condition in the contract if this is not intended to be the case. There is no reference to title guarantee on either the front or back pages of the SCPC form and it is suggested that to avoid doubt a special condition dealing with title guarantee should always be added to a contract drawn using the SCPC. An indication of the type of guarantee given must also be shown on the front of the Standard Conditions contract form. If the key words are omitted from the contract, no guarantee will be implied. The extent of the guarantee can also be altered by express agreement. The guarantees apply not only on the transfer of freehold or leasehold property but can also apply on the grant of a lease (see Chapter 22) and on the transfer of personal property including intellectual property and rights in shares.

*Full title guarantee*

**3.8**     Where the phrase 'full guarantee' is used the transferor warrants that:

(a) he has the right to dispose of the property in the manner purported (s 2(1)(a));

(b) he will at his own cost do all he reasonably can to give his transferee the title he purports to give (s 2(1)(b));

(c) he disposes of the whole interest where that interest is registered (s 2(3)(a));

(d) he disposes of the whole lease where the interest is leasehold (s 2 (3)(b)(i));

(e) he disposes of a freehold where it is unclear from the face of the documents whether the interest is freehold or leasehold (s 2(3)(b) (ii));

(f) in the case of a subsisting lease he gives covenants that the lease is still subsisting and that there is no subsisting breach which might result in forfeiture (s 4(1));

(g) in the case of a mortgage of property which is subject to a rent charge or lease, that the mortgagor will observe and perform the obligations under the rent charge or lease (s 5);

(h) that the person giving the disposition is disposing of it free from all charges and incumbrances (whether monetary or not) and from all other rights exercisable by third parties, not being rights which the transferor does not and could not reasonably be expected to know about (s 3).

Note that (h) above will extend to matters which pre-date the transferor's ownership of the property.

## Limited guarantee

**3.9**     Where limited title guarantee is given the above covenants apply except for (*h*) above which is replaced by the following:

Covenants that the transferor has not charged or incumbered the property by a charge or incumbrance which still exists, that he has not granted any third party rights which still subsist and that he is not aware that anyone else has done so since the last disposition for value (s 3(3)).

### *Transferee's knowledge*

**3.10**     Whichever guarantee is given the transferor is not liable for anything to which the disposition is expressly made subject or which, at the time of the disposition is within the actual knowledge of the transferee or which is a necessary consequence of facts then within the actual knowledge of the transferee (s 6). Knowledge imputed by section 198 of the Law of Property Act 1925 is expressly excluded from the definition of the word 'knowledge' within the Act. In order to limit the seller's potential liability under the covenants it is essential that he discloses to the buyer all known incumbrances over the property (see Chapter 5). Disclosure through a special condition in the contract is desirable in order to be able to prove that these matters were within the buyer's actual knowledge at the date of the disposition.

### *Modification and exclusion of the guarantees*

**3.11**     The extent of the title guarantee depends on the use of the key phrases 'with full guarantee' or 'with limited guarantee' in the contract. The extent of the guarantees given by these phrases can be modified by express words in the contract, or excluded altogether. In the case of modification of the title guarantees in registered land, the Land Registration Rules 1995 (SI 1995 No 140) require the transfer to set out any modifications or variations to the covenants by reference to the section of the 1994 Act which is being amended. Since in freehold transactions any modification of the covenants will not be shown on the register of title, it may be necessary for the buyer to keep a copy of the contract for sale or certified copy of the purchase deed in order to have a record of the covenants which were given to him by his seller.

### *Assignment of guarantee*

**3.12**     The title guarantees run with the land and are enforceable by the buyer's successors in title against his immediate predecessor.  A potential buyer of registered land may need to raise a specific enquiry of his seller to find out whether the title guarantees were modified or excluded during the course of the transaction under which the present seller bought the land, since in freehold transactions no record of any modification of the covenants appears on the register of the title. For this reason a copy of the contract for sale or purchase deed may need to be kept in order to have a record of the covenants which have been given.

*Leases*

**3.13**    The title guarantees apply on both the grant and assignment of a lease. On the grant of a short lease the seller/landlord may consider it inappropriate to give any covenants to the tenant. However, on the grant of a long residential lease or commercial lease at a premium the buyer may wish to have the benefit of covenants given by the seller/landlord. On the grant of a sub-lease it would be unwise for the grantor to give his tenant the benefit of more covenants than he himself received on the grant of the head-lease. Where either full or limited title guarantee is given in the case of the assignment of a subsisting lease the seller gives covenants that the lease is still subsisting and that there is no subsisting breach which might result in forfeiture (s 4). Unless expressly modified this provision could render a seller liable under the covenants for a technical breach of eg a repairing covenant under the lease being sold. Standard Condition 3.2.2 and SCPC Condition 3.2.2 modify this implied covenant by providing that a leasehold property is sold subject to any subsisting breach of a condition or tenant's obligation relating to the physical state of the property which renders the lease liable to forfeiture. Standard Condition 3.2.3 and SCPC Condition 3.2.2 contain a similar provision relating to sub-leases.

*Remedies*

**3.14**    A breach of the covenants is actionable as a breach of contract. Once completion has taken place, or a third party eg a lender, has acquired an interest in the property, it is unlikely that rescission would be granted. Damages will therefore be the most usual remedy for breach, but a seller could be required eg to execute a further document to perfect the title.

*Options*

**3.15**    Where there is an option, the contract for the disposition is, by section 13 of the Law of Property (Miscellaneous Provisions) Act 1994, deemed to have been entered into on the grant of the option, the nature of the title guarantee will therefore be governed by the date of the option agreement itself. Where the option is dated before 1 July 1995 covenants will therefore be implied by virtue of section 76 of the Law of Property Act 1925 (as amended) and not under the 1994 Act. Contracts which are made in pursuance of option agreements dated on or after 1 July 1995 are governed by the 1994 Act in accordance with the above paragraphs.

*Full or limited guarantee?*

**3.16**    If a full guarantee is given without modification the seller is guaranteeing the title not only throughout his own period of ownership but also back through the periods of ownership of his predecessors without limit. This is a potentially onerous obligation to undertake, even for a sole absolute owner of a registered absolute freehold title. However, in practice, very few problems have arisen under the previous legislation relating to covenants for title contained in section 76 of the Law of Property Act 1925 (as amended), as evidenced by the conspicuous paucity of modern reported case law on the subject. It is therefore unrealistic to suppose that the new covenants will cause any greater problems than did their predecessors. In which case it should be perfectly safe for a sole owner of an apparently unimpeachable title to give his buyer an unqualified full title guarantee. The same reasoning applies to co-owners who hold the whole of the legal and equitable interest in the land for their own benefit. Sellers who hold the land as true trustees (ie other than as co-owners for their own benefit), PR's, donors, settlors and selling mortgagees are not however in a position to give a full title guarantee and should consider to what extent they are prepared to give an unqualified limited guarantee which, despite its limited nature, still imports more extensive obligations on the seller(s) than were required under the now repealed section 76 of the Law of Property Act 1925.

PRs and selling mortgagees will usually have no knowledge of the property or its title before it came into their hands and may therefore feel that the only covenant which they are prepared to give is a covenant that they themselves have not encumbered the property, or alternatively (and particularly in the case of selling mortgagees) no covenants at all. Similarly, a donor or settlor both of whom are effectively making a gift of the property may consider it inappropriate to give any covenants to the recipient of the gift. The covenants have equal application irrespective of whether or not value is given for the transaction, so the fact that the property is a gift does not affect the donor's potential liability under the covenants. As noted above, modifications of the covenants must be expressly set out in the contract and in the case of registered land, the purchase deed. Where no covenants are given this fact should also be expressly stated in the contract to alert the buyer to this fact and also to override the effect of Standard Condition 4.6.2 which provides that where the contract is silent the seller will sell with full title guarantee.

*Creation of mortgage*

**3.17**    A mortgagee will frequently insist that the borrower gives a full title guarantee in the mortgage deed, irrespective of whether the property to be charged has the benefit of full or limited title guarantee.

# The Protocol

**3.18**    The terms of the Protocol assume that the Standard Conditions of Sale will be used as the basis of the contract between the parties. If this is not to be so, it is the seller's solicitor's duty to inform the buyer's solicitor of this fact at the outset of the transaction. Certain requirements of the Protocol, such as the supply of office copy entries as evidence of title in registered land, are reflected in the drafting of the Standard Conditions of Sale. Thus if the conditions are to be amended in a way which would involve the solicitor in a departure from Protocol procedures this too needs to be notified to the other solicitor at an early stage in the transaction. It is suggested that in order to avoid delay and mis-understanding, the amendment to the general conditions which effects the departure from Protocol is specifically drawn to the attention of the other solicitor in correspondence between them.

## Incorporation of Standard Conditions of Sale by reference

**3.19**　Some solicitors choose to reproduce their contracts for the sale of land on a word processor, incorporating the Standard Conditions of Sale by reference, in preference to using the printed form of contract. Where this is done, the full text of the general conditions from the Standard Conditions of Sale should be supplied as part of the contract to ensure that the contract is complete, that all its terms are readily accessible to both parties, and that the contract satisfies section 2 of the Law of Property (Miscellaneous Provisions) Act 1989 which requires all the terms agreed by the parties to be incorporated within a written contract (see Chapter 13 below). A contract which expressly incorporates the Standard Conditions by reference (eg 'The Standard Conditions of Sale (4th ed) are deemed to be incorporated within this agreement. Where there is conflict between those Conditions and this agreement, the terms of this agreement will prevail.'), but without the full text of the Conditions being supplied as part of the contract, may still satisfy section 2 (*B Ltd v T Ltd* (1991)). Similar comments apply when using the SCPC.

## Amendment of the Standard Conditions of Sale

**3.20**　Not all the Standard Conditions of Sale will be appropriate for use in every transaction. Thought should therefore be given to the application of the Conditions in the circumstances of the particular transaction, and amendment made to those which are inappropriate. In all cases, amendments should be restricted to those which are essential to meet the circumstances of the individual case. Particular care should be taken over amendments when the Protocol is being used (see 3.18 above). Similar comments apply when using the SCPC.

## Open contract rules

**3.21**　When a contract makes no reference to a particular matter, the contract is said to be 'open' on that point and is therefore governed by the relevant common law or statutory provisions. Some of the open contract rules, such as the rules for deduction of title in unregistered freeholds, are satisfactory in operation, and are normally used without variation. Others, for example the time for completion, which, by the open contract rule is set at 'a reasonable time after contract' are less satisfactory and are frequently altered in practice. The Standard Conditions of Sale and SCPC make some amendments to the less satisfactory of the open contract rules, but it should not be assumed in every transaction that the Standard Conditions or SCPC will contain an amendment which is appropriate to the circumstances of the particular case.

## Special conditions

**3.22** Even where the Standard Conditions of Sale or SCPC have been adopted without amendment, some special conditions will usually be required to deal with the particular circumstances of the transaction in hand. Even in the most straightforward transaction special conditions are frequently needed to deal with the following matters:

- title;
- deposit;
- completion date;
- title guarantee;
- incumbrances;
- fixtures and fittings;
- VAT.

Examples of special conditions to meet particular circumstances are contained in Chapter 24.

## Drafting the contract

**3.23** Drafting the contract is the seller's prerogative, since only he can say what he is prepared to sell to the buyer and on what terms. In practice, however, the relative bargaining strengths of the parties will rarely permit the seller to present the buyer with a contract containing terms which are exclusively to the seller's advantage. Some form of compromise between the parties is inevitable. The seller must seek to protect his own interests while at the same time presenting the buyer with a contract which entices the buyer to proceed with the transaction. A party who seeks to draw or amend the contract in order totally to protect his own interests will at best protract the transaction unnecessarily, or at worst lose the sale altogether.

Additional special conditions should be added to the contract only where they are both relevant and necessary. Since it is important that the client should understand the terms of the contract being entered into, it is preferable to draft such special conditions as are necessary in clear, concise, modern English.

## Value Added Tax

*The charge to VAT*

**3.24** With effect from 1 April 1989 (in some cases 1 August 1989) the

Finance Act 1989 brought certain property transactions within the charge to VAT. Residential property is normally exempt, as also is the transfer of the freehold of an existing building which is more than three years old, but the sale of the freehold of a new commercial building within the first three years after its completion attracts VAT at the standard rate. A seller or landlord usually has the right to elect whether to charge VAT on the sale or grant of a commercial lease. The contract for the sale of the freehold of a new or recently constructed commercial building will need to include provisions relating to the payment of VAT and all commercial leases should contain a comprehensive VAT clause in case the landlord for the time being chooses to tax the rent.

*Example clause*

**3.25**    An example of a VAT clause for inclusion in a lease is set out below:

'(a) To pay to the Landlord by way of additional rent VAT at the rate for the time being in force chargeable in respect of any rent or other payment made or other consideration provided by the Tenant under the terms of or in connection with this lease and in every case where the Tenant covenants to pay an amount of money under this lease such amount shall be regarded as being exclusive of all VAT which may from time to time be legally payable thereon.

(b) In every case where the Tenant has agreed to reimburse the Landlord in respect of any payment made by the Landlord under the terms of or in connection with this lease that the Tenant shall also reimburse any VAT paid by the Landlord on such payment [unless the VAT is recovered/recoverable by the Landlord].

(c) Any reference to VAT in this lease shall include any tax of a similar nature that may be substituted for or levied in addition to it.'

*Standard Condition 1.4 and SCPC Condition 1.4*

**3.26**    The Standard Conditions and SCPC provide for VAT as follows in Condition 1.4:

>   '1.4.1    Any obligation to pay money includes an obligation to pay any value added tax chargeable in respect of that payment.
>
>   1.4.2    All sums made payable by the contract are exclusive of value added tax.'

Residential property is normally exempt from VAT, and this condition is satisfactory for use in that context or in a contract for the sale of a freehold commercial building which at the time of contract is more than three years old, which property is similarly exempt from the charge to VAT. In most other commercial transactions, whether freehold or leasehold, the VAT position will need to be considered carefully and an express special condition added to the contract to deal with the VAT consequences of the transaction. Where VAT is payable on the transaction, stamp duty is assessed on the total price paid, including the VAT element of the price. If there is any doubt as to the relevance of VAT to the transaction, a specialist book on the subject should be consulted.

**3.27**   The Standard Commercial Property Conditions provide for VAT as follows:

'1.4.1   The seller

(a) warrants that the sale of the property does not constitute a supply that is taxable for VAT purposes

(b) agrees that there will be no exercise of the election to waive exemption in respect of the property, and

(c) cannot require the buyer to pay any amount in respect of any liability to VAT arising in respect of the sale of the property, unless condition 1.4.2 applies.

1.4.2   If, solely as a result of a change in law made and coming into effect between the date of the contract and completion, the sale of the property will constitute a supply chargeable to VAT, the buyer is to pay to the seller on completion an additional amount equal to that VAT in exchange for a proper VAT invoice from the seller.

1.4.3   The amount payable for the chattels is exclusive of VAT and the buyer is to pay to the seller on completion an additional amount equal to any VAT charged on that supply in exchange for a proper VAT invoice from the seller.'

Additionally Part 2 Condition A provides:

'A1.1   Conditions 1.4.1 and 1.4.2 do not apply.

A1.2   The seller warrants that the sale of the property will constitute a supply chargeable to VAT at the standard rate.

A1.3   The buyer is to pay to the seller on completion an additional amount equal to the VAT in exchange for a proper VAT invoice from the seller.'

Condition 1.4 in Part 1 of the Standard Commercial Property Conditions is applicable where no VAT arises out of the transaction and contains a warranty from the seller to that effect with provisos for the effect of any change in the law between contract and completion which would have the result of bringing the transaction into charge. Condition 1.4.3 deals exclusively with the VAT position of chattels which are sold with the property.

Where VAT is chargeable Condition 1.4 should be excluded from the contract and use may then be made of Condition A1 which contains basic provisions for VAT. Alternatively the parties may prefer to draft their own terms dealing with this matter in greater detail.

Condition A2 of Part 2 of the Standard Commercial Property Conditions then deals with transfers as a going concern as follows:

'A2.1   Condition 1.4 does not apply.

A2.2   In this condition 'TOGC' means a transfer of a business as a going concern treated as neither a supply of goods nor a supply of services by virtue of Article 5 of the Value Added Tax (Special Provisions) Order 1995.

A2.3   The seller warrants that it is using the property for the business of letting to produce rental income .

A2.4   The buyer is to make every effort to comply with the conditions to be met by a transferee under article 5 (1) and 5(2) for the sale to constitute a TOGC.

A2.5 The buyer will on or before the earlier of :

(a)  completion date, and

(b)  the earliest date on which a supply of the property could be treated as made by the seller under the contract if the sale does not constitute a TOGC,

notify the seller that paragraph (2B) of article 5 of the VAT (Special Provisions) Order 1995 does not apply to the buyer.

A2.6 The parties are to treat the sale as a TOGC at completion if the buyer produces written evidence to the seller before completion that it is a taxable person and that it has made an election to waive exemption in respect of the property and has given a written notification of the making of such election in conformity with article 5(2) and has given the notification referred to in condition A2.5.

A2.7 The buyer is not to revoke its election to waive exemption in respect of the property at any time .

A2.8 If the parties treat the sale at completion as a TOGC but it is later determined that the sale was not a TOGC, then within five working days of that determination the buyer shall pay to the seller :

(a)  an amount equal to the VAT chargeable in respect of the supply of the property in exchange for a proper VAT invoice from the seller, and

(b)  except where the sale is not a TOGC because of an act or omission of the seller, an amount equal to any interest or penalty for which the seller is liable to account to HM Customs and Excise in respect of or by reference to that VAT.

A2.9 If the seller obtains the consent of HM Customs and Excise to retain its VAT records relating to the property, it shall make them available to the buyer for inspection and copying at reasonable times on reasonable request during the six years following completion.'

This optional condition in Part 2 of the Standard Commercial Property Conditions may be used in place of the other VAT provisions where the sale comprises investment property run as a business. Consideration should be given to the adequacy of these provisions or whether specially drafted provisions should be included in the contract. A detailed discussion of VAT is beyond the scope of this book.

References to HM Customs and Excise should now be amended to read: 'HM Revenue and Customs'.

## Unfair contract terms

*Introduction*

**3.28**  The Unfair Contract Terms in Consumer Contracts Regulations (SI 1994 No 3159) implementing EC Council Directive 93/13 came into effect on 1 July 1995. The Regulations refer to 'goods and services', which phrase, using the conventional construction of these words, does not encompass land.

However, the exclusions from the Regulations (Schedule 1) do not mention land as being excluded from their effect and the French text from which the English regulations derive clearly does embrace land within the scope of the Directive. It is therefore uncertain whether the Regulations do affect English land transactions. The third edition of the Standard Conditions of Sale has not been amended to reflect the requirements of the Regulations and makes no reference to them. Despite the uncertainty over the application of the Regulations, an awareness of their contents is advisable and voluntary compliance with them sensible and, in the case of special conditions individually drafted for inclusion in a particular contract, not too difficult to achieve. A summary of the Regulations is set out below.

*When do the Regulations apply?*

**3.29**    Subject to the caveat in the preceding paragraph about the application of the Regulations to land contracts, the Regulations affect all contracts (oral or written) made between a seller or supplier and a consumer (this phrase applies to individuals only). In the context of a land transaction this means any situation where the seller is acting in the course of a business and where the buyer is a private individual. This means that the Regulations do not affect the normal residential conveyancing transaction where both seller and buyer are private individuals, nor a commercial transaction where both seller and buyer are acting in the course of a business. The following situations are however potentially within the scope of the Regulations:

(a) plot sales by a seller/developer (acting in the course of a business) to a private buyer;

(b) tenancy agreements made between a landlord (in business) and a tenant (private individual);

(c) mortgages where the lender is acting in the course of business and the borrower is a private individual;

(d) contracts for financial services made between a broker (on business) and a private individual.

*Unfair terms*

**3.30**    The burden of proof will lie on the buyer/consumer to show that a term included in the contract which was not individually negotiated between the parties is unfair. A term will be regarded as unfair if, contrary to the requirement of good faith, it causes a significant imbalance in the parties rights and obligations arising under the contract to the detriment of the consumer. Various factors, similar to those contained in the Unfair Contract Terms Act 1977 (which does not apply to land contracts), are contained in Schedule 2 of the Regulations to act as guidelines as to whether 'good faith' exists eg the strength of the bargaining position of the parties, the circumstances surrounding the contract, whether the consumer has received any special inducement, such as a discount, to agree to the term. An illustrative list of terms which may be regarded as unfair is set out in Schedule 3. If a term is held to be unfair, that term is to be treated as void, but the rest of the contract remains binding on the parties, so long as it is capable of continuing without the offending term.

*Plain English*

**3.31**    Regulation 3 requires all contracts to be drafted in plain intelligible language.

# Chapter 4

# Service and Delivery of Documents

## General law

### Law of Property Act 1925

**4.1**    Section 196 of the Law of Property Act 1925 lays down regulations which deal with the service of notices required or authorised to be served under that Act. This section may be expressly incorporated into a contract for the sale of land in order to provide certainty in relation to the service of notices which may need to be issued under special or general conditions of the contract.

Section 196 is limited in its application in that it deals with notices only (not documents) and the normal method of service under section 196(4) is by registered post or recorded delivery. The notice is then deemed to be served at the time when the letter would in the ordinary course of post be delivered.

Where section 196 does not apply a notice is deemed to be served when it is received (*Sun Alliance and London Assurance Co Ltd v Hayman* (1975)).

### Service on corporations

**4.2**    Section 75 of the Companies Act 1985 provides that a document to be served on a company is duly served if left at or posted to the registered office of the company. 'Document' includes notices, orders and other legal process and is not confined to documents required to be served under the Companies Acts. This provision is possibly overridden by the provisions of Condition 1.3 (see below).

### Document exchange

**4.3**    The court approved the use of a document exchange for the service and delivery of documents in non-contentious matters in *John Wilmott Homes v Read* (1985). The time of service of documents served by this method will, subject to contrary agreement, be governed by the rules of the particular document exchange being used. Reference should also be made to the statement of the Council of the Law Society relating to the use of document exchanges (81 LSG 2823).

*Fax*

**4.4**     Use of fax for the transmission of documents, letters and notices is common. It is suggested that service is probably effected when the faxed document arrives at the recipient's terminal (see *Entores Ltd v Miles Far East Corporation* (1995)). Whenever fax is used, the solicitor should bear in mind that the transmission may be intercepted or misdirected to a person other than the intended recipient of the letter or document and that if this occurs, the solicitor may be in breach of his duty of confidentiality to his client. In *Ralux NV/SA v Spencer Mason* (1989), the court held that fax could be a valid method of service of any documents other than originating process, but that to be valid, the sender would have to prove that the document in complete and legible form arrived at the recipient's fax terminal. In view of this heavy burden of proof, the Law Society recommended (*Law Society's Gazette*, 27 November 1991) that in cases where it may be necessary later to prove the service of a document (eg exercise of an option), solicitors should use a conventional method of service (eg post, DX) in preference to fax. Fax cannot be used to effect an exchange of contracts (see *Milton Keynes Development Corporation v Cooper (Great Britain) Ltd* (1993)).

*E-mail*

**4.4.1**     Use of e-mail as a means of communication is common. As yet no case law exists on the time of assumed delivery or status of communications sent in this way. Both the Standard Conditions and the SCPC make provision for service of documents or notices by this method. It is suggested that the comments in para 4.4. above, relating to service by fax have equal application to e-mail. It follows therefore that exchange of contracts cannot take place in this way (although arguably the Law Society's formulae for exchange could be activated by e-mail) and that this method of communication cannot be used in any case where delivery of the original document is essential. In any case where delivery of a document is time critical (eg exercise of an option) it would be unwise to rely on e-mail as the sole method of communication, at least until some judicial authority on the status of this method of communication has been established.

## Standard Condition 1.3

**4.5**     Condition 1.3 provides:

'1.3. *Notices and Documents*
1.3.1     A notice required or authorised by the contract must be in writing.
1.3.2     Giving a notice or delivering a document to a party's conveyancer has the same effect as giving or delivering it to that party.
1.3.3     Where delivery of the original document is not essential a notice or document is validly given or sent if is sent
(a)   by fax, or
(b)   by e-mail to an e-mail address for the intended recipient given in the contract.
1.3.4     Subject to conditions 1.3.5 to 1.3.7, a notice is given and a document delivered when it is received.

1.3.5  (a)  A notice or document sent through a document exchange is received when it is available for collection

     (b)  A notice or document which is received after 4.00pm on a working day, or on a day which is not a working day, is to be treated as having been received on the next working day

     (c)  An automated response to a notice or document sent by e-mail that the intended recipient is out of the office is to be treated as proof that the notice or document was not received.

1.3.6  Condition 1.3.7 applies unless there is proof :

     (a)  that a notice or document has not been received, or

     (b)  of when it was received.

1.3.7  A notice or document sent by the following means is treated as having been received as follows :

     (a)  by first class post: before 4.00pm on the second working day after posting

     (b)  by second class post: before 4.00pm on the third working day after posting

     (c)  through a document exchange : before 4.00pm on the first working day after the day on which it would normally be available for collection by the addressee

     (d)  by fax: one hour after despatch

     (e)  by e-mail: before 4.00pm on the first working day after despatch.'

### Effect of the condition

**4.6**    This condition replaces section 196 of the Law of Property Act 1925 in the context of contracts governed by the Standard Conditions of Sale and provides for service of notices and documents by the methods most commonly in use today, together with a deemed time of service for each particular method.

The deemed time of service of documents and notices is geared to the definition of a 'working day' contained in Condition 1.1.1(m) (see 2.11 above).

Transmission by fax or e-mail are permitted provided that the delivery of the original document is 'not essential'. These methods may therefore be used for the delivery of a draft contract or purchase deed, but it is not permissible within the wording of the condition to exchange contracts or to deliver the engrossment of the purchase deed by these methods (see *Milton Keynes Development Corporation v Cooper (Great Britain) Ltd* (1993)). The condition includes a deemed time for service, thus overcoming the uncertainties which surround this method under the common law.

Similarly, the condition provides for a deemed time of service where a document exchange is used, overcoming difficulties which may be encountered where the rules of different exchanges vary. Again, there is at present no judicial decision relating to the time of service when this method of serving a document or notice is used. It should, however, be noted that the time when exchange of contracts through a document exchange takes place differs from the normal time of service of documents under this condition (see Condition 2.1.1, Chapter 13).

Documents sent in fulfilment of an undertaking where exchange of contracts has taken place using one of the Law Society Formulae must, under the terms of the Formulae, be sent by first class post, through a document exchange, or delivered by hand.

The condition contains a provision (Condition 1.3.2) for valid service to be effected on the solicitor to one of the parties as well as service on that party personally.

Service by a method not expressly mentioned by the condition, eg service by hand, is not precluded by the wording of the condition itself. The time of deemed service, even by a method not specified in the condition, seems still to be governed by Conditions 1.3.4.

## SCPC Condition 1.3

**4.7**    This condition is identical in its wording and effect to Standard Condition 1.3, discussed above except that it contains an extra sub-clause (1.3.8) which defines 'first class post' as 'postal service which seeks to deliver posted items no later than the next working day in all or the majority of cases.' This is designed to cover situations where a party chooses to send documents or letters via a privately-run postal service.

# Chapter 5

# Disclosure of Incumbrances

## The general law

**5.1**   Non-disclosure is an omission to reveal a fact, which, had it been revealed, would have influenced a person's decision to enter into a contract. In some circumstances a non-disclosure by the seller is tantamount to a misrepresentation by silence, in which case it may be appropriate to pursue a remedy under the Misrepresentation Act 1967 (see Chapter 8).

*The duty to disclose*

**5.2**   The general rule applicable to contracts for the sale of land is *caveat emptor*, but this rule is subject to certain qualifications. There is an absolute duty on the seller to disclose latent incumbrances and defects in title. A latent defect is one which is not apparent.

The buyer will be aware of the defect if he actually knew of it or if he could have discovered it by an inspection of the property. An example of such a defect is a public footpath crossing the land.

Although a defect is not latent if the buyer has constructive notice of it under section 198 of the Law of Property Act 1925, the effect of section 24 of the Law of Property Act 1969 is to place a duty on the seller to reveal matters which are registered at the Land Charges Department.

There is no duty to disclose patent defects, but a prudent seller will make a full disclosure. Likewise, a prudent buyer will make a careful inspection of the land in order to discover such matters. Although planning matters perhaps do not fall within the ambit of the word 'title', it seems that where a planning charge exists which is known to the seller and which would materially affect the value of the property, then a duty of disclosure arises (*Sakkas v Donford Ltd* (1982)).

It is an implied term of a contract for the sale of land that the seller is selling free from incumbrances. If this is not to be so, the seller must disclose the incumbrances except where the incumbrances are patent. Where the contract contains an express term that the sale is free from incumbrances, the buyer will be able to rescind the contract if he later discovers an irremovable incumbrance. This will be so even if the buyer knew of the defect at the time of contracting (*Cato v Thompson* (1882)).

If the contract is silent, the buyer will not be able to rescind in respect of a defect which he knew about at the time of entering the contract.

There is generally no duty to disclose a physical defect in the land whether latent or patent, but if the non-disclosure misleads the buyer by rendering the contractual description of the land inaccurate, a remedy in misdescription may lie (*Re Puckett & Smith's Contract* (1902)).

There can normally be no duty to disclose, nor liability arising from, a physical defect which is unknown to the seller, for example an underground watercourse, but the buyer may be able to rescind if he would be prevented from using the land for the purpose for which it was sold (*Re Puckett & Smith's Contract*, above).

The general principles outlined above also apply to registered land except that there is no equivalent in registered conveyancing to section 198 of the Law of Property Act 1925. The Register is open to public inspection but the buyer is not deemed to know of its contents unless he has inspected it or has been sent copies of the entries (but see *Faruqi v English Real Estates Ltd* (1979)). Overriding interests will not, however, be revealed by the Register. The seller is under a duty to disclose latent overriding interests but not those that are patent. There is some doubt whether the rights of occupation of a person living in the property are a latent or patent defect. In practice the seller should disclose all overriding interests of which he is aware in order to avoid future liability under the implied covenants for title.

### Protection of the seller where there is a defect in title

**5.3**     The seller should make a frank and full disclosure of the defect in the contract, continuing the wording of the condition with a phrase such as, 'the buyer shall assume that ...' (in respect of, for example, an invalid execution of a deed); or 'the buyer shall raise no objection or requisition with regard to ...' (in respect of, for example, restrictive covenants mentioned in the title of which no details are available). Provided that the seller has been honest in his revelation of the defect, such a clause should prevent the buyer from rescinding in relation to that particular defect. If the seller has not made a full disclosure of the defect, or has been deliberately fraudulent or has attempted to hide the defect, such a clause will not protect him and equity will refuse his request for specific performance (*Re Scott and Alvarez's Contract (1895); Faruqi v English Real Estates Ltd* (1979)).

The problem created by the defect may be mitigated by an insurance policy taken out by the seller assigned to the buyer on completion.

### Remedies at common law

**5.4**     If the non-disclosure is substantial, the seller may not enforce the contract. The buyer may treat the contract as discharged and may be able to claim damages for breach from the seller. Alternatively the buyer may be able to obtain specific performance with an abatement in the purchase price.

A non-disclosure is 'substantial' if it results in the buyer not getting what he contracted to buy. Examples include:

(*a*) an easement over the property affecting its use and enjoyment;

(*b*) unusual or onerous covenants in a lease where no opportunity to inspect the lease was given;

(*c*) an undisclosed breach of a leasehold covenant which might result in forfeiture of the lease.

If the non-disclosure is not substantial, the buyer may be compelled to complete his purchase subject to an abatement in the purchase price to compensate for the defect.

The buyer should pursue his remedies before completion, when the contract merges in the conveyance. After completion the buyer's only recourse will be to bring an action based on the implied covenants for title under the Law of Property (Miscellaneous Provisions) Act 1994. The buyer cannot hold the seller liable under the implied covenants for any matter which was within the buyer's actual knowledge. It is therefore important for the seller to make a full disclosure of all incumbrances in the contract in order to limit his potential liability under the covenants.

If the non-disclosure amounts to a misrepresentation by silence, an action may be brought under the Misrepresentation Act 1967 (see Chapter 8).

The buyer's remedies may be limited by specific contractual provisions. In particular, the contract may include a clause allowing the seller to rescind where he cannot remove a defect in the title. Such a clause may prevent the buyer from being able to claim specific performance and/or may preclude the buyer's claim for damages for breach of contract. The use of a rescission clause is strictly controlled by the courts, who will not allow a seller who contracted with knowledge of the defect to rely on it (see Chapter 24). No such clause is contained in the Standard Conditions of Sale.

No contractual provision will protect a seller who has constructed or altered the property from tortious liability under section 6 of the Defective Premises Act 1972 (*Hone v Benson* (1978)).

## 5.5 Standard Condition 3.1

'3      MATTERS AFFECTING THE PROPERTY

3.1     *Freedom from incumbrances*

3.1.1   The seller is selling the property free from incumbrances, other than those mentioned in condition 3.1.2.

3.1.2   The incumbrances subject to which the property is sold are:

(a)     those specified in the contract

(b)     those discoverable by inspection of the property before the contract

(c) those the seller does not and could not reasonably know about

(d) entries made before the date of the contract in any public register except those maintained by HM Land Registry or its Land Charges Department or by Companies House

(e) public requirements.

3.1.3 After the contract is made, the seller is to give the buyer written details without delay of any new public requirement and of anything in writing which he learns about concerning any incumbrances subject to which the property is sold.

3.1.4 The buyer is to bear the cost of complying with any outstanding public requirement and is to indemnify the seller against any liability resulting from a public requirement.'

## Effect of the condition

**5.6**     The duty of disclosure imposed on the seller by this condition is wider than the duty required under the general law.

The seller's duty in relation to 'incumbrances' excludes disclosure of those matters which 'the seller does not and could not reasonably know about'. The inclusion of this wording is necessary because the duty of disclosure has been held to extend to matters of which the seller has no knowledge (see *Re Brewer and Hankin's Contract* (1899) and *Celsteel Ltd v Alton House Holdings (No 2)* (1986)).

The usual exclusion from disclosure of matters which are apparent on inspection of the property is included in the wording of the condition. Thus, subject to the buyer's duty to inspect implicitly imposed by Condition 3.2.1 (see below) the seller need not disclose matters which are patent or obvious.

The sale of the property is made expressly subject to entries made before the date of the contract in any public register other than the Land Registry, the Land Charges Department or Companies House. From the seller's point of view this condition (3.1.2(d)) places the onus on him to reveal and expressly mention incumbrances which may be registered at these three named registries (note in particular the requirement to disclose registered charges made by companies). Since local land charges are not within this list, the onus is on the buyer to carry out a local land charges search (probably with enquiries of local authority also) and to ensure its result is satisfactory.

'Public requirement' is defined by Condition 1.1.1(j). The definition includes such matters as an obligation to pay the cost of road works. A requirement is made when the work is done. The cost of complying with a public requirement, whether made before or after the contract, is to be borne by the buyer (Condition 3.1.4). If the buyer fails to comply, the seller may fulfil the requirement himself and recover the costs from the buyer.

By Condition 3.1.4, the seller's duty of disclosure continues until completion in respect of public requirement and written communications concerning incumbrances. Oral communications relating to incumbrances do not fall within this condition. No sanction is imposed on a seller who fails to comply with this condition.

Although the buyer takes the property subject to the matters listed in Condition 3.1.2, the special conditions in the contract may override the general conditions, thus a seller who has expressly contracted to sell with vacant possession but who finds himself unable to give possession, perhaps because a closing order has been registered by the local authority, may be liable for breach of contract (see, for example, *Topfell Ltd v Galley Properties Ltd* (1979), although the contract in this case was not based on either the Law Society Conditions or National Conditions which were the standard forms of contract in use at that time).

It should be noted that Condition 7.1 contains an exclusion clause which attempts to limit the seller's liability for non-disclosure. This condition is discussed in Chapter 8.

Conditions 3.3 (tenancies) and 3.4 (retained land) are discussed in Chapters 20 and 21 respectively.

## Suggested amendments to Condition 3.1

**5.7**     The duty of disclosure imposed on the seller by this condition is heavier than that required by the general law and the seller may therefore consider an amendment to limit this duty. Any such limitation would, however, be construed as an exclusion clause, and as such is subject to the reasonableness test contained in the Unfair Contract Terms Act 1977 (see Chapter 8). In particular, the seller may choose to restrict his duty of disclosure to matters which he knew about before the contract was made, effectively negating the continuing duty of disclosure imposed by Condition 3.1.3.

If the buyer does not have time to make all his searches before exchange of contracts he may consider making the contract conditional on the receipt of satisfactory search replies, although the latter would not be a popular amendment from the seller's point of view. A condition which makes the contract conditional must be carefully worded to ensure its validity at common law (see Chapter 24).

The buyer may prefer to limit his liability to bear the expense of complying with public requirements to those which are imposed after the date of contract only, leaving the seller to bear the responsibility for compliance with those requirements which were in existence before that time (see Condition 3.1.4).

## Standard Condition 3.2

**5.8**     Condition 3.2 provides:

'3.2    PHYSICAL STATE

3.2.1    The buyer accepts the property in the physical state it is in at the date of the contract unless the seller is building or converting it.

3.2.2    A leasehold property is sold subject to any subsisting breach of a condi-

45

tion or tenant's obligation relating to the physical state of the property which renders the lease liable to forfeiture.

3.2.3   A sub-lease is granted subject to any subsisting breach of a condition or tenant's obligation relating to the physical state of the property which renders the seller's own lease liable to forfeiture.'

## Effect of the condition

**5.9**   Condition 3.2.1 implicitly imposes a duty on the buyer to inspect the property before contract and to accept the property in its physical state at the date of the contract, unless the property is in the course of construction. Condition 3.2.1 repeats the *caveat emptor* principle, placing the onus of inspecting the property on the buyer.

Read together with Condition 3.2.1, Conditions 3.2.2 and 3.2.3 have the effect of enabling a limitation to be imposed on the seller's liability under the covenants for title in an assignment of leasehold land (see Chapter 22). It should, however, be noted that in Gordon v Selico (1986) the court refused to allow the sellers to rely on a similarly worded condition contained in the Law Society conditions of sale because of the seller's fraud. The court said that the caveat emptor principle had no application where a buyer had been induced by fraud to enter a contract.

The use of the word 'reasonably' in Condition 3.1.2 (c) suggests that the seller is under some duty to investigate for disclosable incumbrances and cannot ignore suspicious circumstances.

## SCPC Condition 3.1

**5.10**   SCPC Condition 3.1 provides as follows:

2   'MATTERS AFFECTING THE PROPERTY

3.1   Freedom from incumbrances

3.1.1   The seller is selling the property free from incumbrances, other than those mentioned in condition 3.1.2.

3.1.2   The incumbrances subject to which the property is sold are:

(a)   those specified in the contract

(b)   those discoverable by inspection of the property before the contract

(c)   those the seller does not and could not reasonably know about

(d)   matters, other than monetary charges or incumbrances, disclosed or which would have been disclosed by the searches and enquiries which a prudent buyer would have made before entering into the contract

(e)   public requirements.

3.1.3   After the contract is made, the seller is to give the buyer written details without delay of any new public requirement and of anything in writing which he learns about concerning a matter covered by Condition 3.1.2.

3.1.4   The buyer is to bear the cost of complying with any outstanding public requirement and is to indemnify the seller against any liability resulting from a public requirement.'

**5.11**   SCPC Condition 3.2 provides as follows:

'3.2   PHYSICAL STATE

3.2.1   The buyer accepts the property in the physical state it is in at the date of the contract unless the seller is building or converting it.

3.2.2   A leasehold property is sold subject to any subsisting breach of a condition or tenant's obligation relating to the physical state of the property which renders the lease liable to forfeiture.'

3.2.3   A sub-lease is granted subject to any subsisting breach of a condition or tenant's obligation relating to the physical state of the property which renders the seller's own lease liable to forfeiture.

**5.12**   SCPC Condition 3.1 is similar to Standard Condition 3.1. However. SCPC Condition 3.1.2(d) differs from its Standard Condition counterpart favouring the seller by placing the onus on the buyer to make all searches which a prudent buyer would have made before entering into the contract. The buyer is then bound not just by entries which he actually discovers by making searches but also by those which he would have discovered had he made those searches. The wording of this sub-clause raises the issue of which searches should a prudent buyer make? No definitive answer exists to this question since it depends on the circumstances of each individual transaction. Clearly in view of the burden placed on the buyer by this sub-clause the buyer's solicitor will need to err on the side of caution and make or consider making a number of less usual searches depending on the nature of the property. Failure to do so, in circumstances where the failure caused loss to the buyer client could result in the buyer succeeding in a negligence action against his own solicitor.

**5.13**   SCPC Condition 3.2 is identical in its wording to Standard Condition 3.2 (see above).

# Chapter 6

# Grants and Reservations

## The general law

**6.1**  The seller who is selling part of his present property may grant easements, such as rights of way, to the buyer over the seller's retained land. Provision for this grant is usually made expressly in the contract although the grant of new easements will be implied in certain limited cases, for example an easement of necessity for a right of way over land which has no other means of access (*Pinnington v Gallard* (1853); see also *Nickerson v Barraclough* (1981)). An easement may also be implied where such implication is necessary to effect the common intention of the parties, as in the case of a right of support for a party wall (see, for example, *Richards v Rose* (1853)).

Rights enjoyed with the land pass to a buyer under section 62 of the LPA 1925. Where a seller sells part only of his land, section 62 may in particular circumstances operate to create new easements over the land retained by the seller. Further, the doctrine of *Wheeldon v Burrows* (1879) may operate on a disposal of part of land by a seller to give the buyer such rights as are continuous and apparent and (possibly) necessary to the reasonable enjoyment of the land conveyed. Formal contracts usually modify the operation of these rules.

Both section 62 of the LPA and *Wheeldon v Burrows* operate in favour of the buyer only. There is no reciprocal section or rule which will reserve to the seller rights which he has previously enjoyed over the land now being sold unless they are rights of necessity. Thus if the seller wishes to continue to exercise such rights, he must expressly reserve these rights in the contract (see also Chapter 21).

## Standard Condition 3.4

**6.2**  Condition 3.4 of the Standard Conditions of Sale provides as follows:

'3.4   *Retained land*

Where after the transfer the seller will be retaining land near the property:

  (a)   the buyer will have no right of light or air over the retained land, but

  (b)   in other respects the seller and the buyer will each have the rights over the land of the other which they would have had if they were two separate buyers to whom the seller had made simultaneous transfers of the property and the retained land.

The transfer is to contain appropriate express terms.'

*Effect of the condition*

**6.3**     The buyer is precluded from the acquisition of rights of light or air over the seller's retained land to which he might otherwise have become entitled by the operation of section 62 of the Law of Property Act 1925 or under the rule in *Wheeldon v Burrows*. It is unclear whether the condition simply seeks to exclude the acquisition of such rights in the present transfer, or whether it will also prevent such rights from being acquired by prescription in the future. The land retained by the seller should be expressly defined in the contract in order to avoid future arguments about the precise extent of the land which is referred to in this condition. The seller may require the purchase deed to contain reservations in his favour over the land sold off, but he is entitled to insist only on such reservations as would have been implied by section 62 of the Law of Property Act 1925 or by the rule in *Wheeldon v Burrows* if the seller had been buying, rather than selling, the land (*Swanborough v Coventry* (1832)).

The extent of the reservations to which the seller is entitled under the condition is limited and may not be sufficient to preserve the amenities of the seller's retained land. Where the seller requires reservations to be included in the purchase deed an express contractual condition should be inserted to deal with the matter. If the seller does not make express provision for reservations in the contract and then approves a draft purchase deed from the buyer which does not provide for reservations, he might be held to have waived his right to the inclusion of the reservations. Subject to this, the seller is entitled to ask the court to rectify the deed in order to give effect to his entitlement to reservations. An order for rectification cannot be obtained where a third party has acquired rights over the property without notice of the claim for rectification. Subject to the exclusion of rights of light and air, the only rights granted to the buyer will be those to which he is entitled under either section 62 of the Law of Property Act 1925 or the rule in *Wheeldon v Burrows*. These implied rights may be insufficient for the buyer, who should seek to amend this condition by a special condition which will set out fully his entitlement to easements and rights.

## Suggested amendments

**6.4**     In most cases the easements and reservations given by this condition will be inadequate to meet the requirements of the parties on the sale of part of land and express easements and reservations, tailored to fit the particular situation in hand, should be included by special condition. In any event, rights which are to be expressly granted and reserved should be set out in the special conditions in order to avoid subsequent contention.

Sales of part are further considered in Chapter 21.

## SCPC Condition 3.4

**6.5**     SCPC Condition 3.4 contains identical wording to Standard Condition 3.4 and the comments expressed above have equal application to this condition.

# Chapter 7

# Identity of the Property

## The particulars of sale

### Purpose of particulars

**7.1**    The purpose of the particulars of sale is to describe accurately both the physical extent of, and the estate in, the land which is the subject of the contract. (Contrast the conditions of sale, the purpose of which is to set out the terms on which the seller is prepared to sell the land.) The particulars should also mention rights which are attached to the property, the benefit of which will pass with the land, and the incumbrances to which that land is subject and to which the land will remain subject after completion of the present sale. Thus charges, onerous covenants and easements should be referred to in the particulars, but usually, the details of such incumbrances are reserved to the special conditions.

### Error in the particulars

**7.2**    An error in the particulars will be a misdescription which may allow the buyer to rescind the contract. It is therefore essential to set out an accurate description of the land in the particulars. The dangers of following word for word the description of the land contained in an earlier document cannot be overstressed.

### Plans

**7.3**    A plan annexed to the contract may help to identify the property and is necessary where part only of the seller's present land is being sold. Plans must be drawn to comply with Land Registry requirements.

### Registered land

**7.4**    Registered land is normally described in accordance with the description contained in the property register of the title and by reference to the filed plan and title number of the property. To describe land as 'registered land' without any qualification implies that the land is registered with absolute title. Thus if the land is registered with a title other than absolute, this fact must be stated in the particulars in order to avoid liability for misdescription.

The boundaries of registered land, as shown on the filed plan, are general boundaries only and should not be relied on as showing their precise extent. If actual loss is suffered through an error made by the registry in drawing a map or plan, compensation may be payable by the Chief Land Registrar.

## Presumptions relating to boundaries

**7.5**     Where no definite indication of ownership of a boundary exists the following rebuttable presumptions will apply.

### Hedges and ditches

**7.6**     When two adjoining properties are separated by a hedge and single man-made ditch, both hedge and ditch belong to the owner of the land on which the hedge is planted (*Vowles v Miller* (1810)).

### Rivers

**7.7**     The bed of a tidal river belongs to the Crown. The owner of land on each bank of a non-tidal river owns the bed of the river up to the middle of the stream. The right to fish the river belongs to the owner of the river bed unless such right has been alienated.

### Roads

**7.8**     The owner of the land adjoining a road is the owner of the soil of one-half of the road. This general presumption, although applying equally to town and country roads, is only likely to be of assistance nowadays in relation to privately owned roads since various statutes vest the ownership of publicly maintained roads in the highway authority.

### Party walls

**7.9**     Party walls are to be treated as if they were severed vertically, the owner of the land on either side being entitled to such rights of support and user over the rest of the structure as are necessary (Law of Property Act 1925, s 38(1)). The common law provisions relating to the maintenance of such walls are complex and it is advisable for express provisions to be made in the contract.

## Evidence of identity at common law

**7.10**     The seller is required to prove that the physical identity of the property itself equates with the identity of the property as described in the title deeds. If the description of the property in the contract differs from that in the deeds, the buyer is entitled to further evidence in order to establish that the two descriptions are identical.

These obligations may be difficult to satisfy in the case of an older property where the existence and extent of the boundaries is unclear. The conditions of sale often alleviate the seller's obligation to comply fully with these strict rules.

## Contractual conditions relating to identity

**7.11** A condition precluding the buyer from requiring further evidence of identity than is afforded by comparing the contract with the title deeds normally implies that the description in the deeds will substantially identify the property. If this is not the case, the seller will be unable, despite the condition, to enforce the contract (*Flower v Hartopp* (1843)).

This implication is negated by a condition which refers to 'such identity *if any* as is afforded by the deeds'.

A condition which requires the buyer to accept the description in the deeds as being 'conclusive' will preclude the buyer from requiring further evidence of identity, but the seller is unlikely to be able to obtain specific performance if the discrepancy is substantial.

The contract may contain a condition requiring the buyer to accept a statutory declaration as evidence of identity. The buyer can insist on the declaration being made by an independent person unless the contract provides otherwise. A declaration covering a period of twelve years' ownership before the present contract may be of insufficient length where the failure to identify the property occurs in an older deed. Despite the presence of such a condition the buyer may be able to insist on better evidence of identity than that given by a statutory declaration if better evidence can be found (*Bird v Fox* (1853)).

## Misdescription

*Definition*

**7.12** For this purpose a misdescription is an error in the particulars of sale which results in the seller being unable to convey the property which he has identified in the particulars. The particulars of sale form part of the contract; thus misdescription gives rise to an action for breach of contract (contrast misrepresentation and non-disclosure).

The error in the description need not necessarily arise from inaccuracy, but will be such that the buyer is misled by it. Only misstatements of fact are actionable, not mis-judgments of opinion.

Examples of misdescription include:

(a) describing freehold land as leasehold or *vice versa*;
(b) inaccurately describing the measurements of the land;
(c) a wrong statement relating to the rent obtainable from a tenanted property.

*Common law remedies for misdescription*

**7.13**   Where the misdescription is substantial, the buyer may treat the contract as discharged. He is entitled to damages where he can establish fraud. In the absence of fraud his entitlement to damages is unclear. The buyer may usually choose to enforce the contract and take a proportionate abatement in the purchase price, but the seller is unable to enforce the contract at all, even if he agrees to an abatement of the price. A misdescription is substantial if its consequence is that the property which the seller is able to convey differs greatly from that which the buyer agreed to buy. This is a question of fact and it is unclear whether a subjective or objective test should be applied to determine the question.

Where the misdescription is not substantial, the buyer may not rescind, but is entitled to an abatement in the purchase price to compensate for the error (*Watson v Burton* (1956)). The seller may obtain a decree of specific performance provided he agrees to accept an abatement in the purchase price.

Whether or not the misdescription is substantial, the buyer may obtain a decree of specific performance together with an abatement in the purchase price unless:

(a)  the loss cannot be quantified in money terms (*Rudd v Lascelles* (1900)); or

(b)  the contract provides to the contrary; or

(c)  the order would cause great hardship to the seller.

Where the misdescription favours the buyer (so that as a result of the error he obtains more or better land than that which he had contracted to buy), the seller cannot rescind, nor can he claim an increased price for the property. If the misdescription is substantial, the court may refuse the buyer's request for specific performance and instead leave the buyer to sue for breach of contract. In this case substantial damages for loss of bargain would be payable (*Lloyd v Stanbury* (1971)).

The buyer will not be entitled to compensation for the misdescription if he was aware of it at the time when the contract was made or if the error does not affect the value of the property (*Castle v Wilkinson* (1870)).

The buyer should pursue his remedies before completion. At that time the contract merges with the conveyance and normally the only remedy available after completion will be an action on the covenants for title under the Law of Property (Miscellaneous Provisions) Act 1994. Exceptionally, rescission may be available after completion if the misdescription is actionable as a misrepresentation (see Chapter 8). An abatement in the purchase price can only be claimed after completion if the misdescription could not have been discovered before completion.

Despite the above, the seller may be able to avoid specific performance and/or the payment of compensation to the buyer by availing himself of a contractual right to rescind. Whether or not he is able to do this will depend on the construction of the particular clause. Most such clauses allow rescission only if the seller cannot make good title and they are strictly construed (see Chapter 24). No clause of this type is contained either in the Standard Conditions of Sale or the Standard Commercial Property Conditions.

### Clauses excluding liability for misdescription

**7.14**    A clause purporting to exclude liability for misdescription will not be effective to deprive the buyer of his right to rescind if the property differs substantially from its description (*Flight v Booth* (1834)). A clause excluding the buyer's right to compensation or damages may be effective if the buyer seeks specific performance. However, if it is the seller who is seeking the decree the court may still order a reduction in the purchase price. A seller who knew of the error at the time the contract was made will not be able to rely on an exclusion clause (*Re Englefield Holdings Ltd and Sinclair's Contract* (1962)).

## Standard Condition 4.4

**7.15**    Condition 4.4 of the Standard Conditions of Sale provides:

'4.4    *Defining the property*

4.4.1    The seller need not:

(a)    prove the exact boundaries of the property

(b)    prove who owns fences, ditches, hedges or walls

(c)    separately identify parts of the property with different titles further than he may be able to do from information in his possession.

4.4.2    The buyer may, if it is reasonable, require the seller to make or obtain, pay for and hand over a statutory declaration about facts relevant to the matters mentioned in condition 4.4.1. The form of the declaration is to be agreed by the buyer, who must not unreasonably withhold his agreement.'

### Effect of the condition

**7.16**    The uncertainty of the common law rule requiring the seller to identify parts of the property which relate to different titles is overcome by Condition 4.4.1 which relieves the seller of this obligation. Some identification of boundaries may be called for by the buyer, but the seller is not required to define these precisely.

The seller's common law duty to identify the property with the description in the title deeds is slightly alleviated by the condition. If the evidence shown by the deeds is insufficient, the seller must, if so required by the buyer, obtain a statutory declaration to support the evidence of identity. No limit is placed on the length of ownership to be covered by the declaration.

The seller must pay for the declaration, which he must submit to the buyer for approval, before having it sworn. The buyer cannot unreasonably withhold his consent to the form of the declaration. No time limit is imposed either on the seller for submission of the declaration for approval or on the buyer to approve the declaration. It seems that the common law implication that these matters must be dealt with within a reasonable time will therefore apply.

If the buyer finds that the evidence of identity provided by both the deeds and the declaration is still insufficient he cannot be forced to complete (*Re Bramwell's Contract* (1969)).

Condition 7.1 contains an exclusion clause which attempts to limit the seller's liability for misdescription. This condition is discussed in Chapter 8.

## Suggested amendments

**7.17** If it is thought that a statutory declaration may be needed in order to prove the identity of the property, the seller may choose to include a special condition setting out the terms on which he is prepared to give such a declaration. It may be desirable to limit the length of the time to be covered by the declaration to, say, twelve years, although from the buyer's point of view, a declaration which is limited to twelve years' ownership may be inadequate if the mistake in identity occurred in an earlier deed. It may also be sensible to place a time limit on the buyer within which he must approve the form of the declaration, or if he fails to agree within the given time limit, require him to accept the declaration in the form drafted by the seller. The condition as drafted leaves room for argument between the parties since its operation depends on the reasonableness of the buyer in both asking for the declaration and in approving its contents. Any amendment which is made to this condition should seek to remove these areas of doubt.

## SCPC Condition 6.4

**7.18** SCPC 6.4 is in identical wording to Standard Condition 4.3 and the comments above in relation to the Standard Condition have equal application here.

# Chapter 8

# Misrepresentation

## The general law

*Definition*

**8.1**    A misrepresentation is an untrue statement of past or present fact
which induces the formation of a contract and if it is not repeated in the
contract will not form part of the contract. The statement can be made in
writing, by word of mouth, or even by pictures, eg in an estate agent's
brochure (see *Atlantic Estates v Ezekiel* (1991)). Statements of opinion or intention do not fall within this definition and do not give rise to a cause of action,
unless it can be shown that the opinion or intention was never reasonably held
(*Edgington v Fitzmaurice* (1885)). Statements of law are not actionable, but the
distinction between law and fact is sometimes unclear (see, for example, *Solle
v Butcher* (1950)).

Mere silence will not normally constitute a misrepresentation, except where the
silence distorts a positive representation (*Dimmock v Hallett* (1866)). Other
exceptions to this rule are where the contracting parties are in a fiduciary relationship, or in contracts *uberrimae fidei*. The misrepresentation must have
produced a misunderstanding in the mind of the person to whom it was made
(the representee), and that misunderstanding must have been one of the reasons
which influenced the representee's decision to enter the contract. The statement
need not have been the sole or main inducement influencing the decision to
contract, but it must have been one of the factors which influenced that decision. For that reason no action will lie in respect of a misrepresentation if it
can be shown that the representee was unaware of the statement, or did not rely
on it, or knew the statement was untrue. There is a duty on the representor to
correct a statement which, although correct at the time of making it, subsequently becomes untrue.

*Types of misrepresentation*

**8.2**    Since the Misrepresentation Act 1967 there are effectively three categories of misrepresentation:

(a) *innocent*: the party making the statement honestly believed the statement
    to be true and had grounds for so believing;

(b) *fraudulent*: a deliberately dishonest statement made 'knowingly, or
    without belief in its truth or recklessly, careless whether it be true or

false' (*Derry v Peek* (1889));

(c) *negligent*: a statement made carelessly, without its accuracy having been checked, but not a deliberate untruth. Carelessness does not necessarily amount to negligence in the tortious sense of that word.

## *Remedies*

**8.3** A misrepresentation is a statement made during the negotiations leading up to the contract and if it is not repeated in the contract itself, no action for breach of contract will be available.

If the misrepresentation made before the contract is repeated in the contract it becomes a contractual term, in which case an action for breach of contract (usually resulting in damages for breach of warranty) will lie. Alternatively, in this situation section 1 of the Misrepresentation Act 1967 allows the contractual term to be treated as a misrepresentation, and an action may be pursued under the Misrepresentation Act 1967.

Although common law remedies are available, it is usual to pursue a remedy under the 1967 Act where rescission and/or damages may be awarded.

The burden of proof under this Act lies on the party making the statement to prove that he had grounds for believing, and did believe the statement he made was true, up to the time the contract was made, that is, that he was not negligent or fraudulent in making the statement. If this can be proved the representee's remedies are limited to rescission or damages in lieu of rescission under section 2(2) of the Act.

If the statement is found to have been made negligently or fraudulently, then in addition to the remedy under section 2(2), damages may be awarded under section 2(1).

Rescission is an equitable remedy; its award is therefore always in the discretion of the court, but will not be available if the contract has been affirmed, that is, the representee with full knowledge of the misrepresentation expressly or impliedly shows an intention to remain bound by the contract. Affirmation may be implied by lapse of time, where the representee takes no steps to bring the contract to an end.

Rescission is also barred if it is not possible to restore the parties substantially to their pre-contract position, for example where a third party has acquired rights in the land which is the subject matter of the action. The creation of a mortgage by the buyer over the land may thus preclude rescission.

Both subsections potentially give rise to an award of damages, but awards made under both subsections are not cumulative. Despite the fact that the misrepresentation action is conceived out of a contractual situation, the assessment of damages under the Act is made on a tortious basis (*Chesneau v Interhome* (1983); *Archer v Brown* (1985)).

If the buyer discovers the misrepresentation before exchange of contracts, he has the choice of withdrawing from negotiations at that stage before he has suffered any loss. In many cases the buyer will not discover the untruth of the statement until after completion, but the fact that completion has taken place does not prevent an action from being pursued under the 1967 Act.

Where the misrepresentation has been repeated as a contractual term, an action for breach of contract will lie. Otherwise it may be possible to establish that the statement constitutes a collateral contract, or to sue for negligence under the principle established in *Hedley Byrne & Co Ltd v Heller & Partners Ltd* (1964).

An action will lie in the tort of deceit for a fraudulent misrepresentation, but the burden of proof in this action lies on the representee (compare the remedy under the 1967 Act).

### Exclusion clauses

**8.4**    An exclusion clause must be properly incorporated into the contract. Where the contract is written, the parties are deemed to have knowledge of its terms whether or not they have read them (*L'Estrange v F Graucob Ltd* (1934)). In other cases, adequate notice of the clause must have been given at or before the time the contract was made.

The wording of an exclusion clause is strictly interpreted by the courts. The clause must be carefully and clearly drafted, since any ambiguity is construed against the party seeking to rely on the clause. A clause which merely excludes liability for oral misrepresentations will not give protection against written misrepresentations and *vice versa*.

Section 3 of the Misrepresentation Act 1967, as amended by section 8 of the Unfair Contract Terms Act 1977, permits the enforcement of a clause purporting either to restrict liability for misrepresentation, or the remedies for misrepresentation, only in so far as the clause satisfies the reasonableness test laid down in section 11 of the Unfair Contract Terms Act 1977.

The burden of proving reasonableness lies on the party seeking to rely on the exclusion clause.

Reasonableness is to be judged in the light of circumstances which were, or ought reasonably to have been, known to or in the contemplation of the parties when the contract was made. The test is applied subjectively, therefore identically worded clauses may held to be reasonable in the context of one set of circumstances and unreasonable in the context of another (see, for example, *Walker v Boyle* (1982)).

## Standard Condition 7

**8.5**    Condition 7 of the Standard Conditions of Sale provides:

'7.1    *Errors and omissions*

7.1.1    If any plan or statement in the contract, or in the negotiations leading to it, is or was misleading or inaccurate due to an error or omission, the remedies available are as follows.

7.1.2    When there is a material difference between the description or value of the property or of any of the chattels included in the contract as represented and as it is, the injured party is entitled to damages.

7.1.3    An error or omission only entitles the buyer to rescind the contract:

    (a)    where it results from fraud or recklessness, or

    (b)    where he would be obliged, to his prejudice, to accept property differing substantially (in quantity, quality or tenure) from what the error or omission had led him to expect.

7.2    *Rescission*

If either party rescinds the contract:

    (a)    unless the rescission is a result of the buyer's breach of contract the deposit is to be repaid to the buyer with accrued interest.

    (b)    the buyer is to return any documents he received from the seller and is to cancel any registration of the contract.'

## Reasonableness

**8.6**    Condition 7 attempts to limit the rights of the parties in the event of misdescription, misrepresentation or non-disclosure. As an exclusion clause, its validity is subject to the reasonableness test in the Unfair Contract Terms Act 1977 (see para 8.1). There is therefore no guarantee that the clause will give adequate protection to the seller in any given situation. The seller may choose to delete Condition 7.1 from the contract and to substitute his own exclusion clause, but that too would be subject to the reasonableness test. The existence of this test means that there will never be certainty over the validity of an exclusion clause until the clause is actually tested by the court in relation to the facts of the particular contract in which it has been incorporated. However, an argument in favour of the reasonableness of this clause is that it was drafted by the solicitors' profession, for its own use, and after consultation with the members of the profession. It does not therefore fall into quite the same category as an ordinary standard contract term which is imposed by one party on the other allowing no freedom of choice in negotiation of the contract. If this hypothesis is correct, the courts may view the question of reasonableness of this condition slightly more favourably than other standard exclusion clauses.

## Remedies

**8.7**    Under Condition 7.1.2 the buyer is entitled to damages, but not rescission, for any material misrepresentation affecting the description or value of the property. This is so whether the misrepresentation is contained in the contract, plan, or preliminary negotiations. 'Negotiations' include all pre-contract enquiries, whether made on standard forms or otherwise. Where the clause applies, compensation may be sought in respect of both oral and written misrepresentations. The word 'material' is not defined by the condition. The clause gives remedies to the 'injured party', which seems to contemplate that the seller might be the victim of the buyer's misrepresentation as well as *vice* *versa*. The right to rescind where a misrepresentation is recklessly or fraudulently made is preserved by Condition 7.1.3. This condition will also permit rescission if, as a result of the misrepresentation, the buyer is prevented from getting substantially what he contracted to buy or the seller is forced to transfer something substantially different from that which he expected to sell. Condition 7.1.2 is governed by the word 'material', but the expression 'substantial' is used in Condition 7.1.3. Neither word is defined, but it must be assumed that the draftsman would not have chosen to use the different expressions if he had intended them to have an identical meaning. Misrepresentations relating to the condition of the property do not fall within the scope of this clause (see Condition 3.2.1), nor those concerning the amount of rent lawfully recoverable from a tenanted property (Condition 3.3.2). When Conditions 7.1.2 and 7.1.3 are read together, the result is that remedies are precluded only where the misrepresentation was not material or substantial in its effect and was wholly innocent, that is, where the representor did not know and had no means of knowing the truth.

## Misdescription

**8.8**     Conditions 7.1.2 and 7.1.3 also regulate the parties' remedies for misdescription. Both compensation and rescission are excluded where the misdescription is not substantial. If the misdescription is substantial compensation and/or rescission may be available to either party. (See further on misdescription in Chapter 7.)

## Non-disclosure

**8.9**     The word 'omission' in the condition indicates that it is intended that the parties' remedies for non-disclosure are also to be governed by these provisions. The remedies available are similar to those for misdescription, although it should be remembered that a non-disclosure may also amount to a misrepresentation by silence and thus the comments on misrepresentation above may be equally relevant to this situation. (See further on non-disclosure in Chapter 5.)

## Rescission

**8.10**     The parties' rights in the event of rescission are governed by Condition 7.2 which applies whenever rescission occurs (that is, the condition is not limited solely to rescission for misrepresentation). Except where rescission is a result of the buyer's breach of contract (note that misrepresentation is not a breach of contract), the buyer is entitled to the return of his deposit with accrued interest. Accrued interest is defined in Condition 1.1.1(a) (see Chapter 2 above). The buyer is to return documents to the seller and to cancel any registration of the contract, presumably at his own expense.

## Suggested amendments

**8.11**    If a seller chooses to substitute his own version of an exclusion clause in place of Condition 7, such clause will remain subject to the reasonableness test in the Unfair Contract Terms Act 1977; its validity would therefore be uncertain, and the seller must bear in mind that the stricter the exclusion clause he inserts, the harder it will be to satisfy the reasonableness test. The seller may, however, decide to amend Condition 7 to limit its application to make the seller liable only for written statements made by himself or his agents. As presently drafted the seller could be liable for statements made by third parties over whom he had no control. A buyer may prefer to delete this condition in its entirety from the contract, relying instead on his remedies under the general law.

## SCPC Conditions 9.1 and 9.2

**8.12**    Except as noted below SCPC Conditions 9.1 and 9.2 are identically worded to their Standard conditions counterparts and have the same effect. SCPC has one additional sub-clause in condition 9.2 as follows:

> '9.2 (c)   the seller's duty to pay any returned premium under Condition 7.1.2
> (e) (whenever received) is unaffected.'

This additional sub-clause relates the return of an insurance premium which may have been paid by the buyer under the provisions of Condition 7 (see Chapter 12). The reasonableness test contained in the Unfair Contract Terms Act 1977 does not apply to commercial contracts.

# Chapter 9

# Title

## Proof of title

**9.1** The seller, at his own expense, must prove to the buyer that he is entitled to transfer the land which he is contracting to sell, or that he can compel someone else to do so. Traditionally, proof of title was not tendered to the buyer until after contracts had been exchanged, but current practice is to supply the buyer with evidence of title at the draft contract stage of the transaction so that queries arising out of the title (if any) are resolved before exchange.

### *Adverse possession*

**9.2** Where the seller's title is based on adverse possession under the Limitation Act 1980, unless the contract provides to the contrary, he must prove the title of the former owner and show how that title has been extinguished. This is normally done by statutory declaration. Title cannot be commenced with a statutory declaration because it is not a good root of title.

## Condition 4

**9.3** Condition 4 of the Standard Conditions provides for title as follows:

'4.1 *Proof of title*

4.1.1 Without cost to the buyer, the seller is to provide the buyer with proof of the title to the property and of his ability to transfer it, or to procure its transfer.

4.1.2 Where the property has a registered title the proof is to include official copies of the items referred to in rules 134(1)(a) and (b) and 135 (a) of the Land Registration Rules 2003, so far as they are not to be discharged or overridden at or before completion.

4.1.3 Where the property has an unregistered title, the proof is to include:

(a) an abstract of title or an epitome of title with photocopies of the documents, and

(b) production of every document or an abstract, epitome or copy of it with an original marking by a conveyancer either against the original or an examined abstract or an examined copy.

### 4.3 *Timetable*

4.3.1 Subject to condition 4.2 and to the extent that the seller did not take the steps described in condition 4.1.1 before the contract was made, the following are the steps for deducing and investigating the title to the property to be taken within the following time limits:

| *Step* | *Time Limit* |
|---|---|
| 1. The seller is to comply with condition 4.11 | Immediately after making the contract |
| 2. The buyer may raise written requisitions | Six working days after either the date of the seller's evidence of title on which the contract or the date of delivery of the requisitions are raised whichever is the later |
| 3. The seller is to reply in writing to any requisitions raised | Four working days after receiving the requisitions. |
| 4. The buyer may make written observations on the seller's replies | Three working days after receiving the replies |

The time limit on the buyer's right to raise requisitions applies even where the seller supplies incomplete evidence of his title, but the buyer may, within six working days from delivery of any further evidence, raise further requisitions resulting from that evidence.

**9.4** The reference in Condition 4.3 to Condition 4.2 deals with requisitions (see Chapter 15). The drafting of Condition 4 assumes that the normal practice of deduction of title before exchange will occur and the timetable specified in this condition is in effect a default timetable which would only need to be used in cases where the parties had failed to make their own arrangements for deduction and investigation of title. Condition 4.1 emphasises that it is the seller's responsibility to deduce title satisfactorily and at his own cost. This reflects both what currently happens in practice and the ethos of the Home Information Pack provisions. Copies of a registered title are to be official copies.

*Unregistered titles*

**9.5** Condition 4.1.3 requires the seller to supply the buyer with the customary abstract or epitome in the case of unregistered titles. The condition does not specify the contents of the abstract, which will thus be governed by section 44 of the Law of Property Act 1925, unless altered by special condition. A special condition will in any event be required to identify the document which is to form the root of title. By section 45(4) of the Law of Property Act 1925, the buyer may call for production of documents forming part of the title which are not in the custody of the seller, his mortgagee or trustee, provided that the buyer pays the cost of production of such documents. Under Condition 4.1.3 the seller is required at his own expense to produce the originals or marked abstracts of all documents forming part of the title to the buyer. No time limit is specified within which the buyer may call for production, but at common law the buyer's right to verify title expires with his time limit for raising requisitions.

*Time not of the essence*

**9.6**    Time is not of the essence for the delivery of proof of title, but any delay by the seller will be taken into account in assessing relative fault in the event of a delayed completion (see Chapter 21). Since evidence of title is normally delivered to the buyer before exchange of contracts, this is unlikely to cause problems in practice. Time is of the essence in relation to requisitions on title.

## Suggested amendments

**9.7**    Condition 4.1 is suitable for use in most freehold transactions, but requires amendment to meet the special circumstances of a sub-sale, or where the seller's title is awaiting registration at the Land Registry. Both of these matters are discussed in Chapter 24. In the rare cases where title documents are not in the possession of the seller, his lender or trustees, the seller may consider excluding the buyer's right to call for the production of original documents which are not within the custody of these persons. This amendment would have the effect of excluding section 45(4) of the Law of Property Act 1925 which entitles the buyer to call for the production of such documents at his own expense.

## The Protocol

**9.8**    By para 4.4, evidence of title is to be supplied to the buyer with the draft contract.

## SCPC Conditions 4.1 and 4.2

**9.9**    SCPC Conditions 6.1 and 6.3 are identically worded to their Standard Condition counterparts and have the same effect. Comment on the Standard Conditions appears above.

# Chapter 10

# Chattels

## The general law

*Chattels*

**10.1**    Chattels are not part of the land. They will not therefore automatically pass to the buyer with the property and unless otherwise agreed the seller is entitled to remove them before completion. Chattels which are intended to be included in the sale should be itemised in a special condition of the contract. If the price of the chattels is to be additional to the purchase price, this should be made clear in the special condition.

*Appointment of price*

**10.2**    Even where the price of the chattels is included in the purchase price, it may be possible to apportion the purchase price between the chattels and the land. An apportionment of the purchase price may be desirable where its effect is to bring the actual purchase price of the land into the nil band for stamp duty purposes. However, the apportionment must be an honest estimate of the value of the chattels – any over-valuation may be a fraud on the Inland Revenue and thus render the contract illegal (*Saunders v Edwards* (1987)).

Where the purchase price is apportioned, the contract, even though embodied in one document, is effectively two contracts; one for the sale of the land to which the Law of Property Act 1925 applies, and the second for the sale of chattels to which the Sale of Goods Act 1979 applies. Thus, as far as the chattels are concerned, section 12 of the Sale of Goods Act 1979 implies a non-excludable warranty that the seller is selling the chattels free from incumbrances (such as an undischarged hire-purchase agreement). In the event of breach of that warranty, the buyer will have an action in damages against the seller which is quite separate from any right of action which he may have in respect of defects in the land itself.

*Title to chattels*

**10.3**    The goods should be specifically named items and in such an event section 18 of the Sale of Goods Act 1979 will also apply, although this section is capable of exclusion by a contractual term. Section 18 provides that title in specific chattels passes to the buyer at the date of the contract and the risk of loss or damage lies with the buyer from that time. Where section 18 is implied, the buyer should consider insuring the chattels on exchange of contracts.

*Fixtures*

**10.4**    Fixtures attached to the land will pass automatically to the buyer unless expressly excluded by special condition. A special condition should itemise the fixtures which it is intended to remove.

The buyer should raise a pre-contract inquiry with the seller to ascertain whether items such as a greenhouse or central heating systems are still subject to a hire purchase or credit agreement.

Title to fixtures will have passed to the seller as soon as the items became attached to the land (*Re Allen-Mayrick's Will Trusts, Mangnall v Allen-Meyrick* (1966)) despite any outstanding credit agreement; therefore title will pass to the buyer on completion. However, to prevent any future dispute over the owner-ship of such items, the buyer may choose to insert a special condition in the contract requiring the seller to discharge any outstanding incumbrances over the fixtures on or before completion. The inclusion of this condition will at least give the buyer an enforceable remedy against the seller if he should fail to discharge the incumbrance since it its doubtful whether the implied covenants for title under the Law of Property (Miscellaneous Provisions) Act 1994 would cover this matter and Standard Condition 9 has no application to fixtures.

*Distinction between chattels and fixtures*

**10.5**    Since the practical distinction between chattels and fixtures is often unclear, it is important that the parties agree between them precisely which items in the property are to be removed and which are to remain (see *TSB Bank Plc v Botham* (1995)). A list of the agreed items may then be attached to the contract in order to avoid future disputes.

## Standard Condition 10

**10.6**    Condition 10 of the Standard Conditions of Sale provides as follows in respect of chattels:

'10.1    The following provisions apply to any chattels which are included in the contract, whether or not a separate price is to be paid for them.

10.2    The contract takes effect as a contract for sale of goods.

10.3    The buyer takes the chattels in the physical state they are in at the date of the contract.

10.4    Ownership of the chattels passes to the buyer on actual completion.'

*Effects of the Condition*

**10.7**    The effect of this condition is to postpone the passing of title in the chattels to the buyer until completion, thus ousting the effect of section 18 of the Sale of Goods Act 1979. A warranty of freedom from incumbrances will also be implied under section 12 of the Sale of Goods Act 1979, because the contract is expressed to take effect as a contract for the sale of goods. This latter provision applies irrespective of whether the purchase price of chattels has been apportioned from the value of the land. The seller is under a duty to take care of the chattels between contract and completion.

## The Protocol

**10.8**    Under the Protocol, the seller's solicitor is required to ask his client to complete the Fixtures Fittings and Contents form, listing those items which are to be removed from the property and those which are to remain, and indicating whether any additional price is to be paid for items which are to remain at the property. The completed form will then be agreed with the buyer and will form part of the contract.

## SCPC Condition 12

**10.9**    SCPC Condition 9 provides as follows:

'12.1    The following provisions apply to any chattels which are included in the contract.

12.2    The contract takes effect as a contract for the sale of goods.

12.3    The buyer takes the chattels in the physical state they are in at the date of the contract.

12.4    Ownership of the chattels passes to the buyer on actual completion but they are at the buyer's risk from the contract date.'

**10.10**    Although this condition is similar to Standard Condition 10 (see above), it differs in one important respect. Under the SCPC title in the chattels is to pass on actual completion  (as under Standard Condition 10) but risk in the chattels passes to the buyer on exchange. Under Standard Condition 10 risk is deferred until completion. It is likely that this change has been made in the SCPC to reflect the changes made to the insurance of the property (Chapter 12). However, the form of wording of SCPC Condition 12.4 is not satisfactory from the buyer's point of view. If the buyer assumes the risk then he should insure against that risk. It will be extremely difficult for the buyer to obtain cover in respect of chattels which he does not own. SCPC 12.4 should therefore be amended to defer the passing of risk until completion. The wording of Standard Condition 10.3 defers risk and thus could be substituted in a commercial contract.

# Chapter 11

# Deposit

## The general law

**11.1**    Payment of the deposit acts as a part payment of the purchase price. More important than this from the seller's point of view is that the payment is an indication of the buyer's serious intention to be bound by the contract, since the buyer may have to forfeit the deposit if he fails to complete (*Howe v Smith* (1884); *Hinton v Sparkes* (1868)).

*The amount*

**11.2**    Unless the contract expressly provides for the payment of a deposit, none is payable.

It is customary for a payment of 10% of the purchase price to be payable on exchange of contracts. Where the purchase price of chattels is apportioned in the contract the 10% is calculated exclusive of the price of the chattels.

A lower deposit may be negotiated, but *Morris v Duke-Cohan & Co* (1975) suggests that it may be professional negligence for the seller's solicitor to accept a deposit of less than 10% without his client's express authority. Despite this case, it is currently common practice for a deposit of less than 10% to be accepted.

Deposits in excess of 10% are very rare, and cannot be justified in normal circumstances (see *Dojap Investments Ltd v Workers Trust and Merchant Bank Ltd* (1993) where the forfeiture of a 24% deposit was held to be a penalty).

*Preliminary deposits*

**11.3**    The seller's estate agent will often ask the buyer to pay a small pre-contract deposit to him pending negotiation of the contract. There is no legal obligation on the buyer to pay this sum. It does not give the buyer any priority over other prospective buyers, nor does it bind the seller to sell the property to the buyer.

Unless the seller has authorised the estate agent to take a preliminary deposit, the risk of loss of that deposit through the agent's insolvency or misappropriation falls on the buyer (*Sorrell v Finch* (1977)).

If the seller has authorised a deposit to be taken, and held in the capacity of 'agent for the seller', the seller will be liable if the agent defaults. It is unclear what the position would be if such a deposit were authorised to be held in the capacity of 'stakeholder'.

The buyer is entitled to demand the return of his pre-contract deposit at any time, irrespective of whether the seller has authorised such a deposit to be taken, or of the capacity in which it was being held (*Burt v Claude Cousins & Co Ltd* (1971)).

If the buyer is persuaded to pay a preliminary deposit, he should ensure that the sum paid is small (say, £100), and that he obtains a written receipt for the payment which specifies that the payment is made 'subject to contract'.

The contract will normally require the payment of the 10% deposit to be made to the seller's solicitor, in which case the solicitor should check whether a preliminary deposit has been paid and the estate agent should hand such preliminary deposit to the seller's solicitor on exchange. In practice this is often not done, and the agent retains the deposit until completion, when it is credited against the commission payable by the seller.

## New houses

**11.4**   The builder of a new house will similarly demand a preliminary deposit from a prospective buyer. The position here is slightly different from that outlined above, since the terms of payment often reserve a particular plot for the buyer for a specified period, with a guarantee that the purchase price will not be increased for the period of the 'option'. Whether that deposit is returnable if the buyer decides to withdraw depends on the terms on which the deposit is paid.

The buyer should ensure that he fully understands the terms of payment of the deposit, and should obtain a written receipt.

## Dishonoured deposit cheque

**11.5**   Breach of the condition in the contract relating to the payment of the deposit is a fundamental breach of contract. The seller has the option of either keeping the contract alive for the benefit of both parties, or of treating the contract as discharged by the breach, and in either event of suing for damages (*Millichamp v Jones* (1983)).

The contract should be drafted to indicate precisely what the rights of the parties are in the event of dishonour of the cheque. Such a contractual clause will not solve all the problems which may occur with the dishonour of the cheque. An express contractual condition may give the seller the right to withdraw from the contract – but he may remain bound by another contract (for example, to purchase another house) which he had entered in reliance on this one. The only real solution is to specify an infallible method of payment of the deposit. A condition which states that payment of the deposit must be made by solicitor's clients' account cheque, building society cheque, or banker's draft should meet this requirement. Alternatively, the seller may choose to accept the buyer's own cheque, provided that the cheque is endorsed by the buyer's solicitor. This method does not guarantee that the cheque will be met on presentation, but goes a long way towards guaranteeing its creditworthiness, since the buyer's solicitor should only endorse the cheque in a situation where he is sure of his client's financial status. (The buyer's solicitor would be personally liable if the cheque was not met – section 56 of the Bills of Exchange Act 1882.) The use of a deposit guarantee scheme eliminates most problems in connection with the payment of deposits but in practice use of such a scheme is rare. The Standard Conditions of Sale do not provide for the payment of the deposit to be made by this method and if desired a special condition would have to be added to the contract. A lender's deposit free scheme may also be used to guarantee the deposit. The terms of these schemes vary from lender to lender and before accepting the buyer's request to use such a scheme the seller should check that its terms adequately protect the seller, particularly in the case of the buyer's default under the contract.

*Capacity in which the deposit is held*

**11.6**    The deposit may be held in one of three capacities:

- (a)  as agent for the seller;
- (b)  as agent for the buyer;
- (c)  as stakeholder.

It is unlikely that the seller would agree to the deposit being held to the buyer's order; the capacity of 'agent for the buyer' is thus rarely met in practice. In the absence of contrary agreement, solicitors and estate agents receive the deposit as agent for the seller, but an auctioneer holds in the capacity of stakeholder. This general rule can be varied by express contractual condition.

If the deposit is held as agent for the seller, the agent may hand the money to the seller before completion. Thus the seller may use the deposit received on his sale contract towards the money needed for the deposit on his own purchase. This may present the buyer with problems in recovering the money if for some reason the contract does not proceed.

A stakeholder is the principal for both parties. The deposit money can therefore be handed to one party without the consent of the other, but the stakeholder risks liability in damages if he wrongly pays the money to one party. Normally the stake should not be handed over until completion takes place. In this situation the seller is unable to use the deposit obtained from his sale towards the deposit on another transaction, and will have to finance the further transaction from his own funds, or by means of a bridging loan. If the buyer were to consent to the seller's using the deposit to finance his own purchase, it is arguable that the buyer would be protected from losing his money by having a double equitable charge over the seller's present property and over the property which the seller is buying ((1970) 120 NLJ 1128). Such a charge would need to be registered as a C(iii) land charge (or notice or caution in registered land) and could only be enforced by an order for sale of the property.

## Deposit

Most deposits are held by the seller's solicitor either in the capacity of agent for the seller or stakeholder. The money is client's money and must be placed in a clients' account (Solicitors' Accounts Rules 1991, r 2(1)).

Whether the money is held as agent for the seller or stakeholder, interest may be payable under the Solicitors' Accounts Rules 1991, r 20. Where the money is held as stakeholder, interest is payable on the stake money under the Solicitors' Accounts Rules 1991. It is up to the parties to decide which of them is to be entitled to the interest. An appropriate clause must be added to the contract to deal with the payment of interest. The Law Society's recommended form of wording is: 'The stakeholder shall pay to the seller/buyer a sum equal to the interest the deposit would have earned if placed on deposit (less costs of acting as stakeholder)'.

## Estate agents

**11.7**    Preliminary deposits paid to estate agents are discussed at 11.3 above.

The Standard Conditions of Sale provide for the deposit to be held by the seller's solicitor; so an amendment to the standard general conditions will be required if an estate agent is to hold the money. The deposit may be held either as agent for the seller or as stakeholder, but in either case the risk of its loss through the agent's default generally falls on the buyer (*Sorrell v Finch* (1977)). This risk has now been minimised since the introduction of section 16 of the Estate Agents Act 1979 which requires agents to carry insurance to cover clients' money.

Section 13(1) of the Act provides further protection for the buyer since clients' money, being trust money, will not vest in a trustee in bankruptcy, should the agent be made bankrupt.

'Clients' money', which is defined by section 12 of the 1979 Act to include any contract or pre-contract deposit, must be placed in a clients' account (s 14) and is held on trust by the agent for the person who is or will become entitled to the money.

When the deposit is held as agent for the seller the agent must account for the interest earned on any deposit exceeding £500 where the interest earned is or would amount to at least £10 (reg 7 Estate Agents (Accounts) Regulations 1981, SI 1981 No 1520). It seems that there may be no obligation to account for interest earned on a deposit held as stakeholder. It is unclear whether the 1979 Act applies to an estate agent acting in the capacity of auctioneer. Where the deposit is held by an estate agent as stakeholder, the buyer will have to authorise the release of the deposit on completion.

## Fiduciary sellers

**11.8**    Where the sellers are selling as trustees, the money arising from the sale will be trust money and should never be outside the control of the trustees (Law Society's Conveyancing Handbook para B17.5.9). This requirement will be satisfied if the deposit is held by some person as agent for the seller.

*Return of deposit*

**11.9**   A preliminary deposit is returnable to the buyer on demand. If the seller cannot prove his title to the property he must return the deposit with interest, unless the contract provides otherwise (*Hodges v Earl of Litchfield* (1835)).

Where the court refuses a decree of specific performance, or in any action for the return of the deposit, the court may order its return to the purchaser (Law of Property Act 1925, s 49(2); *Universal Corporation v Five Ways Properties* (1979)).

*The unrepresented seller*

**11.10**   Where the seller is not represented by a solicitor or licensed conveyancer, it would be unwise for the buyer to pay his deposit to the seller in person or to an unqualified representative, since such a course of action may present difficulties for the buyer if the contract does not proceed to completion.

The Law Society recommends (Law Society's Conveyancing Handbook para B17.5.8) that the buyer should pay his deposit either to his own solicitor, to be held in the capacity of stakeholder, or to a reputable estate agent as stakeholder. Failing this, the deposit should be placed in a deposit account at a bank or building society in the joint names of the seller and buyer. Payment to the buyer's solicitor represents the safest course of action from the buyer's point of view, but the seller may be reluctant to agree to this. Whichever of these three courses is chosen, a special condition must be inserted in the contract to deal with this matter.

# Standard Condition 2.2

**11.11**   Condition 2.2 of the Standard Conditions of Sale provides for deposits as follows:

'2.2   *Deposit*

2.2.1   The buyer is to pay or send a deposit of 10% of the purchase price and the chattels price no later than the date of the contract.

2.2.2   If a cheque tendered in payment of all or part of the deposit is dishonoured when first presented, the seller may, within seven working days of being notified that the cheque has been dishonoured, give notice to the buyer that the contract is discharged by the buyer's breach.

2.2.3   Conditions 2.2.4 to 2.2.6 do not apply to a sale by auction.

2.2.4   The deposit is to be paid by direct debit or to the seller's conveyancer by a cheque drawn on a solicitor's or licensed conveyancer's client account.

2.2.5   If before completion date the seller agrees to buy another property in England and Wales for his residence, he may use all or any part of the deposit as a deposit in that transaction to be held on terms to the same effect as this condition and condition 2.2.6.

*Deposit*

> 2.2.6 Any deposit or part of a deposit not being used in accordance with condition 2.2.5 is to be held by the seller's conveyancer as stakeholder on terms that on completion it is paid to the seller with accrued interest.'

*Amount*

**11.12** A full deposit of 10% of the purchase price is required by Condition 2.2.1. Money payable for chattels is expressly mentioned by the condition, and the 10% will be calculated inclusive of the price of the chattels, but allowing credit for any preliminary deposit paid before exchange. The money is due not later than the date of the contract.

If a deposit of less than 10% of the purchase price has been agreed, this will have to be dealt with by special condition. Condition 6.8.3 (see Chapter 18) does acknowledge the possibility of a less than 10% deposit being taken by requiring that the balance of the 10% becomes immediately payable on service of a completion notice.

Where the sale is by private treaty or by auction, except where Condition 2.2.5 applies, the deposit is to be held by the seller's conveyancer in the capacity of stakeholder.

*Method of payment*

**11.13** Except in auction contracts payment is to be made by direct credit or solicitor's or licensed conveyancer's client account cheque only. The solicitor's cheque must be from client account, and it must be drawn on a clearing bank (see Condition 1.1.1 (c) and Chapter 2). In the unlikely event that such an instrument is not met, Condition 2.2.2, reflecting the decision is *Millichamp v Jones* (1983), gives the seller the choice of treating the contract as being discharged by the buyer's breach. To exercise this option he must serve notice on the buyer within seven working days of the dishonour. The wording of the condition releases the seller from any obligation to make a second presentation of the cheque. The option of treating the contract as discharged will apply only if the time limit is honoured and if payment has been tendered in accordance with the condition. If the buyer's own cheque is accepted by the seller and then dishonoured, this right would seem not to be available. Although not expressly mentioned by the condition, the seller will probably also have the option of suing on the cheque because of the separate cause of action arising out of the cheque itself.

*Use of deposit money in related transaction*

**11.14** Condition 2.2.5 permits the seller to use part or all of the deposit payable by the buyer towards the deposit payable by the seller in a related transaction. 'Related transaction' is defined as meaning the purchase of a property in England and Wales for the seller's residence. This is subject to the proviso that the money which is used by the seller to fund his own deposit is held by its recipient on terms to the same effect as those contained in Condition 2.2.5, that is, the seller's purchase contract will also have to incorporate Condition 2.2.5 or very similar wording. Although not expressly stated by the condition, such part of the deposit as is to be used by the seller in his related transaction will temporarily be held by the seller's solicitor as agent for the seller, the balance, if any, being held under the terms of Condition 2.2.6 as stakeholder.

This condition reflects the widespread practice of using the seller's sale deposit towards the deposit on his purchase, thus eliminating or reducing the amount of bridging finance needed by the seller. Some protection is given to the buyer by specifying that the seller may only use the deposit for the one purpose set out in Condition 2.2.5. Nevertheless, the buyer may not be enthusiastic about the inclusion of this condition, since if the deposit is used by the seller in this way, he has no immediate recourse to the money if the seller defaults on completion. The money may have passed through several transactions in the chain and be in the hands of an ultimate recipient whose identity is unknown to the buyer, and over whom the buyer has no control, nor from whom he has any right to demand the repayment of the money. In such a situation, the buyer's only recourse would be to sue the seller for the return of the deposit under section 49 of the Law of Property Act 1925, the success of such an action depending on the seller's solvency. Alternatively, and provided the buyer had registered his interest as a lien, the buyer could recover his deposit through a court order for the sale of the property.

*Interest*

**11.15**   Where any deposit (or part of a deposit) is held as stakeholder under Condition 2.2.6, interest on the stake money is payable to the seller. 'Accrued interest' is defined in Condition 1.1.1(a) (see Chapter 2 above). Interest on money held either as agent for the seller or as stakeholder is in any event payable under the Solicitors' Accounts Rules 1991.

*Sale by tender*

**11.16**   The condition is inappropriate for use in a sale by tender.

## Suggested amendments

**11.17**   To widen the condition slightly, the seller may consider accepting payment by means of a building society cheque which should be a safe method of payment, but if this is done, or if it is decided to allow payment by the buyer's personal cheque, a special condition to specifically incorporate Condition 2.2.2 should be added. If this is not done, the option of treating the contract as discharged on dishonour of the cheque will not be available to the seller.

Payment by the methods specified in Condition 2.2.4 does not apply to auction contracts where, unless amended by special condition, the buyer's own cheque (with its attendant risks) may have to be accepted by the seller.

A special condition will be necessary to deal with the method of payment of the deposit on a sale by tender.

A special condition will also be necessary if a deposit of less than 10% is to be accepted on exchange. A similar amendment would be required if more than the customary 10% deposit was to be paid, but this situation is extremely rare (see 11.2 above).

A buyer would prefer to amend Conditions 2.2.5 and 2.2.6 to prevent the use of the deposit by the seller in his related purchase transaction.

A special condition will be necessary to deal with the payment of the deposit, where the seller is represented by an unqualified person (see 11.10 above).

## SCPC Condition 2.2

**11.18**    SCPC Condition 2.2 provides as follows:

'2.2 Deposit

2.2.1    The buyer is to pay a deposit of 10% of the purchase price no later than the date of the contract.

2.2.2    Except on a sale by auction the deposit is to be paid by direct credit and is to be held by the seller's conveyancer as stakeholder on terms that on completion it is paid to the seller with accrued interest.'

**11.19**    The SCPC, like its Standard Condition counterpart, provides for a 10% deposit to be paid on exchange and if a different sum is to be payable , the condition will need to be amended. Payment is to be made by direct credit, as defined by Condition 1.1.1(g). The difficulties of complying with this condition where exchange takes place late in the afternoon have been discussed in Chapter 2, and an amendment to the condition to avoid breach of the condition where the deposit money cannot physically be transmitted until the working day following the day of exchange is recommended.

**11.20**    The SCPC condition differs from its Standard condition counterpart in that it makes no provision for a leapfrogging deposit (see Standard condition 2.2.5). In the context of a commercial transaction this omission is not significant and wording similar to Standard condition 2.2.5 could be used in a commercial contract if needed.

**11.21**    Since money paid under a commercial contract using the SCPC is only to be paid by direct credit, there is no need for the conditions to contain provisions relating to referred cheques and these provisions (found in SCS) are omitted from the SCPC deposit condition but do appear in SCPC Condition 2.3, dealing with auctions, where a cheque may be tendered for the deposit. If it is contemplated in a sale by private treaty that money will be paid other then by direct credit, the wording of SCPC 2.3, as it relates to referred cheques could be deemed by special condition to apply to all money paid under the contract. Such an amendment should however only be necessary where funds are not payable by either direct credit or solicitor's clients' account cheque.

In all other respects the wording of SCPC 2.2 mirrors its Standard Condition counterpart and the comments relating to Standard Condition 2.2 (above) have equal application.

# Chapter 12

# Insurance

## The general law

*Introduction*

**12.1**    On exchange of contracts the beneficial interest in the property passes to the buyer although the legal estate remains vested in the seller until completion.

Any gain accruing to the property after exchange will belong to the buyer. Likewise, the risk of any loss or damage must be borne by him, unless it can be shown that the loss or damage is attributable to the seller's lack of reasonable care (*Clarke v Ramuz* (1891)).

Before contracts are exchanged, the buyer should be advised of the insurance risk and steps taken to ensure that a valid insurance policy will cover the property with effect from the date of exchange.

Where the purchase is being financed with the assistance of a building society mortgage, the mortgagee will normally insure the property. Reference should be made to the particular society's standing instructions to check its procedure on insurance. Some societies will effect cover from the date of issue of the mortgage offer; others will do so only on the issue of the advance cheque unless requested to do so earlier. The latter will need to be notified that exchange has taken place.

The sum insured under the policy will often be greater than the purchase price of the property since the cost of rebuilding may exceed the market value of the property as it now stands.

The seller is under no legal obligation to keep up his insurance after exchange but will often maintain the policy until completion.

*Statutory provisions*

**12.2**    If loss or damage is suffered and the buyer has failed to insure, provided the seller still has a valid policy, it may be possible for the buyer to claim the benefit of that policy under section 47 of the Law of Property Act 1925.

Three conditions must be satisfied before section 47 will operate in favour of the buyer:

(a) the contract does not exclude the operation of the section;

(b) the buyer pays a proportionate part of the premium from the date of the contract;

(c) the insurance company has consented to the buyer's interest in the policy.

It is unlikely in practice that section 47 will be of much assistance to the buyer, since if he has not taken out his own insurance, he has probably also not taken the trouble to notify the seller's insurers of his interest in the policy.

Where the damage is caused by fire, the buyer might be able to establish that he is a 'person interested' in the seller's policy under section 83 of the Fires Prevention (Metropolis) Act 1774 and call on the insurer to apply the insurance money to rebuilding the property. The application of this Act is not confined to London (*Re Barker, ex parte Gorley* (1864)), but there is no modern authority in favour of the proposition that the buyer is a 'person interested' within the section.

Unless either section 47 or the 1774 Act applies, the buyer has no right to the proceeds of any insurance policy maintained by the seller.

Even if the property is totally destroyed between exchange of contracts and completion, the buyer is still bound to complete, with no abatement in the purchase price, since the doctrine of frustration does not apply to freehold land. The House of Lords' decision in *National Carriers Ltd v Panalpina (Northern) Ltd* (1981) shows that the doctrine of frustration can apply to a leasehold estate, in which case the provisions of the Law Reform (Frustrated Contracts) Act 1943 would apply.

Where the buyer does complete the contract, the seller will have suffered no loss and will be unable to claim on his insurance policy, or if his claim has already been met, he will be under an obligation to repay the insurance proceeds to his insurers (*Castellain v Preston* (1863)). Property insurance is indemnity insurance, therefore the seller can recover no more than his actual loss.

The above paragraphs relate only to property insurance. The buyer should take out his own insurance for house contents with effect from the date when he moves into the property.

### Double insurance

12.3    In most cases the buyer will take out his own policy on exchange, and the seller will not cancel his policy until completion. For this period the property is covered by both parties, and if during this time the property is damaged or destroyed, problems can arise over double insurance (see (1980) LS Gazette, p 376). Most insurance policies contain a 'rateable proportion' clause, under which only a proportionate part of the sum insured will be claimable in the event of there being double insurance. The Law Society Conditions of Sale (1984 revision) contained a clause which was designed to overcome this difficulty by providing that if the buyer's insurance proceeds were reduced by the application of a rateable proportion clause, the purchase price of the property was to abate by a sum equal to the reduction which the buyer suffered at the hands of his insurance company. This clause, which is reproduced below, did not apply where the seller was obliged to use his insurance proceeds to reinstate the property, but would apply if the seller, not being under an obligation to do so, chose to apply the insurance proceeds towards reinstatement. The clause as drafted was never litigated, but there is no apparent reason why it should not work. This clause, or similar wording, may be considered for inclusion in a contract in order to avoid the hazards of double insurance.

The clause provides:

'(1) If the property is destroyed or damaged prior to actual completion and the proceeds of any insurance policy effected by or for the (buyer) are reduced by reason of the existence of any policy effected by or for the (seller), the purchase price shall be abated by the amount of such reduction.

(2) Sub-condition (1) shall not apply where the proceeds of the (seller's) policy are applied towards the reinstatement of the property pursuant to any statutory or contractual obligation.'

## Standard Condition 5.1

**12.4** The Standard Conditions of Sale deal with the matter in this way:

'5.1  *Responsibility for property*

5.1.1  The seller will transfer the property in the same physical state as it was at the date of the contract, (except for fair wear and tear) which means that the seller retains the risk until completion.

5.1.2  If at any time before completion the physical state of the property makes it unusable for its purpose at the date of the contract:

(a) the buyer may rescind the contract

(b) the seller may rescind the contract where the property has become unusable for that purpose as a result of damage against which the seller could not reasonably have insured, or which it is not legally possible for the seller to make good.

5.1.3  The seller is under no obligation to the buyer to insure the property.

5.1.4  Section 47 of the Law of Property Act 1925 does not apply.'

*Effect of the Condition*

**12.5** Section 47 of the Law of Property Act 1925 is expressly excluded by the condition. This removes the uncertainties of that section from the contract. The seller is generally under no obligation to insure. If the buyer requires the seller to keep his policy on foot until completion, a special condition to this effect will have to be added to the contract. In such a case, the seller would probably require the special conditions to provide that the buyer pays a proportionate part of the premium due under the policy.

The seller is under a duty (Condition 5.1.1) to transfer the property in the same physical state as it was at the date of the contract (see also Condition 3.2.1). No exclusion or reservation is mentioned under Condition 5 for property which is in the course of construction, where, if this condition is interpreted literally, a most unsatisfactory result is achieved for the buyer and an amendment to the condition would be required in such circumstances.

The risk in the property remains with the seller until completion (Condition 5.1.1), so relieving the buyer of his obligation to insure, but since the seller is expressly also relieved of the duty to maintain his insurance, most buyers continue to make arrangements to insure the property from the time of exchange of contracts. Since it is unlikely that in practice the seller will cancel his insurance policy until completion, it is probable that between exchange and completion two policies will exist, both covering the same property, continuing the possibility of problems over double insurance.

If before completion the property is damaged to the extent that it is not usable for its purpose at the date of the contract, the buyer is entitled under Condition 5.1.2(a) to rescind the contract. The buyer would presumably choose to exercise this right only where he had not insured the property, or where he encountered difficulty in enforcing his policy. No conditions are attached to the buyer's rights to rescind, but some argument may arise between the parties over whether the property is 'unusable' within the terms of the condition. Rescission by the seller in such circumstances is permitted only where the damage has been caused by a risk against which the seller could not reasonably have insured, or where the damage is such that it is not legally possible for the seller to restore the property to its former condition. No time limit is imposed on either party during which they may exercise the right to rescind. The rights and obligations of the parties on rescission are dealt with by Condition 7.2 (see Chapter 19).

Although the intention behind this condition is sensible in that it removes the anachronistic concept that the risk in the property automatically passes to the buyer on exchange, the wording may give rise to some difficulty in interpretation. The text of the condition follows the recommendations expressed by the Law Commission in their paper *Transfer of land – passing of risk from vendor to purchaser* (CM 109). A similar clause is included in *Precedents for the Conveyancer* (cl 16–62 at p 8217), which may be considered as an alternative to this condition. Although the *Conveyancer* clause is much longer than Standard Condition 5.1.2, it does require the seller to maintain his insurance policy until completion, and also specifies a time limit within which rescission must take place.

Where the buyer takes possession of the property before completion, he is, by Condition 5.2.2, obliged to insure the property. It seems therefore that if the property were rendered unusable between exchange and completion, the buyer could not exercise his right to rescind under Condition 5.1.2.

If the property is leasehold, the seller will be obliged to maintain his insurance policy if the terms of the lease require the tenant to insure (Condition 8.1.3; Chapter 22).

Condition 5.1 has proved to be the most controversial of all the conditions in the Standard Conditions of Sale and is unpopular with many practitioners. The problems which the condition was designed to resolve are only in part cured, owing to the unhappy wording of the condition itself. If the condition is used, it is suggested that at the very least a time limit is imposed during which the parties must choose whether or not to exercise the right to rescind. Many practitioners prefer to delete this condition altogether, so reverting to the common law position where risk passes to the buyer on exchange, carrying with it the obligation for the buyer to insure the property. Some lenders also prefer this condition to be deleted since the consequences of the common law position are at least known, whereas the precise interpretation of Condition 5.1 is speculative. The main adverse consequences of reverting to the common law position are, firstly, that the buyer has to incur the expense of taking out a policy, and, secondly, that if the property were to be damaged, problems might be encountered with double insurance. Neither of these arguments is tenable: the buyer would in any event have to take out a policy on completion – to take it out on exchange of contracts adds very little extra to the total bill. Problems of double insurance can (in the rare case of there being such a problem) be resolved by inserting a clause similar to Law Society Condition 11(1).

## Suggested amendments

**12.6**    If the buyer wants the seller to maintain his insurance policy, a special condition to this effect will need to be added to the contract. The buyer should be given the right to inspect the policy, and to have his interest noted on the policy, in return for payment of a proportionate part of the premium (if so required by the seller).

Where the property is in the course of construction a special condition requiring the seller to complete the building works in accordance with agreed plans or specifications will override the first part of Condition 5.1.1. In these circumstances it may be reasonable for the seller to bear the risk in the property until completion and for the buyer not to insure the property himself.

A buyer may not be entirely happy with the wording of Condition 5.1.2 and may wish to amend this clause to clarify the word 'unusable', and possibly to negate the seller's right to rescind.

## The Protocol

**12.7**    Paragraph 5.21 of the Protocol requires the buyer's solicitor to check that building insurance arrangements are in place before exchange.

# SCPC Condition 7.1

**12.8**  SCPC Condition 7.1 provides as follows:

'7.1  *Responsibility for insuring*

7.1.1 Conditions 7.1.2 and 7.1.3 apply if:

    (a)  the contract provides that the policy effected by or for the seller and insuring the property or any part of it against loss or damage should continue in force after the exchange of contracts, or

    (b)  the property or any part of it is let on terms under which the seller (whether as landlord or as tenant) is obliged to insure against loss or damage.

7.1.2 The seller is to:

    (a)  do everything required to continue to maintain the policy, including the prompt payment of any premium which falls due

    (b)  increase the amount or extent of the cover as requested by the buyer, if the insurers agree and the buyer pays the additional premium

    (c)  permit the buyer to inspect the policy, or evidence of its terms, at any time

    (d)  obtain or consent to an endorsement on the policy of the buyer's interest, at the buyer's expense

    (e)  pay to the buyer immediately on receipt, any part of an additional premium which the buyer paid and which is returned by the insurers

    (f)  if before completion the property suffers loss or damage:

        (i)  pay to the buyer on completion the amount of policy moneys which the seller has received, so far as not applied in repairing or reinstating the property, and

        (ii)  if no final payment has been received, assign to the buyer, at the buyer's expense, all rights to claim under the policy in such form as the buyer reasonably requires and pending execution of the assignment, hold any policy moneys received in trust for the buyer.

    (g)  on completion:

        (i)  cancel the insurance policy

        (ii)  apply for a refund of the premium and pay the buyer, immediately on receipt, any amount received which relates to a part of the premium which was paid or reimbursed by a tenant or third party.

    The buyer is to hold the money subject to the right of that tenant or third party.

7.1.3  The buyer is to pay the seller a proportionate part of the premium which the seller paid in respect of the period from the date when the contract is made to the date of actual completion, except so far as the seller is entitled to recover it from a tenant.

7.1.4   Unless condition 7.1.2 applies:

    (a)   the seller is under no obligation to insure the property

    (b)   if payment under a policy effected by or for the buyer is reduced, because the property is covered against loss or damage by an insurance policy effected by or for the seller, the purchase price is to be abated by the amount of that reduction.'

7.1.5   Section 47 of the Law of Property Act 1925 does not apply.'

**12.9**   Condition 7.1 represents one of the most noticeable differences between the Standard conditions and the SCPC. Under the Standard Conditions, risk in the property remains with the seller until completion (reversing the normal open contract position on insurance), whereas the SCPC take the traditional approach of risk passing to the buyer on exchange. Although many will welcome the SCPC's reversion to the conventional insurance position there are some circumstances in which this change will adversely affect the buyer. For example, an institutional buyer, purchasing for investment purposes, will not wish to assume any risk in the property until completion, and in this situation the insurance provisions contained in Standard Condition 5.1 will be more suitable, and a clause to that effect would invoke the provisions of SCPC 7.1.2 and 7.1.3.

**12.10**   Where SCPC is used unamended, the buyer takes the risk in freehold property on exchange and thus must insure the property from that time. Although, by SCPC 7.1.4(a) the seller is under no obligation to insure, in most cases he will have an existing policy covering the property which he would be unwise to cancel until after completion. Thus between exchange and completion there will be two policies on foot, covering the same property and the problems associated with double insurance might therefore arise if a claim was made. SCPC Condition 7.1.4(b) attempts to resolve this problem by providing for an abatement of the purchase price in these circumstances. SCPC Condition 7.1.4(b) is a plain English version of the condition which previously existed as Law Society condition 11(1) (para 12.3 above). The wording of the new version is less exact than the old Law Society condition 11(1), it is unclear, for example, what is meant by the word 'reduced'. As noted above, the effect of an abatement condition, such as Law Society Condition 11(1) and SCPC 7.1.4(b) has never been litigated and its precise effect is uncertain. It should be noted that where chattels are included in the sale, the risk in the chattels also passes to the buyer on exchange (SCPC Condition 12, Chapter 10).

**12.11**   SCPC Conditions 7.1.2 and 7.1.3 make provision for those cases where Condition 7.1.4 is removed from the contract and risk remains with the seller. Under this condition it appears that the buyer can request the seller to note the buyer's interest on the policy, at the buyer's expense . The buyer is not bound by the condition to pay a proportionate part of the premium but would need to do so if requested by the insurers following an increase in cover requested by the buyer under Condition 7.1.2(b).

**12.12**   If the property suffers loss or damage between exchange and completion, and the property is insured under the seller's policy, the buyer does not have the right to rescind the contract but the seller is obliged to pay to the buyer on completion the amount received by the seller under the policy. If by completion date no final payment has been received by the seller from the insurer, the seller is to transfer to the buyer at the buyer's expense the seller's rights under the policy. In either of these situations the buyer is to pay a proportionate part of the insurance premium. This provision may be considered unsatisfactory by a buyer who may not wish to complete on a property which is unusable, nor will he wish to become involved in protracted negotiations with the seller's insurer relating to the amount due under the policy. The buyer may therefore prefer to add a special condition allowing him to rescind the contract if the property becomes unusable owing to damage by an insured risk between contract and completion.

## Existing leases

**12.13**   Standard Condition 8.1.3 places an obligation on the seller to comply with any insurance provision in the lease which requires the tenant to insure the property. SCPC 10.1.3 is identical in wording and effect.

## Property transferred subject to a lease

**12.14**   SCPC 7.1.2 and 7.1.3 also deal with property which is transferred subject to a lease where the seller is obliged to insure against loss or damage.

# Chapter 13

# Exchange of Contracts

## Effect of exchange

**13.1**    A contract for the sale of land is normally drawn up in two identical parts; each party signing one part. The contracts are then physically exchanged, so that the seller receives the part of the contract signed by the buyer and *vice versa*.

Only when contracts have been exchanged does a binding contract exist between the parties, from which neither party will normally be entitled to withdraw (*Eccles v Bryant and Pollock* (1948)).

Since the buyer will not normally be able to change his mind about the transaction once exchange has taken place, it is essential that he has concluded his financial arrangements for the purchase (for example, by accepting a satisfactory mortgage offer) before committing himself to the contract. Steps should also have been taken to ensure that the property will be adequately insured from the time of exchange, since at common law the risk of loss or damage to the property passes to the buyer at this time (see Chapter 12).

A completion date will usually be agreed by the parties immediately before exchange, the date being inserted into the contract at the time of exchange.

An exchange of contracts is not the only method of bringing a legally binding contract into existence. A single document embodying the contractual terms, and signed by both parties will become binding and enforceable as soon as the second signature has been appended to the document (*Smith v Mansi* (1962)). The most usual reason for only having one document is that the same solicitor is acting for both parties – itself a relatively uncommon occurrence since r 6 Solicitors Practice Rules 1990 severely restricts the circumstances in which this can happen.

## Statutory requirements

**13.2**    Section 2 of the Law of Property (Miscellaneous Provisions) Act 1989 requires all contracts for the sale of land, or for the disposition of an interest in land, to be in writing. 'Interest in land' and 'disposition' have the same meanings as they have under the Law of Property Act 1925. The writing must contain all the terms which have been agreed by the parties and must be signed by both parties; or, 'if the document is drawn up in two parts, as will normally be the case with a contract prepared by a solicitor and intended to come into existence through an exchange of contracts, each party must sign one part. If the writing does not contain all the terms agreed by the parties, it is possible to join a second document to the first one in order to supply the missing terms (but see *Firstpost Homes Ltd v Johnson* (1995)). It may be possible under section 2 for one document which is signed and which contains more or less all the contract terms to refer to another document in order to pick up a stray missing term, or for a contract to be drawn up which refers to, say, the Standard Conditions of Sale, without setting out those conditions in full. In this case the general conditions from the standard contract for sale will be read into the contract as if they were written out in full in the document itself. An exchange of correspondence between the parties will not normally satisfy section 2 (*Commission for the New Towns v Cooper* (1995)). Failure to comply with section 2 means that no contract has come into existence and the court has no power to enforce the oral agreement between the parties.

Because of the stringent requirements of section 2, care will need to be exercised with collateral contracts, options, or side letters issued in connection with a contract for the sale of land. To be valid and enforceable these too may need to satisfy the requirements of writing and signature by both parties (see *Record v Bell* (1991); *Walford v Miles* (1992)). However in *Pitt v PHH Asset Management Ltd* (1993) it was held that an oral lock-out agreement was a valid collateral contract and did not need to satisfy section 2. Similarly in *McCausland v Duncan Lawrie* (1995) it was held that a variation of a contract did not need to satisfy section 2. Equitable mortgages will also need to be in writing to satisfy the section (*United Bank of Kuwait v Sahib* (1996)).

Privileged leases, that is, those granted for a term not exceeding three years, at the best rent without a fine, and taking effect in possession, are excluded from the requirements of the section. Contracts which are governed by the Financial Services Act 1986 are also exempt, as are auction contracts. This latter exception should be carefully noted, because an auction contract is valid and enforceable even if oral. The contract will be concluded with the fall of the auctioneer's hammer, and there is no need for either party to sign a memorandum of the sale.

## Authority to make a contract

**13.3**    Neither a solicitor nor an estate agent has implied authority to sign a binding contract on behalf of his client (*Suleman v Shahisavari* (1989)). This general principle should be distinguished from the Court of Appeal's decision in *Domb v Isoz* (1980), where, provided the solicitor does have express authority to contract, he may use that authority to effect an exchange of contracts by whatever method he thinks fit.

An auctioneer acting as such does have authority, on normal agency principles, to bind his client to a contract of sale which is entered into at the time of the auction or shortly afterwards. The auctioneer is also the agent of the buyer at the time of the contract of sale but not otherwise (see Chapter 23).

The above rules may be varied by contrary agreement.

## Contract races

**13.4**    A seller may send out identical draft contracts to several prospective buyers on the understanding that he will sell to the first buyer whose signed contract and deposit cheque is received at the seller's solicitor's office. In this situation it may be that a contract exists from the moment when the successful buyer's contract is received by the seller, without the need for a formal exchange of contracts (*Daulia v Four Millbank Nominees Ltd* (1978)). Where a contract race is involved the seller's solicitor must comply with Solicitors' Practice Rule 1990 Rule 6A which requires the seller's solicitor to inform each buyer's solicitor that contracts have been submitted to more than one buyer. Such information, if given orally, must be confirmed in writing. If the seller refuses to allow his solicitor to disclose this information to the buyers, the solicitor must cease to act for the seller forthwith. Further, the solicitor must not accept instructions to act for both seller and buyer or for more than one prospective buyer where a contract race is involved.

## Registration of the contract of sale

**13.5**    A contract for the sale of land falls within the definition of an 'estate contract' and is therefore capable of registration. Failure to register will render the contract void against a subsequent purchaser of the legal estate for money or money's worth. Actual knowledge of the contract by the subsequent purchaser is irrelevant.

The consequence of non-registration may be that the buyer loses his right to the property which he had contracted to buy, although he would have an action for breach of contract against the seller. The buyer's solicitor may be liable to his own client in negligence.

The risk of the seller's selling the property elsewhere is usually considered to be very slight and, for this reason, most solicitors choose not to register the contract. Registration should however be effected in sub-sale contracts (registration against the name of the seller in the main contract) or if there is to be a long delay between exchange of contracts and completion, or if the buyer suspects the seller. Such a registration should be cancelled immediately upon completion.

## Standard Condition 2.1

**13.6**    The Standard Conditions of Sale provide for the formation of the contract in Condition 2 as follows:

'2.1 *Date*

2.1.1    If the parties intend to make a contract by exchanging duplicate copies by post or through a document exchange, the contract is made when the last copy is posted or deposited at the document exchange.

2.1.2    If the parties' conveyancers agree to treat exchange as taking place before duplicate copies are actually exchanged, the contract is made as so agreed.'

### Time of exchange

**13.7**    Condition 2.1.1 deals with the date of the contract when exchange is effected by post or through a document exchange. The time when the contract is effective under this condition is different from the deemed time of service of documents under Condition 1.3 (see Chapter 4).

Where the contract comes into existence by any method other than by post or document exchange, Condition 2.1.2 applies and the date of the contract is as agreed by the parties.

Personal exchange is not dealt with by the condition. Exchange by this method is infrequent nowadays, but when used presents no practical problems, and the omission of a reference to this method of exchange is not significant.

### Suggested amendments

**13.8**    Previous versions of the Conditions of Sale contained an authority for the solicitor to effect an exchange of contracts. This is absent from the current edition of the Standard Conditions of Sale. Although such a clause would not strictly form part of the contract, since it deals with matters which take place before the contract comes into existence, the solicitor always needs his client's authority to effect an exchange, and the inclusion of a clause in the contract which refers to this matter serves as a useful reminder but is not essential.

## The Protocol

**13.9**    Paragraph 8 of the Protocol states:

'On exchange the buyer's solicitor shall send or deliver to the seller's solicitor:

8.1    The signed contract with all names, dates and financial information completed.

8.2    The deposit provided in the manner prescribed in the contract. Under the Law Society's Formula C the deposit may have to be sent to another solicitor nominated by the seller's solicitor.

8.3    If contracts are exchanged by telephone, the procedure laid down by the Law Society's Formulae A, B or C must be used and both solicitors must ensure (unless otherwise agreed) that the undertakings to send documents and pay the deposit on that day are strictly observed.

8.4    The seller's solicitor shall, once the buyer's signed contract and deposit are held unconditionally, having ensured that the details of each contract are fully completed and identical, send the seller's signed contract on the day of exchange to the buyer's solicitor in compliance with the undertaking given on exchange.

8.5    Notify the client that contracts have been exchanged.

8.6    Notify the seller's estate agent or property seller of exchange of contracts and the completion date.'


## The effects of exchange

**13.10**    On exchange, a binding contract exists from which, normally, neither party may withdraw without incurring liability for breach.

The beneficial ownership in the property passes to the buyer who becomes entitled to any increase in value of the property, but also bears the risk of any loss or damage, hence the need to ensure that insurance of the property is effective from the moment of exchange (note that under Condition 5.1 the risk in the property remains with the seller until completion, thus displacing this common law rule).

The seller retains the legal title to the property until completion, but holds the beneficial interest on behalf of the buyer. During this period the seller is entitled to remain in possession of the property and to the rents and profits (unless otherwise agreed). He must also discharge the out-goings until completion. He owes a duty of care to the buyer and will be liable to the buyer in damages if loss is caused to the property through neglect or wanton destruction (*Clarke v Ramuz* (1891); *Phillips v Lamdin* (1949)). This duty continues so long as the seller is entitled to possession of the property and does not terminate because the seller vacates the property before completion (*Lucie-Smith v Gorman* (1981)).

Both parties have a lien over the property – the buyer to the extent of the deposit paid, the seller for the balance of the purchase price. Such liens are enforceable only through a court order for the sale of the property, provided that, as against third parties, they are protected by registration or by holding the title deeds to the property.

Protection of the lien by registration is not normally considered to be necessary, but should be undertaken immediately if problems arise between the parties in the period between contract and completion.


## After exchange

**13.11**    The client, estate agent and buyer's lender should all be informed that exchange has taken place, and the completion date should be entered in the solicitor's diary or file prompt system.

Any deposit held by the seller must immediately be paid into clients' account.

If any preliminary deposit has been held by an estate agent, the agent should be asked to send such sum to the seller's solicitor, who is normally required under the contract to hold 'the deposit', that is, the whole of the amount specified in the contract as the contractual deposit (see Condition 2, Chapter 11). The agent may be reluctant to part with the money, preferring to hold it on account for any commission due to him.

If not already done, the seller should then deduce title to the buyer.

## Between exchange and completion

**13.12**   There will frequently be an interval of about four weeks or less between exchange of contracts and completion. During this time the seller must deduce his title to the buyer (if he has not already done so), and answer any queries raised by the buyer's investigation of that title. The buyer has to draft the purchase deed (subject to the seller's approval), attend to his final searches, and draft the mortgage deed (where appropriate).

Most of the work involved in these procedural steps will fall on the buyer's solicitor, but he will rely on the co-operation of the seller's solicitor in order to be able to complete the necessary steps by the agreed completion date. Many transactions will proceed quite smoothly from exchange to completion, but it is useful for both parties to have a 'timetable' for the procedural steps, to ensure that as far as possible completion does take place on time.

*Common law timetable*

**13.13**   The open contract rules lay down an incomplete timetable for the procedural steps:

| | | |
|---|---|---|
| Abstract to be delivered | – | Within a reasonable time after exchange of contracts. |
| Requisitions to be delivered | – | Within a reasonable time after delivery of the abstract. |
| Completion | – | To take place within a reasonable time. |

Since no specific time limits are imposed at common law this implied timetable is of little practical use and is only relied on where the parties have not made specific provisions relating to these matters in the contract.

## Standard Condition 4.3

**13.14**   Condition 4.3 of the Standard Conditions of Sale contains a timetable listing the various procedural steps which have to be taken between contract and completion and specifying time limits by which these steps must be achieved. The object of this timetable is to lay down a framework which will ensure the smooth progress of the transaction from exchange to completion on the agreed date. Most transactions will proceed smoothly whether or not the time limits are strictly adhered to, but a further function of these limits is to ascertain the degree of fault attributable to each party in the event of a delayed completion when interest on the balance of the purchase price will become payable. It is for this reason that the time limits are of practical importance in the transaction and should where possible be observed.

The timetable is as follows:

'4.3.1 Subject to condition 4.2 and to the extent that the seller did not take the steps described in condition 4.1.1 before the contract was made, the following are the steps for deducing and investigating the title to the property to be taken within the following time limits:

| Step | Time Limit |
|---|---|
| 1. The seller is to comply with condition 4.1.1 | Immediately after making the contract |
| 2. The buyer may raise written requisitions | Six working days after either the date of the contract or the date of delivery of the seller's evidence of title on which the requisitions are raised whichever is the later |
| 3. The seller is to reply in writing to any requisitions raised | Four working days after receiving the requisitions |
| 4. The buyer may make written observations on the seller's replies | Three working days after receiving the replies |

The time limit on the buyer's right to raise requisitions applies even where the seller supplies incomplete evidence of his title, but the buyer may, within six working days from delivery of any further evidence, raise further requisitions resulting from that evidence. On the expiry of the relevant time limit the buyer loses his right to raise requisitions or make observations.

4.3.2 The parties are to take the following steps to prepare and agree the transfer of the property within the following time limits:

| Step | Time Limit |
|---|---|
| A. The buyer is to send the seller a draft transfer | At least twelve working days before completion date |
| B. The seller is to approve or revise that draft and either return it or retain it for use as the actual transfer | Four working days after delivery of the draft transfer |
| C. If the draft is returned the buyer is to send an engrossment to the seller | At least five working days before completion date |

4.3.3 Periods of time under conditions 4.3.1 and 4.3.2 may run concurrently.

4.3.4 If the period between the date of the contract and completion date is less than 15 working days, the time limits in conditions 4.2.2, 4.3.1 and

4.3.2 are to be reduced by the same proportion as that period bears to the period of 15 working days. Fractions of a working day are to be rounded down except that the time limit to perform any step is not to be less than one working day.'

*Effect of the condition*

**13.15**　The fall-back date for completion under Condition 6.1.1 is set at twenty working days after the date of the contract. The time limits in Condition 4 will fit together to meet this completion date provided that the normal practice of delivering the draft purchase deed at the same time as requisitions on title is observed. Provided that requisitions and draft purchase deed are dealt with concurrently, a completion date fifteen days after exchange can be achieved without altering the condition. If the various steps listed in the condition were each to be taken consecutively, completion date would need to be at least thirty-four days after the date of exchange. Condition 4.3.3 permits the time limits for delivery of requisitions and draft purchase deed to run concurrently; if they are not made to run concurrently, the timetable does not work to achieve its goal of completion twenty working days after the date of the contract. The method of calculation of the limits changes within the timetable itself; for example, requisitions – *within* six working days of delivery of the abstract; draft purchase deed – at least twelve working days *before* completion, making it difficult at first sight to appreciate that the time limits within the two sub-conditions do fit together as a single unit.

Where the time fixed for completion is less than fifteen working days after the date of the contract, an adjustment to the limits is necessary in order to make the timetable work. The formula for doing this is given in Condition 4.3.4, although the actual calculation of the reduced limits still has to be made by the solicitors concerned. A similar formula could be used to extend the time limits in Condition 4.3.1 where the completion date has been set at more than twenty working days from exchange. The limits in Condition 4.3.2 are geared backwards from completion date (as opposed to forwards from exchange), and so would not need to be altered to fit an extended completion date. Although in these circumstances such an adjustment may not be considered worthwhile, strict observance of the limits (whether extended or not) should still be made because if completion is delayed, compliance with the limits will minimise a party's liability to pay compensation for the delay.

The time limits within this condition are all assessed by reference to the definition of a 'working day' contained in Condition 1.1.1(m).

If the evidence of title delivered by the seller is incomplete, the onus is on the buyer to draw the defect to the seller's attention within the time limit given for raising requisitions. If he fails to do this, he will lose his right to query the title. Provided the buyer does point out the imperfection to the seller, the seller must, by the proviso to Condition 4.3.1, deliver further evidence to complete his title, and the buyer then has a further six working days in which to raise requisitions on that further evidence. Item 3 of Condition 4.3.1 states that the seller is to reply to *any* requisition raised within four working days after receiving the requisition. This limit presumably also applies to requisitions on the further evidence of title raised under the proviso. Similarly, although the proviso does not expressly say so, it is assumed that the three working day time limit for making observations on replies contained in item 4 of Condition 4.3.1 will apply to the buyer's observations on the seller's replies to supplementary requisitions. If imperfect evidence of title is initially delivered by the seller, there is thus the possibility of two separate time limits, both applying to requisitions, running simultaneously in the transaction. If supplementary requisitions have to be raised, following delivery of further evidence of title, the timetable within Condition 4 will need to be watched carefully; the timetable as drafted is closely knit, and may not be met if the seller does not respond quickly to the buyer's request for further evidence of title. The wording of the proviso to Condition 4.3.1 overcomes the problem of the application of time limits where initially an imperfect abstract is delivered (*Ogilvy v Hope-Davies* (1976)). The time limits contained within this condition are absolute, and unless extended by agreement between the parties, the buyer will lose his right to query the seller's title unless he raises his requisitions and further observations within the specified limits. In many cases title is deduced to the buyer at the pre-contract stage of the transaction, and a contractual condition forces the buyer to raise his requisitions before exchange of contracts. In such cases the time limits within this condition become superfluous.

## SCPC Conditions 6.3.1 – 6.3.4

**13.16**   The provisions contained in the SCPC relating to the date of the contract and to the timetable of events between exchange and completion are identical to those contained in the Standard Conditions and which are discussed above. In so far as the timetable of events between exchange and completion is concerned, the fact that this schedule does not fit together when there is a shorter or longer gap than normal between exchange and completion is of less significance under the commercial conditions because compensation for late completion (SCPC 9.3) under the SCPC is not dependent on the concept of relative fault. An amendment to the conditions to make the timetable fit the parties' agreed completion date is therefore unnecessary.

# Chapter 14

# Requisitions on Title

## The general law

*Purpose of requisitions*

**14.1**    The buyer has the right, within a reasonable time after the delivery of the abstract, to raise requisitions of the seller in order to clarify any queries which have arisen through the buyer's examination of the abstract of title.

The seller must answer the requisitions within a reasonable time (*Re Stone & Saville's Contract* (1962)). If the seller does not comply with the time limit for delivery of his abstract, the buyer is not bound by any time limit imposed on the delivery of his requisitions.

A requisition relating to the seller's ability to convey can be raised at any time, notwithstanding the imposition of common law or contractual time limits. In the same way a query relating to a matter not revealed by the abstract can be raised at any time. The buyer must make his observations on the seller's replies to requisitions within a reasonable time.

*The nature of requisitions*

**14.2**    The nature of the requisitions should, in theory, be confined to specific matters of title and the buyer is not entitled to ask, nor the seller required to answer, enquiries of a general nature (see *Re Ford & Hill* (1879)). In practice, requisitions are commonly raised in relation to administrative matters (for example, asking the seller to supply a completion statement) and the standard form of requisitions on title provides a convenient medium by which these matters may be settled. It is also usual at this stage to ask the seller to confirm that the answers which he gave to pre-contract enquiries are still correct.

Few title problems emerge from an examination of a registered title. Those which exist will probably be in relation to undischarged incumbrances which appear on the Charges register or in relation to overriding interests.

A sale of a registered title which is expressly made subject to the entries on the register of the title will not prevent the buyer from raising a requisition asking for full details of documents referred to in the register (*Faruqi v English Real Estates Ltd* (1979)).

If the seller has a good title and has prepared his abstract carefully there should similarly be few requisitions which need to be raised in conjunction with an unregistered title.

Only requisitions relating to title are subject to the constraints of a time limit imposed by the contract. Those relating to the form of the conveyance are not so limited. The distinction between 'title' and 'conveyance' is in theory clear, but in practice it is sometimes difficult to distinguish between the two. A general definition of a requisition relating to 'conveyance' is that such a requisition is capable of being complied with either by the seller himself, or by the seller enforcing against some other person a right vested in the seller. Examples of 'conveyance' requisitions include a query relating to whether a mortgagee should be joined as a party to the purchase deed, or about the appointment of an additional trustee.

The distinction between the two types of requisition is important in that where a requisition is subject to a time limit, which is not complied with, the buyer may lose his right to make an objection to the title on that ground. The seller's right to rescind where the buyer persists in making a requisition with which the seller cannot comply is limited to requisitions on title only. (See Chapter 24.)

At common law there is no right to raise requisitions relating to planning matters. This is not a serious limitation on the buyer's rights since such enquiries are conventionally dealt with before exchange of contracts.

### Waiver of objections to title

**14.3**    The buyer may lose his right to object to a matter of title if he has not complied with the time limit for raising requisitions. At common law, where the time for raising requisitions is simply 'within a reasonable time of delivery of the abstract', it will be difficult to decide at what precise moment the buyer loses his rights.

The buyer may expressly waive his right to object to the title, or may do so impliedly. The following acts by the buyer will be evidence (but not necessarily conclusive evidence) of implied waiver:

(a) Entry into possession of the property.
(b) The tender of a draft purchase deed after requisitions have been raised and answered, and no further objections made to the answers. (The delivery of the draft purchase deed simultaneously with the requisitions will not necessarily amount to waiver.)
(c) An attempt by the buyer to re-sell the property. (If the seller voluntarily answers requisitions which are made out of time he may be held to have waived his contractual rights to decline to answer and will be obliged to deal with the buyer's observations on his replies.)

### Buyer's remedies if requisitions not answered

**14.4**    If the seller refuses to answer requisitions at all, or his answers are not to the buyer's satisfaction, a summary remedy is provided under section 49 of the Law of Property Act 1925.

The section is intended to settle disputes between the parties relating to individual problems arising out of the abstract. It should not normally be used to seek a declaration in general terms as to the validity of the seller's title, although actions framed in such general terms have been allowed under the section (*Re Hargreaves & Thompson's Contract* (1886); *Re Bramwell's Contract, Bramwell v Ballards Securities Investments Ltd* (1969)). The court will not, however, allow an action under the section where the area of dispute is the enforceability of the contract itself (*Re Sandbach & Edmondson's Contract* (1891)).

The court may make whatever order it thinks fit in order to resolve the dispute, including an order for costs. Alternatively, the buyer may choose to discontinue his purchase.

## Standard Condition 4.3

**14.5**    The Standard Conditions of Sale provide:

'4.3.1 Subject to condition 4.2 and to the extent that the seller did not take the steps described in condition 4.1.1 before the contract was made, the following are the steps for deducing and investigating the title to the property to be taken within the following time limits:

| *Step* | | *Time Limit* |
|---|---|---|
| 1. | The seller is to comply with condition 4.1.1 | Immediately after making the contract |
| 2. | The buyer may raise written requisitions | Six working days after either the date of the contract or the day of delivery of the seller's evidence of title on which the requisitions are raised whichever is the later |
| 3. | The seller is to reply in writing to any requisitions raised | Four working days after receiving the requisitions |
| 4. | The buyer may make written observations on the seller's replies | Three working days after receiving the replies |

The time limit on the buyer's right to raise requisitions applies even where the seller supplies incomplete evidence to his title, but the buyer may, within six working days from delivery of any further evidence, raise further requisitions resulting from that evidence. On the expiry of the relevant time limit the buyer loses his right to raise requisitions or make observations.'

*Effect of the condition*

**14.6**    The buyer's time limit for raising requisitions runs either from the date of the contract or from the day of delivery of the seller's evidence of title. Thus if evidence of title is delivered before exchange of contracts, the buyer has six working days from exchange within which to raise his requisitions. 'Delivery' is governed by Condition 1.3 (see Chapter 4).

The buyer loses his right to raise requisitions or to make observations on the seller's replies if he does not comply with the time limits in this condition. He may also suffer the penalty of having to pay compensation to the seller if, as a result of the buyer's delay at this stage of the transaction, completion is delayed. For both of these reasons, compliance with the time limits in Condition 4.3.1 is advisable.

There is no right under the condition to raise requisitions about planning matters or about persons who are in actual occupation of the property. Both of these matters, if relevant to the transaction, should have been dealt with pre-exchange; therefore their omission here should not seriously prejudice the buyer.

If the evidence of title delivered by the seller is incomplete, the onus is on the buyer to draw the defect to the seller's attention within the time limit given for raising requisitions. Should he fail to do this, he will lose his right to query the title. Provided the buyer does point out the imperfection to the seller, the seller must, by the proviso to the condition, deliver further evidence to complete his title, and the buyer then has a further six working days in which to raise requisitions on that further evidence. Item 3 of Condition 4.3.1 says the seller is to reply to any requisition raised within four working days after receiving the requisition. This limit presumably also applies to requisitions on the further evidence of title raised under the proviso. Similarly, although the proviso does not expressly say so, it is assumed that the three working day time limit for making observations on replies contained in item 4 of Condition 4.3.1 will apply to the buyer's observations on the seller's replies to supplementary requisitions. If imperfect evidence of title is initially delivered by the seller, there is the possibility of two separate time limits, both applying to requisitions, running simultaneously in the transaction.

As drafted, the condition makes no distinction between requisitions relating to title and those relating to conveyance; thus the common law rule applies to the latter and the time limits stipulated in the condition will not be relevant.

The condition refers to requisitions arising out of the 'evidence of title' and does not specifically mention requisitions arising out of documents which were delivered to the buyer before exchange of contracts. It seems therefore that the common law will apply to such requisitions and, provided that the contract expressly or impliedly provides for the seller to show a good title, the buyer may raise requisitions on documents delivered to him before exchange and may insist that defects revealed by those documents are corrected. In practice the right to raise requisitions in these circumstances is often precluded by a special condition. Where evidence of title is delivered before exchange, the time limit of six working days applies to requisitions in so far as the right to raise requisitions is not barred by contractual condition.

No provision is made for the submission of queries after the delivery of observations on the seller's replies to requisitions. The common law implication that further queries must be sent and answered within a reasonable time will therefore apply.

## The Protocol

Under the Protocol, the buyer must raise his requisitions as soon as possible after exchange, and in any case, within the time limits stipulated in the contract for the raising of requisitions (para 9.1). By para 9.2 of the Protocol, the seller is under a duty to reply to requisitions as soon as possible. Further observations and replies are not mentioned.

## SCPC Condition 6.3

**14.8**    The wording and effect of SCPC 4.1 is identical to that contained in Standard Condition 4.3, discussed above.

# Chapter 15

# Possession Before Completion

## The general law

**15.1**   Except by agreement between the parties, there is no right for the buyer to take possession of the property before completion. The seller will normally be reluctant to allow the buyer into possession, since it may prove difficult to persuade him to vacate the property and, once he has gained possession, the buyer may lose his incentive to complete the transaction quickly.

*Tenant or licensee?*

**15.2**   In the absence of contrary agreement, a buyer who takes possession does so as a tenant at will, and in the case of residential property the seller will be able to regain possession of his property only if either the buyer voluntarily moves out or the seller obtains a court order.

No such danger exists in relation to business premises since a tenant at will of premises falling within the Landlord and Tenant Act 1954 Part II cannot claim the protection of that Act (*Hagee (London) Ltd v A B Erikson and Larsen* (1976)).

No security of tenure will arise under the Landlord and Tenant Act 1954 Part II if the agreement between the parties constitutes a licence to occupy and not a tenancy. The test of exclusive occupation is no longer paramount in distinguishing between a licence and a tenancy and care must be exercised in framing the terms of the 'licence' in order to avoid its being construed as a tenancy (*Street v Mountford* (1985); see also *AG Securities v Vaughan* (1988) and *Antoniades v Villiers and Bridger* (1988)). It was decided in *Bretherton v Paton* (1986) that on the breakdown of a tentative agreement for the sale of a house the proposed buyer in possession before completion became a Rent Act protected tenant. This application of the *Street v Mountford* principle is a matter of some concern if a prospective buyer is let into possession before a formal contract is entered into, since *Street v Mountford* makes it clear that what the parties call the arrangement between them or their intentions (as to licence or tenancy) are not the determining factors.

If a licence to occupy has been terminated by the seller, he may seek a summary order for possession against the buyer. A court order for possession is always required in the case of residential property: section 2 of the Protection from Eviction Act 1977.

During the period between exchange of contracts and completion the seller holds the legal estate on trust for the buyer, and is liable for any damage suffered by the property during this time (*Clarke v Ramuz* (1891)). This general duty of care imposed on the seller is not affected or altered by the fact that the buyer has taken possession of the property. The seller should therefore ensure that the terms of the agreement under which the buyer takes possession clearly state that as from the date of entry into possession the responsibility for loss or damage lies with the buyer who will indemnify the seller against all such loss or damage.

### Rights and duties of the buyer

**15.3**    Entry into possession is a notional completion and so from the date of entry the buyer is entitled to receive the income of the property (that is, the rent, if any) from the part of the property which the buyer does not occupy. He becomes liable for the outgoings on the property and must pay the seller interest on the balance of the purchase price at the contract rate, or if none, the general equitable rate (see Chapter 18).

No interest or 'rent' is payable before the date of actual completion if the seller's title turns out to be defective (*Winterbottom v Ingham* (1845); *Cantor Art Services Ltd v Kenneth Bieber Photography Ltd* (1969)). Unless the contract provides to the contrary, or the buyer makes express objection at the time of entry, the buyer will by taking possession be deemed to have accepted the seller's title and will lose the right to object to any defect of which he had knowledge at that time (*Re Gloag & Miller's Contract* (1883)).

The buyer is probably not entitled to create any tenancies or to carry out extensive alterations during his period of occupation. Minor alterations, with the seller's consent, may be effected, but the buyer should be wary of spending money on improving the property before he has ascertained the validity of the seller's title. If the seller withdraws from the contract on the grounds that he cannot make good title, the application of a contractual rescission clause may prevent the buyer from recovering from the seller the money spent on such improvements. If completion is to be delayed, the buyer of unregistered land may protect his contract by registration of a C(iv) land charge against the estate owner (normally the seller).

The equivalent registered land entry could also be considered in such circumstances, but is not crucial, since by taking possession the buyer will acquire an overriding interest.

### Liens

**15.4**    The seller has an equitable lien over the property which endures until the purchase price is paid in full. The buyer has a similar lien to safeguard the return of the deposit (with interest), any instalments of the purchase price, and any interest paid under the contract. The buyer will lose his lien if the sale goes off due to the buyer's fault.

Such liens, if unsupported by the deposit of title deeds, must be protected by the entry of a notice or caution in registered land in order to bind a subsequent purchaser (or by a C(iii) land charge in unregistered land). The non-registration of the buyer's lien over registered land will not be fatal since by going into possession he will acquire an overriding interest. A lien can only be enforced by a court order for the sale of the property.

## Standard Condition 5.2

**15.5**   The Standard Conditions of Sale, Condition 5.2, provide:

'5.2   *Occupation by buyer*

5.2.1   If the buyer is not already lawfully in the property, and the seller agrees to let him into occupation, the buyer occupies on the following terms.

5.2.2   The buyer is a licensee and not a tenant. The terms of the licence are that the buyer:

(a) cannot transfer it

(b) may permit members of his household to occupy the property

(c) is to pay or indemnify the seller against all outgoings and other expenses in respect of the property

(d) is to pay the seller a fee calculated at the contract rate on the purchase price and the chattels price (less any deposit paid) for the period of the licence

(e) is entitled to any rents and profits from any part of the property which he does not occupy

(f) is to keep the property in as good a state of repair as it was in when he went into occupation (except for fair wear and tear) and is not to alter it

(g) is to insure the property in a sum which is not less than the purchase price against all risks in respect of which comparable premises are normally insured

(h) is to quit the property when the licence ends.

5.2.3   On the creation of the buyer's licence, condition 5.1 ceases to apply, which means that the buyer then assumes the risk until completion.

5.2.4   The buyer is not in occupation for the purposes of this condition if he merely exercises rights of access given solely to do work agreed by the seller.

5.2.5   The buyer's licence ends on the earliest of: completion date, rescission of the contract or when five working days' notice given by one party to the other takes effect.

5.2.6   If the buyer is in occupation of the property after his licence has come to an end and the contract is subsequently completed he is to pay the seller compensation for his continued occupation calculated at the same rate as the fee mentioned in condition 5.2.2(d).

5.2.7   The buyer's right to raise requisitions is unaffected.'

*Effect of the condition*

**15.6**    The provisions of this condition do not apply to purchasers who are sitting tenants.

A buyer who enters into possession under the terms of this condition is stated to become a licensee and as such will acquire no security of tenure and may be evicted by the seller using the summary possession procedures mentioned in 15.2 above. Until the decisions in *Street v Mountford and Bretherton v Paton* (see 15.2 above) there would have been no doubt that the statement that the buyer 'be the licensee and not the tenant' meant exactly that, and there was no danger that a tenancy (which might be subject to security of tenure) might inadvertently be created in this situation. Since these two decisions the position may be less clear, although it was recognised in *Street v Mountford* that legal relationships which would or might negative a tenancy include occupancy under a contract for the sale of land. Had the arrangement in *Bretherton v Paton* been followed by a formal contract using this condition, the buyer (being already in possession as tenant) would not have been treated as a licensee.

Interest is payable at the contract rate on the remainder of the purchase price, (including the price of chattels) less the deposit paid. Instalments of the purchase price which have been paid on or before the buyer's entry into possession are not excluded from the interest provision. Where the buyer pays an instalment of the price as a term of his being allowed into possession, this condition should be amended so that the buyer is liable to pay interest only on the outstanding balance of the purchase price. Unless the contract is discharged or rescinded the buyer remains liable for interest until actual completion unless, before actual completion, the buyer's licence to occupy has been terminated by the service of notice under Condition 5.2.3.

During his occupation the buyer is entitled to keep the rent (if any) arising from the property, but must pay or indemnify the seller against all outgoings. The buyer must take out his own insurance over the property at this time (if he has not already done so). The policy must comply with the terms of Condition 5.2.2(g). Since the terms of Condition 5.2.2(g) are rather general, the buyer may be advised to seek the seller's agreement to the buyer's proposed policy before it is taken out. The seller has no right to inspect the buyer's policy under this provision and no specific sanction for breach of Condition 5.2.2(g) exists, except that the seller could choose to terminate the licence under Condition 5.2.5. The buyer assumes the risk in the property when he takes up occupation and retains that risk until completion, notwithstanding that he may have given up possession of the property. If the seller continues to maintain his own insurance policy at this time, problems with double insurance might occur if damage was sustained to the property (see Chapter 12).

The buyer must keep the property in as good a state of repair as it was in when he took up occupation. There is no obligation on him to improve the property, and he is specifically prohibited from altering it.

The licence created is non-assignable and may be used only by the buyer and his household.

At common law a buyer who enters into possession is deemed to have accepted the seller's title. This rule is abrogated by Condition 5.2.7.

The licence to occupy terminates immediately on contractual completion date or upon rescission of the contract, or may be brought to an end by either party giving five working days' written notice to the other. The notice will be served in accordance with the provisions of Condition 1.3 (Chapter 4). Since the buyer's licence to occupy ends automatically on completion date (as defined in Condition 6.1.1), there can be no double charge to interest if completion is delayed. The compensation provisions of Condition 7.3.2 apply between completion date and the day of actual completion. Thus if the buyer is in occupation and completion is delayed, he will pay his licence fee until contractual completion date (at which time his licence to occupy terminates), and from then until actual completion, compensation assessed under Condition 7.3.2. If the buyer remains in occupation between contractual completion date and the date of actual completion, his status – and the terms of his occupancy – seem to be undefined except that by Condition 5.2.6 the obligation to pay a licence fee is expressly maintained.

Condition 5.2.4 resolves an ambiguity which had occurred in previous editions of the Conditions by making it clear that a buyer who is given access to the property solely for the purpose of doing work agreed by the seller is not deemed to be in occupation under the terms of this condition and is thus not subject to the obligation to pay a licence fee under Condition 5.2.2(d). Where rights of access are given under this provision, the seller would be advised to have a written agreement with the buyer setting out the terms of the access arrangement, eg times of permitted access, specifying precisely the works to be done, provisions for remedying damage caused by the buyer, termination of the arrangement, and insurance provisions for the property during this time.

## Suggested amendments

**15.7**    If the buyer will be paying instalments of the purchase price in addition to the deposit, he should amend this condition so that he is not required to pay interest on those instalments which have been paid if he goes into possession before completion. The seller may wish to specify in detail the type of property insurance cover to be obtained by the buyer, and may wish to have the right to inspect that policy. If double insurance will be a problem during the period of the buyer's occupation, a clause to resolve this may be included (see Chapter 12). Where the buyer is permitted access solely for the purpose of doing works to the property, a separate agreement detailing the terms of the access arrangement would provide certainty for the parties.

## Standard Commercial Property Conditions

**15.8**    The current edition of the Standard Commercial Property Conditions contains no provisions for the buyer to take possession before completion.

The previous edition of the Conditions contained a clause broadly similar to Standard Condition 5.2 (above), the terms of which are too general for most commercial requirements. If the buyer of commercial property is to take up occupancy before completion a specific clause or clauses should be added to the contract and tailored to suit the needs of the particular circumstances.

# Chapter 16

# The Purchase Deed

## Drafting the deed

**16.1**    The buyer usually prepares the purchase deed and bears the cost of doing so (*Poole v Hill* (1840)).

The seller is entitled under section 48(1) of the Law of Property Act 1925 to reserve the right to submit a form of purchase deed to the buyer, but, except in the case of building estates, rarely does so.

Where the buyer is buying a house in the course of construction on a building estate the seller normally requires the purchase deed to be in standard form, so that all the houses on the estate enjoy the benefit and suffer the burden of identical easements and are subject to identical covenants. In such a case it is common for the contract to stipulate that the purchase deed must be prepared in accordance with the draft annexed to the contract, or even that the seller will supply the engrossment.

A draft purchase deed should be complete in itself and should not require reference to any other document for the purposes of preparing the engrossment (Opinion of the Council of the Law Society, Law Society's Digest, Supp. 160(c)).

At one time the draft purchase deed was not submitted until after the seller had answered the buyer's requisitions. Thus the tender of the draft purchase deed suggests that the buyer is satisfied with the seller's title and is evidence that the buyer has waived the right to raise further objections to the title.

The modern practice is to submit the draft purchase deed for the seller's approval at the same time as requisitions are raised. If a time limit is imposed under the contract for the delivery of requisitions (see Condition 4.1.1), the buyer is entitled to deliver requisitions (and to raise further requisitions) until the expiry of that time limit notwithstanding that the draft purchase deed may already have been delivered. There is therefore no danger of waiver in such a case. If, unusually, the contract does not specify a time limit for the delivery of requisitions, the buyer should make clear to the seller that the draft purchase deed is delivered subject to the buyer's right to raise requisitions. This will prevent any misunderstanding between the parties over acceptance of the seller's title.

The deed must be in the form prescribed by the Land Registration Rules and set out in the schedule to those Rules. Alterations and additions to the prescribed forms may be made only if necessary or desirable and if permitted by the Rules or by the Chief Land Registrar.

## Contents of the deed

**16.2**   This paragraph does not contain a full discussion of the contents of the purchase deed. It is intended here only to give a brief summary of some of the areas which give rise to difficulty, with particular reference to those matters which are dealt with in Conditions 4.1.2 and 4.5.

The purchase deed must reflect the terms of the contract. Neither party can insist on the inclusion of particular words unless either the contract or the general law makes provision for their inclusion. If the purchase deed does not reflect the contract, the court may order rectification in order to correct the error in the deed. Rectification is a discretionary remedy and will not be awarded, *inter alia*, where a third party who has acquired rights in the land would be prejudiced by the order.

*Parties*

**16.3**   All persons whose concurrence is necessary to vest the legal estate contracted to be sold to the buyer must be joined as parties to the deed.

The seller may not impose a condition on the buyer that he shall accept a title made with the concurrence of a person entitled to an equitable interest in the property (such as a beneficiary) (Law of Property Act 1925, s 42(1)).

The correct course of action where this problem arises under a trust is for the seller to appoint a further trustee of the legal estate, and for the trustees to convey.

Where land is settled land under the Settled Land Act 1925 the tenant for life will normally convey, the trustees of the settlement also being made parties to the deed in order to give a valid receipt for the purchase price.

If the seller has been adjudicated bankrupt, his trustee in bankruptcy will convey, and the bankrupt will not be a party to the deed. However, where a limited company has gone into liquidation, the company, not the liquidator, will normally transfer the property. The liquidator must be joined as a party in order to give a receipt for the purchase price, but he does not hold the legal estate in the land unless, unusually, a vesting order has been made under section 538 of the Companies Act 1985.

If the buyer is concerned that someone other than the seller, who is in occupation of the property, may have an equitable interest in the property, a possible solution to the problem is to require that person to be joined as a party to the purchase deed.

*Plans*

**16.4**    The buyer may not insist on the use of a plan if the contract sufficiently identifies and adequately describes the land without one.

Where the property is referred to as being 'more particularly delineated on the plan', in the event of dispute over the extent of the property the plan will prevail over the description in the body of the purchase deed. The converse is true if the plan is described as being 'for identification purposes only'. If the plan is to predominate over the verbal description of the property, the plan must be drawn to scale and must be on a scale large enough to clearly identify the property (*Re Sharman's Contract* (1936)). The use of a plan is considered to be essential where part only of the seller's present estate is to be conveyed to the buyer.

Registered titles are usually transferred by reference to the plan filed at HM Land Registry. A separate plan will, however, be required if only part of the seller's title is being transferred. Plans must be signed by the parties to the purchase deed but need not be witnessed.

Measurements or plans stated in the body of the deed must be shown in metric values (Units of Measurement Regulations 1986 (as amended)).

Markings on the plan must comply with Land Registry requirements.

*Title guarantee*

**16.5**    Under the Law of Property (Miscellaneous Provisions) Act 1994 the buyer will obtain the benefit of certain implied covenants for title if the key phrase 'the seller transfers with full/limited title guarantee' is included in the purchase deed. If this phrase is not used no covenants are implied. The extent of the covenants can be expressly modified by contractual condition as repeated in the purchase deed. In registered land any modification of the covenants must be set out expressly in the purchase deed and refer to the section of the 1994 Act which is being modified. Except in the case of leasehold land, a modification of the covenants is not shown on the register of the title so that a buyer will need to keep a certified copy of either the contract or purchase deed as evidence of the modification. Such evidence may need to be produced to a buyer on a subsequent sale of the property. The nature and extent of the covenants is discussed in Chapter 3.

*Indemnity covenants*

**16.6**    Where restrictive covenants have been imposed on the land but the covenantor's liability is limited to seisin (ie ownership) no indemnity covenant is required. If the covenants are not so limited the seller should require the buyer to enter into an indemnity covenant in the purchase deed.

The burden of a positive covenant does not run with freehold land and the only method of enforcing such a covenant is through a chain of indemnity covenants. Even in the absence of an express contractual condition requiring an indemnity covenant, a person who buys with notice of a restrictive covenant may only obtain a decree of specific performance against the seller if he undertakes to enter into a covenant for indemnity.

Where land is sold subject to restrictive covenants but the seller will not after completion retain any interest in the land sold, his only entitlement is to a covenant for indemnity and not to a covenant to observe and perform (*Re Poole and Clarke's Contract* (1904)). Even where the seller will after completion retain some interest in the land sold a covenant to observe, perform and indemnify may be construed as a covenant for indemnity only, unless the wording of the covenant makes clear that its object is to benefit the land retained by the seller (*Reckitt v Cody* (1920)).

*Acknowledgement and undertaking*

**16.7** If any of the seller's title deeds to unregistered land are not to be handed to the buyer on completion (such as a probate, or documents relating to land retained by the seller), a purchase deed relating to unregistered land should contain an acknowledgement by the seller of the buyer's right to production of the retained deed(s). Production may be requested in writing by the buyer at his expense, for the purpose of inspecting the deeds and comparing an abstract against the original, and for production of the deeds at any court hearing in the United Kingdom. In addition to the acknowledgement, sellers other than those acting in a fiduciary capacity will also give an undertaking for the safe custody of the deeds. The undertaking confers a right to damages if the deeds are lost or defaced except by fire or other inevitable accident.

These rights, conferred by section 64 of the Law of Property Act 1925, arise only if the acknowledgement and/or undertaking are given by a person who retains the deeds. If, for example, the seller's mortgagee retains possession of the deeds, he will give an acknowledgement to the buyer, but an express covenant should be taken from the seller to give an undertaking as soon as the deeds come into his possession.

The burden of the obligation imposed by section 64 runs with the deeds, and the benefit with the land except into the hands of a lessee at a rent. Thus once given, the clauses need not be repeated in subsequent documents.

These clauses are unnecessary in a transfer of registered land.

# Execution

**16.8** The seller must always sign the purchase deed in order to transfer the legal estate. The buyer's signature is required if he gives a covenant in the deed, and is always necessary, even in the absence of such a covenant, in the case of a transfer of registered land.

The rules relating to the execution of deeds by individuals are contained in section 1 of the Law of Property (Miscellaneous Provisions) Act 1989. The section applies to all deeds, not just those concerning land. A deed is valid provided three conditions are fulfilled:

(a) the deed must make it clear on the face of it that it is intended to be a deed;

(b) the document must be signed by the individual in the presence of a witness (there are special provisions for signature in front of two witnesses where the individual is himself incapable of signing the document); and

(c) the deed must be delivered.

Words such as 'signed as a deed by X and delivered' will show that the document is intended to be a deed. Section 1 makes it a legal requirement that a deed is witnessed, but there is no restriction on who may be the witness. Deeds must be delivered in order to be effective, but solicitors and licensed conveyancers are conclusively presumed to have authority to deliver a deed on the client's behalf. An authority to deliver another person's deed need no longer be given by deed.

Plans which are intended to form part of the conveyance or transfer must be signed by the parties but need not be witnessed.

Section 130 of the Companies Act 1989 provides that a company need no longer have a common seal. In line with this development, there follows the provision that a company has the option of not sealing a deed. If a seal is not used, the document must make it clear on its face that it is intended to be executed by the company, and if it is to be a deed, must use express words to show that it is a deed (this is similar to section 1 of the Law of Property (Miscellaneous Provisions) Act 1989 in relation to individuals). A form of wording which may be appropriate for use by companies which do not wish to use their common seal is as follows: 'executed as a deed by X plc on signature by A director and B secretary and delivered'. Delivery by the company will be presumed on execution, and provided the rules outlined above are followed, the buyer will still be able to rely on the protection given by section 74 of the Law of Property Act 1925.

## Sub-sales

**16.9**    At common law the buyer may require the seller to execute a transfer to the buyer's nominee (for example a sub-purchaser) provided that the buyer bears any additional expense. The seller may refuse to convey directly to a sub-purchaser only if the contract entitles him to do so, or the personal qualifications of the original buyer are material to the contract. If the land to be transferred is subject to covenants on which the seller would remain liable after completion, the seller may insist that the original buyer joins in as a party to the purchase deed in order to give an indemnity covenant (*Curtis Moffat Ltd v Wheeler* (1929)).

Whether or not the land is affected by covenants, the original buyer should always join in the deed between the seller and sub-purchaser in order to 'direct' the seller to transfer, and to release his equitable interest, and thus to give the sub-purchaser the benefit of the covenants implied under The Law of Property (Miscellaneous Provisions) Act 1994.

## Standard Condition 1.5

**16.9.1**  Standard Condition 1.5 provides as follows:

'The buyer is not entitled to transfer the benefit of the contract.'

Unless this provision is deleted from the contract it will prohibit sub-sales. Since sub-sales can be used as a vehicle for fraud the seller may prefer to leave this Condition in place unless the buyer can demonstrate a good reason for its removal.

The disadvantage to the buyer of the inclusion of such a clause is that two transfers become necessary and two amounts of stamp duty land tax may become payable, with a consequent increase in legal fees.

## SCPC Condition 1.5

**16.9.2**  SCPC condition 1.5 provides as follows:

'1.5.1   The buyer is not entitled to transfer the benefit of the contract.

1.5.2   The seller may not be required, to transfer the property in parts or to any person other than the buyer.

**16.9.3**  This condition effectively prevents sub-sales or the assignment of the benefit of the contract under the SCPC.

## Standard Conditions 4.3.2 and 4.6

**16.10**  Conditions 4.3.2 and 4.5 of the Standard Conditions of Sale provide for the following procedure:

'4.3.2   The parties are to take the following steps to prepare and agree the transfer of the property within the following time limits:

| Step | | Time Limit |
|---|---|---|
| A. | The buyer is to send the seller a draft transfer | At least twelve working days before completion date |
| B. | The seller is to approve or revise that draft and either return it or retain it for use as the actual transfer | Four working days after delivery of the draft transfer |
| C. | If the draft is returned the buyer is to send an engrossment to the seller | At least five working days before completion date |

4.6   *Transfer*

4.6.1 The buyer does not prejudice his right to raise requisitions, or to require replies to any raised, by taking any steps in relation to preparing or agreeing the transfer.

4.6.2     Subject to condition 4.6.3 the seller is to transfer the property with full title guarantee.

4.6.3     The transfer is to have effect as if the disposition is expressly made subject to all matters covered by condition 3.1.2.

4.6.4     If after completion the seller will remain bound by any obligation affecting the property which was disclosed to the buyer before the contract was made, but the law does not imply any covenant by the buyer to indemnify the seller against liability for future breaches of it:

(a) the buyer is to covenant in the transfer to indemnify the seller against liability for any future breach of the obligation and to perform it from then on, and

(b) if required by the seller, the buyer is to execute and deliver to the seller on completion a duplicate transfer prepared by the buyer.

4.6.5     The seller is to arrange at his expense that, in relation to every document of title which the buyer does not receive on completion, the buyer is to have the benefit of:

(a) a written acknowledgement of his right to its production, and

(b) a written undertaking for its safe custody (except while it is held by a mortgagee or by someone in a fiduciary capacity).'

### Effect of the conditions

**16.11**    Under Condition 4.3.2 the responsibility for the preparation of the purchase deed rests with the buyer. Since under step B of the condition the seller is to retain the draft for use as an engrossment if he approves it as drawn, the draft supplied by the buyer will have to be of engrossment quality. 'A draft transfer' is mentioned by the condition, but as a matter of good practice the buyer should supply the seller with two draft copies in case amendments are needed. The time limits imposed by this condition are calculated backwards from completion date and are discussed at 13.23 above.

The word 'transfer' is defined by Condition 1.1.1(l) to include a conveyance and an assignment.

The preparation of the purchase deed (lease) on the grant of a new lease is dealt with by Condition 8 (see Chapter 22).

The condition does not specify the form of the purchase deed. This may therefore be left to the buyer's discretion provided that it accurately reflects the terms of the contract. In registered land the buyer's freedom to choose the form of the deed is restricted by the requirements of the Land Registration Rules. Where the present conveyance will induce first registration of title the buyer may either draft a conveyance in conventional form or a transfer.

Condition 4.6.4 concerns indemnity covenants. Under this condition the buyer is required to perform existing covenants and to indemnify the seller against future breach. In the event of a breach of covenant by the buyer, the seller could obtain an injunction to restrain the breach.

This condition is limited to an indemnity for *future* breaches only. It also provides that the seller may require the buyer to execute and deliver to the seller (at the latter's expense) a duplicate transfer. This provision will mainly be of use when the transaction is a sale of part so that in addition to taking an indemnity covenant from the buyer in respect of existing covenants, the buyer is also entering new covenants directly with the seller which benefit the land retained by the seller. In these circumstances it is useful for the seller to have a copy of the executed purchase deed as evidence of the existence and extent of the covenants entered into by the buyer. The word 'obligation' extends the scope of the clause beyond restrictive and positive covenants and could extend to a personal liability of the seller which will endure beyond completion of the present transaction. This provision applies only where the seller will himself retain liability under an obligation after completion. If in any other circumstances the seller requires the buyer to execute a duplicate transfer, an express condition will need to be added to the contract. In order to draw this provision to the buyer's attention it may be advisable to refer specifically to it in the special conditions, even in circumstances where the seller's right to the duplicate transfer derives directly from Condition 4.6.4.

No implied covenant to observe and perform the terms of a lease is given by an assignee to his assignor (Landlord and Tenant (Covenants) Act 1995, s 14) and if the assignor requires such an indemnity from the assignee it must be given expressly. The 1995 Act only applies to leases granted on or after 1 January 1996. In relation to the assignment of leases granted before this date, indemnity is implied under section 77 of the Law of Property Act 1925 provided value is given for the transaction.

The intention of Condition 4.6.3 is to save the buyer from having to repeat clauses from the contract in the purchase deed by deeming the transfer to have effect as if it were made expressly subject to the matters to which the property is sold including items identified as such by Special Condition in the contract eg incumbrances, reservations, tenancies. Indemnity covenants to be given by the buyer and a modification of the covenants for title by the seller would seem not to be covered by the wording of this condition and so should still be expressly set out in the purchase deed. In registered land any modification of the implied covenants must in any event be set out expressly in the purchase deed to meet the requirements of the Land Registration Rules. Where clauses from the contract are not repeated in the purchase deed, a copy of the contract will need to be kept to provide future evidence of its contents.

Condition 4.6.1 clarifies the general law relating to the waiver of the right to raise requisitions by providing that the buyer is not deemed to have accepted the seller's title not to have waived his right to raise requisitions merely because he has delivered a draft purchase deed or engrossment to the seller. This condition acknowledges the common practice of delivery of the draft purchase deed at the same time as requisitions are delivered. The condition should however be read in conjunction with Condition 4.2.3 which makes time of the essence in relation to the delivery of requisitions.

Condition 4.6.5 reflects the general law in requiring the seller to provide an acknowledgement and undertaking in respect of title deeds which will be retained by him on completion (see 16.7 above). An acknowledgement and undertaking is unnecessary in registered land since once the buyer has become the registered proprietor of the land, previous documents affecting the land are generally irrelevant. The seller is required, at his own expense, to procure an acknowledgement from the person who has the current custody of the deeds (for example, a mortgagee).

Condition 4.6.2 deals with the covenants for title which are implied by the Law of Property (Miscellaneous Provisions) Act 1994 and says that in the absence of provision in the contract the seller will transfer with full title guarantee. A full title guarantee is not suitable for use in all situations and therefore this condition will normally be overridden by an express term of the contract. The nature of the title guarantee and any modification of it should be expressly stated in the purchase deed. A full discussion of the implied covenants given by the 1994 Act is set out in Chapter 3.

## Suggested amendments

**16.12**    Condition 4.3.2 will need to be amended if the seller wishes to reserve the right to prepare the purchase deed himself (in estate conveyancing, for instance).

Condition 4.6.2, dealing with title guarantee is easily overlooked since it is more usual to find this matter dealt with by special rather than by general condition. An amendment to this condition to provide for limited title, guarantee and/or some modification of the covenants will frequently be required.

Where an acknowledgement and undertaking are relevant to the transaction, and the seller holds the property in a fiduciary capacity, the buyer may wish to amend Condition 4.6.4 to provide that the seller gives a covenant in the conveyance that he will (if required by and at the expense of the buyer) give an undertaking for safe custody as and when the documents to which the covenant relates come into his possession.

## The Protocol

**16.13**    Paragraph 9.1 of the Protocol requires the buyer's solicitor to send two copies of the draft purchase deed to the seller's solicitor 'as soon as possible after exchange and in any case within the time limits contained in the Standard Conditions of Sale'. The seller's solicitor must approve and return the draft purchase deed 'as soon as possible after receipt' (para 9.2). The form of the deed is not mentioned by the Protocol. On receipt of the approved draft purchase deed, the buyer's solicitor is to engross it and (if necessary) to obtain the buyer's signature to the deed before sending it to the seller's solicitor 'in time to enable the seller to sign it before completion without suffering inconvenience' (para 9.3).

## SCPC Condition 6.3.2

**16.14**   SCPC Condition 6.3.2 is identical in wording and effect to Standard Condition 4.3.2, discussed above.

## SCPC Condition 6.6

**16.15**   SCPC Condition 6.6 provides as follows:

'6.6.1   The buyer does not prejudice its right to raise requisitions, or to require replies to any raised, by taking any steps in relation to the preparation or agreement of the transfer.

6.6.2   Subject to condition 6.6.3 the seller is to transfer the property with full title guarantee.

6.6.3   The transfer is to have effect as if the disposition is expressly made subject to all matters covered by condition 3.1.2.

6.6.4   If after completion the seller will be bound by any obligation affecting the property and disclosed to the buyer before the contract was made, but the law does not imply any covenant by the buyer to indemnify the seller against liability for future breaches of it:

(a) the buyer is to covenant in the transfer to indemnify the seller against liability for any future breach of the obligation and to perform it from then on, and

(b) if required by the seller, the buyer is to execute and deliver to the seller on completion a duplicate transfer prepared by the buyer.

6.6.5   The seller is to arrange at its expense that, in relation to every document of title which the buyer does not receive on completion, the buyer is to have the benefit of:

(a) a written acknowledgement of the buyer's right to its production, and

(b) a written undertaking for its safe custody (except while it is held by a mortgagee or by someone in a fiduciary capacity).'

**16.16**   SCPC 6.6 is similar in wording and effect to Standard Condition 4.6. Indemnity is only required in respect of obligations which have been disclosed to buyer before exchange of contracts.

# Chapter 17

# Completion

## The completion statement

**17.1**  The buyer's solicitor will ask the seller's solicitor to send a completion statement showing the exact amount of money due on completion, how that amount is calculated and to whom the seller requires the money to be paid. This request will usually be made at the time when the buyer's solicitor raises his requisitions on title, but the seller may not be in a position to prepare the statement at that time because, for example, he may not yet have received the last receipts for outgoings from his client. The statement should, however, be sent to the buyer's solicitor as soon as is possible in order to allow time to organise the necessary finances. As a matter of courtesy the seller should supply the buyer's solicitor with two copies of the completion statement because the latter will need to send one copy to his own client.

The statement will show the amount of the purchase price, giving credit for any deposit paid, and adjustments to that price to take account of the income and outgoings on the property, the amount, if any, to be paid for chattels and fittings, and in appropriate cases a figure representing interest on the balance of the purchase price.

Where the only money payable on completion is the balance of the purchase price, a formal completion statement is often dispensed with (see *Carne v Debono* (1988)).

## Apportionments

**17.2**  In order to be able to settle all the financial matters relating to the property on completion, income and outgoings may be apportioned between the parties as at the date of actual completion. Thus, if the seller has paid the water rates on the property for a period which extends beyond the date of actual completion, the buyer will be asked to reimburse the seller with the amount of the charge which relates to the period from the day following actual completion until the end of that payment period. A proportionate allowance in favour of the buyer should be made where the sum to be apportioned has not yet been paid by the seller. Apportionments are usually made on a daily basis and are shown on the completion statement, payment being made at completion.

Apportionments should be made of both 'income and outgoings' of the property, this phrase being generally accepted to include rent and ground rent, water and drainage rates, and possibly service charges. In practice the apportionment of water rates is rarely dealt with at completion, it being considered better practice for the parties to settle these accounts directly with the authority concerned after completion has taken place. Amounts due or owing to the client in respect of council tax (in the case of residential property) or business rates (commercial property) should also be dealt with directly with the authority concerned. After completion a letter should be written to the appropriate authority, informing it of the change of ownership and requesting that an apportioned account should be sent direct to the client for settlement by him. Not only do local authorities prefer this practice, it also relieves the seller's solicitor of a tedious calculation.

Many local authorities will now send to the buyer, with the replies to his local authority search and enquiries, a form on which the change of ownership of the property can be notified after completion.

Service charges, the amount of which may vary depending on the amount of expenditure incurred, may be difficult to apportion and may instead have to be dealt with by an undertaking given on completion that the buyer will pay or the seller reimburse (or as appropriate) a proportionate amount of the service charge when it is ascertained. (See Chapter 22.)

The buyer's solicitor will expect to inspect or have handed over to him on completion the receipts or demands relating to sums which have been apportioned on the completion statement. The seller's solicitor may choose to send these receipts or demands to the buyer's solicitor with the completion statement, asking him to hold them to the seller's order until completion. This will give the buyer's solicitor the opportunity to check the figures on the completion statement and will ultimately save time at completion itself.

## Payment

**17.3**    There is no reason why payment of completion money should not be made by the solicitor's clients' account cheque or a building society cheque but payment by such methods is very rare in practice. The usual method of payment is by banker's draft or telegraphic transfer. Where the seller has to discharge an existing mortgage on the property and/or to complete his purchase of another property on the same day, it may be convenient for him to ask the buyer to bring to completion two or more drafts so that the appropriate proportions of the purchase price can be applied directly to the discharge of the mortgage or purchase of the new property without having to bank the money and draw further drafts.

If completion is to take place through the post, a specially crossed banker's draft can be posted to the seller's solicitor but it is usual practice, and in these circumstances safer, for the money to be transmitted by telegraphic transfer or direct credit. By these methods the money is remitted directly to the seller's solicitor's bank by transfer from the buyer's solicitor's clients' account to the seller's solicitor's clients' account. The seller's solicitor's bank is asked to tele-phone their customer as soon as the money is received by them; the seller's solicitor will then telephone the buyer's solicitor confirming receipt of the money. This method of transferring money is potentially very quick, but where a transfer between different banks (as opposed to different branches of the same bank) is required, a delay is sometimes experienced.

## Liens

**17.4**    The seller has an equitable lien over the property which lasts until he receives payment of the purchase price in full despite the fact that he may have given up possession of the property. Unless the seller retains the title deeds, such lien cannot be enforced against a subsequent buyer unless it is registered as a notice or caution (C(iii) land charge in unregistered land), the only method of enforcement being an order for sale of the property. The seller's lien is over the property, not the title deeds, and in the absence of an express condition in the contract which permits retention of the deeds, the seller must hand over the title deeds to the buyer as soon as completion has taken place. This is irre-spective of whether the purchase price has been paid in full at that time. The Law Society's Code for completion by post contains an undertaking that the seller's solicitor will send the title deeds to the buyer's solicitor by first class post or document exchange on the day of completion. Any purported retention of the title deeds by the seller's solicitor would be a breach of this undertaking, unless a variation of the Code to this effect had been agreed in writing between the solicitors to the parties before completion.

## Time and place

**17.5**    The date for completion is usually agreed between the parties before exchange of contracts and inserted in the contract as a special condition on exchange, although the Standard Conditions contain a fall-back date for completion if this matter is inadvertently overlooked. In residential conveyancing transactions a completion date four weeks after exchange is considered to be normal practice, but there is an increasing trend in practice for the interval between exchange and completion to be shorter than this. If there is to be a long interval between exchange and completion the buyer should consider protecting his contract by registering a notice against the registered proprietor (C(iv) land charge unregistered against the name of the current estate owner in unregistered land).

By convention, completion takes place at the offices of the seller's solicitor or, if the seller is to discharge a mortgage on completion, and his solicitor does not also act for the mortgagee, at the offices of the seller's mortgagee's solicitor.

If it is not convenient for the buyer's solicitor or a member of his staff to attend completion personally, he may appoint another solicitor in the seller's locality to act as his agent for this purpose. The agent should be given full written instructions for completing the purchase.

The Law Society's Code for completion by post sets out the procedure to be followed in this situation. Completion by post is the normal method currently in use.

## Completing a chain of transactions

**17.6**    The buyer may have to complete the sale of his present property before completing his purchase, so that he can apply the proceeds of sale towards the purchase price of his new house. Ideally both transactions should be completed on the same day in order to avoid either the buyer being homeless or the need to obtain bridging finance. A similar situation may apply to the seller and so a chain of transactions builds up, all of which are due to be completed on the same day. In such a situation the timing of the completions needs to be planned carefully so that the transaction at the bottom of the chain is completed first, probably quite early on the morning of completion day, and the purchase price, or part of it, will then be applied to each consecutive link in the chain, until the last transaction in the line is completed later in the day. If all the solicitors involved in the chain work within travelling distance of one another, it may be convenient to arrange for them all to meet at the office of one of them, in which case, provided nothing goes wrong, all the completions will take place within a fairly short space of time. Alternatively, completion may be effected through the post, using direct transfers to remit the money, completion being confirmed by a telephone call to the buyer's solicitor as soon as it has taken place.

## Completion checklist

**17.7**    Before completion the buyer's solicitor should have written out either for himself or his agent (who may be the seller's solicitor) a checklist of the matters to be dealt with at completion itself. Although the actual requirements on completion will vary with each transaction, when completing an unregistered purchase of the whole of the seller's present land the buyer's solicitor would generally expect to have to deal with most of the matters listed below:

*Verify the deeds*

**17.8**    Where the land being bought is already registered, verification of title is strictly speaking unnecessary since the Register itself reflects the true state of the title.

If this has not been done at an earlier stage in the transaction the abstract or epitome relating to unregistered land should be checked against the original deeds. If any of the deeds are not handed over on completion the abstract or epitome should be marked up as evidence of the examination of the original.

*Demands and receipts for outgoings*

**17.9**   If not already done, the seller should produce for inspection the demands and receipts for outgoings on the property so that the buyer's solicitor can check the figures against those shown on the completion statement. Where an apportionment on the completion statement results in the buyer paying a sum of money to the seller, a receipt for such payment should be obtained.

An undertaking from the seller to discharge the outgoings on the property up to the date of completion may be given where no apportionment has been made. Demands for outgoings, which will ultimately have to be paid by the buyer, should be handed over to him.

*The deeds*

**17.10**   The buyer will have ascertained by means of his requisitions on title which deeds are to be handed to him at completion. The seller will normally have prepared a schedule of the deeds which should be checked by the buyer and will ask the buyer to sign a copy of the schedule as evidence of receipt of the deeds.

Included in the schedule will be the transfer to the buyer, which, although usually drafted and engrossed by the buyer, should still be checked. In particular, the seller's signature and the presence of a witness's signature should be inspected. The transfer should then be dated with the date of completion.

In registered land, unless there are pre-registration deeds, only the transfer will be handed over on completion and an undertaking to discharge the seller's mortgage(s) (where appropriate).

*Memorandum on retained documents*

**17.11**   Where any document forming part of an unregistered title is not to be handed over on completion, the buyer may require a memorandum of the present transaction to be indorsed on the retained deed. Section 200 of the Law of Property Act 1925, which cannot be excluded by contractual condition, gives the right to such an indorsement where the conveyance to the buyer contains restrictions of user or contains rights over retained land. Although it is not obligatory for the buyer to insist on his rights under the section, it is in any event regarded as good conveyancing practice to require the memorandum to be indorsed, since it may provide protection for the buyer against a subsequent fraudulent or mistaken conveyance by the seller of the same property. A similar procedure should be carried out where the transaction comprises an assent or conveyance from personal representatives. In this case the donee or buyer should require the personal representatives to indorse a memorandum of the transaction on the grant in order to obtain the protection afforded by section 36 of the Administration of Estates Act 1925. In all cases an examined copy of the indorsed memorandum should be placed with the buyer's title deeds.

*Undertakings*

**17.12** The buyer may require the seller to supply an undertaking relating to the discharge of outgoings on the property. The seller's mortgagee will frequently not agree to sign the vacating receipt on the seller's mortgage until he actually receives the redemption money which, unless the mortgagee attends completion, will not occur until after completion has taken place. It will not therefore usually be possible for the sealed DSI (or receipted mortgage) to be handed to the buyer at completion. The buyer should require the seller's mortgagee's solicitor to give a written undertaking in relation to this matter. A solicitor is personally liable on an undertaking given by him, he must therefore ensure that he does not commit himself to do anything which he either cannot or is not prepared to do. The form by wording recommended by the Law Society should normally be used.

An undertaking to discharge the seller's mortgage may be accepted from a licensed conveyancer but should not be accepted from an unqualified person.

*Purchase price*

**17.13** The buyer's solicitor, having dealt with the matters listed above, will hand the purchase price, as calculated in accordance with the completion statement, to the seller. When completion is taking place through the post, the money may have been sent to the seller's solicitor's clients' account by direct transfer, but in cases of personally attended completion payment is usually made by banker's draft. The seller, if he has to discharge an existing mortgage, or if he requires part of the purchase price to be applied to his own purchase, may have asked the buyer to draw two or more separate bankers' drafts in favour of different payees to make up the total sum.

*Receipts for money*

**17.14** The purchase deed will usually contain a receipt clause which, provided the buyer pays his money to the seller's solicitor, will act as a receipt and good discharge of payment of the purchase price (Law of Property Act 1925, ss 67–69), and no separate receipt for the money is required. If the money is not paid to a solicitor a separate receipt for the payment may be desirable. In so far as the money paid on completion does not represent the purchase price itself, for example where it is in respect of apportionments of outgoings or money paid for chattels, a separate receipt should always be obtained.

*Keys*

**17.15** Sometimes the buyer's solicitor will collect the keys to the property at completion. More frequently the parties will either have dealt with this matter themselves, or the keys will be held by the estate agent who will release them to the buyer on receipt of a telephone call from the seller's solicitor confirming that completion has taken place.

*Release of deposit*

**17.16**   Where the deposit has been held by some person as stakeholder, the buyer should provide a written release of that deposit on completion. If the seller's solicitor has been acting as stakeholder this requirement is often not insisted upon, but such a release will be necessary in other cases.

*The effect of completion*

**17.17**   In unregistered conveyancing the legal estate in the seller's land passes to the buyer on completion. Vacant possession is also normally given at this time. In registered conveyancing the legal estate does not pass to the buyer until the buyer's name has been entered on the proprietorship register of the title at HM Land Registry.

On completion the contract merges with the conveyance or transfer, in so far as the two documents cover the same ground, after which the only remedy usually available will be to bring an action on the covenants for title under the Law of Property (Miscellaneous Provisions) Act 1994.

# After completion

*The seller*

**17.18**   The client should be informed that completion has taken place. Where relevant the seller's estate agent should also be informed of completion so that the keys may be released to the buyer (if not handed over at completion). The estate agent's account for commission may have to be paid. The seller's mortgage should be discharged in accordance with any undertaking given on completion and the balance of the proceeds of sale dealt with in accordance with the seller's instructions.

*The buyer*

**17.19**   The client and his mortgagee should be informed that completion has taken place. File copies of documents (such as the purchase deed and concurrent mortgage) should be made up to correspond with the originals.

*S*tamp duty land tax may be payable, depending on the amount of the consideration and the presence of a certificate of value in the deed. This must be paid within thirty days of the execution of the deed. Late payment attracts penalties. Where a life policy has been assigned as collateral security for the loan, the assurance company should be notified of the assignment in order to comply with the Policies of Assurance Act 1867. Any entry which has been made to protect the contract should be discharged.

Where unregistered land has been acquired under a conveyance on sale (but not voluntary conveyance or assent), the transaction induces first registration of title and an application for registration must be made within two months of completion, failing which the conveyance of the legal estate becomes void. An application for the registration of the transfer of registered land, the discharge of the seller's mortgage and the registration of the buyer's mortgage should be made within the priority period of thirty working days afforded by the mortgagee's and/or the buyer's pre-completion Land Registry search. This point is often overlooked.

Title deeds should be sent to the buyer's mortgagee, or if no mortgage is involved, dealt with in accordance with the client's instructions, for example placed in the solicitor's strong room or deposited with the client's bank.

The local authority will need to be notified of the change of ownership.

Account should be rendered to the client for any money remaining in the solicitor's hands.

*Interest on the deposit*

**17.20** Contractual conditions (such as Standard Condition 2.2.6) may require the payment of interest on the deposit. If the buyer is entitled to the interest, and the seller holds the deposit, this matter will have to be taken into account in assessing the amount due on completion. Condition 2.2.6 is discussed in Chapter 11.

## Standard Conditions 6 and 7.4

**17.21** The Standard Conditions of Sale make the following provisions for completion:

'6.      COMPLETION

6.1     *Date*

6.1.1   Completion date is twenty working days after the date of the contract but time is not of the essence of the contract unless a notice to complete has been served.

6.1.2   If the money due on completion is received after 2.00pm, completion is to be treated, for the purposes only of conditions 6.3 and 7.3, as taking place on the next working day as a result of the buyer's default.

6.1.3   Condition 6.1.2 does not apply and the seller is treated as in default if:

(i)     the sale is with vacant possession of the property or any part of it, and

(ii)    the buyer is ready, able and willing to complete but does not pay the money due on completion until after 2.00pm because the seller has not vacated the property or that part by that time.

6.2     *Arrangements and place*

6.2.1   The buyer's conveyancer and the seller's conveyancer are to co-operate in agreeing arrangements for completing the contract.

6.2.2   Completion is to take place in England and Wales, either at the seller's conveyancer's office or at some other place which the seller reasonably specifies.

6.3 *Apportionments*

6.3.1 Income and outgoings of the property are to be apportioned between the parties so far as the change of ownership on completion will affect entitlement to receive or liability to pay them.

6.3.2 If the whole property is sold with vacant possession or the seller exercises his option in condition 7.3.4, apportionment is to be made with effect from the date of actual completion; otherwise, it is to be made from completion date.

6.3.3 In apportioning any sum, it is to be assumed the seller owns the property until the end of the day from which apportionment is made and that the sum accrues from day to day at the rate at which it is payable on that day.

6.3.4 For the purpose of apportioning income and outgoings, it is to be assumed that they accrue at an equal daily rate throughout the year.

6.3.5 When any sum to be apportioned is not known or easily ascertainable at completion a provisional apportionment is to be made according to the best estimate available. As soon as the amount is known, a final apportionment is to be made and notified to the other party. Any resulting balance is to be paid no more than ten working days later, and if not then paid the balance is to bear interest at the contract rate from then until payment.

6.3.6 Compensation payable under condition 5.2.6 is not to be apportioned.

6.4 *Amount payable*

The amount payable by the buyer on completion is the purchase price and the chattels price (less any deposit already paid to the seller or his agent) adjusted to take account of:

(a) apportionments made under condition 6.3;

(b) any compensation to be paid or allowed under condition 7.3.

6.5 *Title deeds*

6.5.1 As soon as the buyer has complied with all his obligations on completion the seller must hand over the documents of title.

6.5.2 Condition 6.5.1 does not apply to any documents of title relating to land being retained by the seller after completion.

6.6 *Rent receipts*

The buyer is to assume that whoever gave any receipt for a payment of rent or service charge which the seller produces was the person or the agent of the person then entitled to that rent, or service charge.

6.7 *Means of payment*

The buyer is to pay the money due on completion by direct credit and, if appropriate, an unconditional release of a deposit held by a stakeholder.

7.4    *After completion*

Completion does not cancel liability to perform any outstanding obligation under this contract.'

## Completion date

**17.22**  'Completion date' is defined by Condition 1.1.1(d) as either the date specified in the agreement, or the date contained in Condition 6.1.1. The contract will usually specify a completion date by special condition, such date frequently being closer to the date of exchange of contracts than the twenty working days allowed in Condition 6.1.1. Unless a notice to complete has been served, time is not of the essence of the contract. This provision is normally satisfactory to both parties and its inclusion prevents this matter being over-looked inadvertently in cases where the common law would otherwise deem time to be of the essence, such as the sale of a business as a going concern.

## Time and place

**17.23**   If the money due on completion is not paid by 2.00 pm on the day of completion, the buyer may be liable to compensate the seller for the delay by paying interest on the balance of the purchase price. Whether or not compensation becomes payable will depend on the calculation of relative fault under the provisions of Condition 7.3 (see Chapter 18). Because the definition of a working day does not apply to the calculation of compensation under Condition 7.3, a buyer who delays in completing by 2.00 pm on a Friday, will be deemed not to have completed until the following Monday, and may be liable for three days' interest, even though the seller actually received the money later on the preceding Friday afternoon. The imposition of the 2.00 pm time limit enables the seller either to deposit his money in the bank before the close of business or to use the sale proceeds towards the purchase price of another transaction which is to be completed on the same day. If the seller is involved in a chain of transactions a special condition in the contract may be needed to fix a time limit earlier than 2.00 pm so that the seller is able to comply with the time limit under his own purchase contract. Although the provisions of Condition 6.1.2 apply to all working days, not just to completions which are due to take place on the last working day of the week, the condition has no application if the contract provides for vacant possession to be given on completion and the seller has not vacated the property by 2.00 pm on the day of actual completion (Condition 6.1.3).

Completion must take place in England and Wales, but may be at the seller's solicitor's office or another place 'reasonably' specified by the seller (Condition 6.2). Where the seller's solicitor does not also act for the seller's mortgagee, the wording of this condition would allow completion to take place at the mortgagee's office. Similarly, in a chain of transactions, it may some-times be convenient to arrange to complete several links in the chain at a venue which is convenient to all the solicitors involved. The condition does not state when or how the seller must notify the buyer of his choice of completion venue, although this is a matter which is normally dealt with in the answers to the buyer's requisitions on title. The buyer is not entitled to choose the venue for completion.

*Apportionments*

**17.24** Apportionments (Condition 6.3.1) are to be made on contractual completion date unless the property is to be sold with vacant possession or the seller has exercised his option to take the income of the property under Condition 7.3.4 (Chapter 18), when, in both cases, the apportionments are made as at the date of actual completion. The phrase 'income and outgoings' is generally accepted to include rent, water and drainage rates, ground rents and rentcharges, but not sums of a capital nature nor fire insurance premiums. Service charges under leases may fall within this definition, and seem implicitly to be included by the reference in Condition 6.3.5 to the provisional apportionment of sums which are not easily ascertainable. Leasehold insurance premiums probably also fall within the definition. Council tax is a liability which does not attach to property and is not within this definition so will have to be dealt with directly with the local authority concerned. Business rates on commercial property are also better dealt with direct with the authority concerned rather than by attempted apportionment on completion. Apportionments are to be made on a daily basis (Conditions 6.3.3 and 6.3.4). This provision overcomes problems caused where payment periods for a sum to be apportioned are of unequal length over a calendar year. The condition does not specify how or when the parties are to account to each other for the apportioned sums, but it is usual for those sums to be included in the completion statement and so dealt with on actual completion.

Service charges under leases may be apportioned under Condition 6.3.5 which provides for a provisional apportionment to be made if the actual amounts are not known or easily ascertainable. This condition is discussed in Chapter 22. Although the condition is of most relevance to service charges its application is not confined to service charges alone and the condition can be used to make a provisional apportionment of any sums where the actual figures are not available by completion. This will include the apportionment of outgoings relating to freehold property as well as to leasehold.

Condition 6.6 is discussed in Chapter 22.

## Methods of payment

**17.25** It is unclear from Condition 6.1.2 whether the completion money will be deemed to have been received by 2.00 pm on the day of completion if by that time it has reached the seller's solicitor's bank account under the direct transfer system, but the seller has not by that time been notified by his bank of the arrival of the money. From a buyer's point of view it can be argued that the bank received the money as the seller's agent, and thus the seller would be deemed to have received the money, even if he was not aware of its arrival at the bank. Where money is sent by direct transfer it is important for both parties to keep a check on the time of arrival of the funds at the seller's bank in order to avoid disputes over deemed late completion. A release of deposit should be provided whenever the deposit is held by some person in the capacity of stake-holder. Although required by Condition 6.7 it is often not insisted upon where the deposit is held by the seller's solicitor. Unless amended by special condition, payment by cheque, cash, or banker's draft, are not permitted methods.

### Post-completion liabilities

**17.26**   A non-merger clause is provided in Condition 7.4, thus overcoming difficulties which would otherwise be encountered by the existence of the rule that the contract and purchase deed merge on completion.

This clause applies to any obligations which have not been performed by the time of completion, not just to obligations to pay money.

### Lien

**17.27**   A seller is only entitled to a lien over the documents of title if the buyer has failed to comply with some obligation under the contract. If a seller completes despite not having received the purchase price in full, he will, if he wishes to enforce payment through his lien over the property, have to protect the lien by registration. The condition does not apply on a sale of part of unregistered land where the seller will retain the title deeds. As worded, the condition seems to require the seller to hand over the originals of, for example, a probate or general power of attorney, since neither of these documents necessarily relates to land retained by the seller.

### Amount payable

**17.28**   Condition 6.4 defines how the amount payable by the buyer on completion is to be calculated. The amount to be tendered includes apportionments and any compensation calculated under Condition 7.3. The buyer cannot force the seller to complete unless the amount tendered by the buyer complies with this condition.

## Suggested amendments

**17.29**   Completion date will normally be dealt with by a special condition in preference to relying on the fall-back date in Condition 6.1.1.

If it is thought desirable to make time of the essence of the contract, this too will have to be done by special condition. Because the compensation provisions under Condition 7.3 are assessed on the concept of relative fault, raising the possibility of either party being liable to pay compensation, it is not advisable for the seller to make time of the essence for the sole purpose of providing the buyer with an incentive to complete on the contractual date.

The time of completion (2.00 pm) may have to be altered by special condition where the transaction forms part of a chain.

If the buyer wishes to make payment by any method other than that specified in Condition 6.7, he will have to seek the seller's agreement to an amendment of this condition. The range of banks through which payment may be made on completion is sufficiently wide to meet the requirements of most transactions and so would probably only need alteration where the buyer wishes to make payment through a foreign bank. Payment by cheque or banker's draft is not permitted under the condition as drafted.

The choice of the place of completion is left to the seller. If the buyer was suspicious about the rights of non-owning occupiers in the property and wished to complete at the property itself in order to ensure that vacant possession would be surrendered, he would have to seek the seller's agreement to this by special condition.

The conditions do not contain a provision permitting the buyer to call for a memorandum of the current transaction to be indorsed on the seller's retained deeds. Such a provision may be desirable in the case of dispositions of unregistered land by personal representatives or sales of part of unregistered land to guard against the possibility of a subsequent fraudulent re-conveyance of the same property. The need for a memorandum has largely been eroded by the extension of compulsory registration of title (in registered land the register is conclusive and the unregistered title deeds become irrelevant for this purpose). Where the buyer feels that he does wish the seller to indorse a memorandum on retained title deeds, he can probably insist on this under the provisions of either section 200 of the Law of Property Act 1925 (sales of part) or section 36 of the Administration of Estates Act 1925 (dispositions by PRs). These statutory provisions do not, however, permit the buyer to inspect and/or retain a copy of the indorsement, and if these rights were to be insisted on, they would have to be given to the buyer by special condition in the contract itself.

# The Protocol

**17.30** Paragraph 11 of the Protocol deals with completion and provides that where completion is to take place by post, unless otherwise agreed the Law Society's Code for Completion is to be used. The buyer's solicitor is to notify the seller's solicitor as soon as possible, and at the latest by the morning of completion day, how the completion money is to be sent to the seller's solicitor and the steps which have been taken to send the money. As soon as the seller's solicitor is satisfied that the completion money has been received, he is to authorise the release of the keys to the buyer and notify the buyer's solicitor that this has been done. The seller's solicitor must also ensure that his client is aware of the need to notify the local and water authorities of the change of ownership of the property.

# SCPC Conditions 8 and 7.4

**17.31**    SCPC Conditions 6 and 7.4 provide as follows:

'8.1    *Date*

8.1.1    Completion date is twenty working days after the date of the contract but time is not of the essence of the contract unless a notice to complete has been served.

8.1.2    If the money due on completion is received after 2.00 p.m., completion is to be treated, for the purposes only of conditions 8.3 and 9.3, as taking place on the next working day as a result of the buyer's default.

8.1.3    Condition 8.1.2 does not apply if:

(a) the sale is with vacant possession of the property or any part of it, and

(b) the buyer is ready, able and willing to complete but does not pay the money due on completion until after 2.00pm because the seller has not vacated the property or that part by that time.

8.2    Place

Completion is to take place in England and Wales, either at the seller's conveyancer's office or at some other place which the seller reasonably specifies.

8.3    Apportionments

8.3.1    Subject to condition 8.3.6 income and outgoings of the property are to be apportioned between the parties so far as the change of ownership on completion will affect entitlement to receive or liability to pay them.

8.3.2    The day from which the apportionment is to be made ("apportionment day") is:

(a) if the whole property is sold with vacant possession or the seller exercises its option in condition 9.3.4, the date of actual completion, or

(b) otherwise, completion date.

8.3.3    In apportioning any sum, it is to be assumed that the buyer owns the property from the beginning of the day on which the apportionment is to be made.

8.3.4    A sum to be apportioned is to be treated as:

(a) payable for the period which it covers, except that if it is an instalment of an annual sum the buyer is to be attributed with an amount equal to 1/365th of the annual sum for each day from and including the apportionment day to the end of the instalment period

(b) accruing –

(i) from day to day, and

(ii) at the rate applicable from time to time.

8.3.5    When a sum to be apportioned or the rate at which it is to be treated as accruing is not known or easily ascertainable at completion, a provisional apportionment is to be made according to the best estimate available. As soon as the amount is known, a final apportionment is to be made and notified to the other party. Subject to condition 8.3.8, any resulting balance is to be paid no more than ten working days later, and if not then paid the balance is to bear interest at the contract rate from then until payment.

8.3.6   Where a lease of the property requires the tenant to reimburse the landlord for expenditure on goods or services, on completion:

(a) the buyer is to pay the seller the amount of any expenditure already incurred by the seller but not yet due from the tenant and in respect of which the seller provides the buyer with the information and vouchers required for its recovery from the tenant, and

(b) the seller is to credit the buyer with payments already recovered from the tenant but not yet incurred by the seller.

8.3.7   Condition 8.3.8 applies if any part of the property is sold subject to a lease and either:

(a) (i)   on completion any rent or other sum payable under the lease is due but not paid

(ii)   the contract does not provide that the buyer is to assign to the seller the right to collect any arrears due to the seller under the terms of the contract, and

(iii)   the seller is not entitled to recover any arrears from the tenant, or

(b) (i)   as a result of a rent review to which condition 5 applies a reviewed rent is agreed or determined after actual completion, and

(ii)   an additional sum then becomes payable in respect of a period before the apportionment day.

8.3.8

(a) The buyer is to seek to collect all sums due in the circumstances referred to in condition 8.3.7 in the ordinary course of management, but need not take legal proceedings or distrain.

(b) A payment made on account of those sums is to be apportioned between the parties in the ratio of the amounts owed to each, notwithstanding that the tenant exercises its right to appropriate the payment in some other manner.

(c) Any part of a payment on account received by one party due to the other is to be paid no more than ten working days after the receipt of cash or cleared funds and, if not then paid, the sum is to bear interest at the contract rate until payment.

8.4   Amount payable

The amount payable by the buyer on completion is the purchase price (less any deposit already paid to the seller or its agent) adjusted to take account of:

(a) apportionment made under condition 8.3

(b) any compensation to be paid under condition 9.3

(c) any sum payable under condition 7.1.2 or 7.1.3.

8.5      Title deeds

8.5.1      As soon as the buyer has complied with all its obligations on completion the seller must hand over the documents of title.

8.5.2      Condition 8.5.1 does not apply to any documents of title relating to land being retained by the seller after completion.

8.6      Rent receipts

The buyer is to assume that whoever gave any receipt for a payment of rent which the seller produces was the person or the agent of the person then entitled to that rent.

8.7      Means of payment

The buyer is to pay the money due on completion by direct credit and, if appropriate, by an unconditional release of a deposit held by a stakeholder.'

SCPC Condition 7.4 provides:

'Completion does not cancel liability to perform any outstanding obligation under the contract.'

**17.32** SCPC Conditions 8 and 9.4 are similar in wording and effect to their counterparts in the Standard conditions, the following differences should however be noted.

**17.33** Apportionments under the Standard Conditions are made on the basis that the seller owns the property throughout the day of actual completion. The converse situation applies under the SCPC and the day of completion is treated as belonging to the buyer.

**17.34** The method by which apportionments are to be calculated under SCPC condition 8.3.4 is not clear from the wording of the condition itself. It is thought that the wording is intended to achieve the result that apportionments should be calculated on a daily basis (ie x divided by 365) irrespective of the fact that the payment being apportioned may be payable eg quarterly. Since apportionments are notoriously difficult both to calculate and agree the lack of clarity in the wording of this sub-clause is unhelpful. It is suggested that the wording of Standard Condition 8.3.4 might provide a suitable alternative to this clause.

**17.35** Conditions 8.3.6–8.3.8 represent an expanded version of Standard Condition 6.3.5, dealing with recovery of estimated service charges and apportionment in relation to tenanted property.

# Chapter 18

# Late Completion

## Common law provisions

*Effect of delay*

**18.1**    Where completion takes place after the date fixed by the contract, the purchase price is adjusted to take account of the delay, the object of this adjustment being to put the parties in the position in which they would have been had the contract been completed on time.

Where the delay has been caused by the buyer he is entitled to keep the income from the property (if any) for the period between contractual completion date and the date of actual completion, but must reimburse the seller for outgoings on the property during this period and must also pay interest to the seller on the balance of the purchase price for the period of the delay.

Instead of paying interest at the general equitable rate or contractual rate (see below) the buyer may place the balance of the purchase price on deposit with a bank and, having given notice of the deposit to the seller, pay to him the interest actually earned while the money is on deposit. This course of action is rarely taken by the buyer since, if he is financing his purchase with the aid of a mortgage he will not have the funds available to place on deposit. If the delay is caused by the seller's wilful default he is entitled to claim interest on the balance of the purchase price or to keep the net income, whichever represents the lesser figure. These common law entitlements are often varied by express contractual condition.

## Rate of interest

**18.2**    Where no rate of interest is specified in the contract, the rate payable is the 'general equitable rate' which, according to *Esdaile v Stephenson* (1822), is a mere 4% per annum.

However, the courts are now taking a more realistic view of the rate of interest to be implied into a contract; for example, in *Bartlett v Barclays Bank Trust Co Ltd* (1980), the rate was assessed on the basis of the figure allowed on the court's short term investment account under section 6(1) of the Administration of Justice Act 1965. Alternatively the court might now fix the rate of interest by reference to the base rates of the major clearing banks.

*Occupation before completion*

**18.3**    If the buyer goes into possession of the property before completion he becomes entitled to the income from any part of the property which he does not occupy, must bear the outgoings on the property, and must pay the seller interest on the purchase price from the date of his entry into occupation until actual completion.

A buyer in possession cannot escape his obligation to pay interest by placing the balance of the purchase price on deposit (*Re Priestley's Contract* (1947)).

Where it is thought that the buyer may wish to go into possession before completion a low contractual interest rate may be a disincentive to the buyer to complete on the contractual date.

*Fixing the contractual interest rate*

**18.4**    The purpose of the contractual rate is two-fold. Firstly, it provides an incentive to the buyer to complete on time by making the expense of delay costly. Secondly, it compensates the seller for the delay. A rate which was excessive might be construed by the courts as a penalty and thus void, but this would depend on the circumstances of the transaction and the relative bargaining strength of the parties.

If the buyer delays completion, the seller may have either to raise bridging finances in order to complete his own purchase on time, or to pay interest under his own purchase contract if completion of that contract is also delayed.

If the delay is caused by the seller, the buyer may encounter similar problems in that he may either have to pay interest on the contract for the sale of his own house or, if he completes that contract on time, to pay for alternative accommodation and storage charges for his furniture for the period of the delay. The contractual rate of interest must be fixed bearing these potential losses in mind. A figure of 3–4% above the base rate of one of the major clearing banks, and which fluctuates with that bank's base rate, is commonly used in residential conveyancing contracts. A fixed percentage figure is less advisable since it may put one of the parties at a severe disadvantage if interest rates change substantially between exchange of contracts and actual completion.

*Time of the essence*

**18.5**    There will be a breach of contract if the contract is not completed on the due date, whether or not time is of the essence. Time is not generally of the essence unless either the parties expressly stipulate that conditions as to time must be strictly complied with, or the nature of the subject matter or the surrounding circumstances show that time should be considered to be of the essence. Where the sale is of a business as a going concern, time will impliedly be of the essence under the 'subject matter' exception since delay in completion could have a detrimental effect on the goodwill attached to the business. In *Pips (Leisure Productions) Ltd v Walton* (1981), it was held that this rule would also apply to the sale of a wasting asset, which in the Pips case was a twenty-one year lease. In the absence of very special circumstances time is not impliedly of the essence in the sale of an ordinary dwelling house with vacant possession. However, it was suggested in *Raineri v Miles* (1981), that time might impliedly be of the essence where the sale forms part of a chain of trans-actions. The fact that a specific completion date is inserted in the contract does not of itself mean that time is of the essence of that date. The addition of the phrase 'on or before', inserted before the date, will not affect this.

Even where time is initially of the essence this condition may be waived expressly or impliedly by the conduct of the parties. Negotiations taking place after contractual completion date in an attempt to conclude the completion of the transaction may have this effect (*Luck v White* (1973)).

Where, however, delay to a particular date is agreed by the parties, time having been of the essence of the original date, time will become of the essence of the substituted date (*Buckland v Farmar & Moody* (1978)).

If time was not originally of the essence, or that particular stipulation has been waived, time may be made or re-made of the essence by giving reasonable notice to the party in default. The time fixed for performance in the notice must be reasonable, in that it must give the defaulting party a fair opportunity of being able to perform his obligations by the new completion date. Thus the more onerous the obligations under the contract, the longer the notice to be given.

## Notice to complete

**18.6**    Once the completion date has passed by, the party not in default may be able to serve notice on the other party requiring him to complete within the time limit specified in the notice. At common law two requirements are essential for the service of a valid notice to complete:

- (a)  the notice must allow a reasonable time for completion;
- (b)  the party serving the notice must himself be ready, able and willing to complete.

Compliance with these requirements can give rise to difficulties since a date for completion which is considered to be 'reasonable' by the innocent party may not be viewed as such by the party in default or by the court. Express contrac-tual conditions can remove the severity of these requirements, for example a condition which specifies an exact period for compliance with a completion notice will oust the common law requirement for reasonableness.

Where the contract sets out a procedure for the service of a notice to complete, the requirements of that condition must be strictly adhered to, failing which the notice will be invalid under the condition, although it may still be valid at common law provided it satisfies the requirements outlined above. In order to avoid any doubt about the application of the common law, a notice served under a standard contractual condition should expressly refer to the condition under which it is served.

Although it is not necessary to serve a completion notice before applying to the court for an order for specific performance, a notice cannot be served after such an order has been obtained (*Singh v Nazeer* (1978)).

An effective notice to complete cannot be served unless the party serving the notice is 'ready, able and willing' to complete (*Re Barrs Contract, Moorwell Buildings Ltd v Barr* (1956)). Thus if requisitions are outstanding or the seller has failed in his duty of disclosure, he will not be able to serve notice until he has attended to these matters. It seems, however, from *Cole v Rose* (1978) that the failure of a party to attend to minor administrative details (such as arranging a time for completion) will not prevent him from being in a position to serve a completion notice, but in the same case the existence of an undischarged mortgage prevented the service of a valid notice.

A seller who is in breach of his duty to take proper care of the property between contract and completion may still serve a notice to complete (*Prosper Homes Ltd v Hambros Bank Executor and Trustees Co Ltd* (1979)).

In *Bechal v Kitsford Holdings Ltd* (1988), a seller was held to be 'ready able and willing' to complete although he was guilty of misdescribing the property. A notice to complete served by him was therefore valid and the buyer was left to pursue his remedy for misdescription through seeking an abatement to the purchase price.

Probably a notice, once served, cannot be withdrawn except with the agreement of both parties (see *Quadrangle Development and Construction Co Ltd v Jenner* (1974)).

## Damages

**18.7**   Any delay in completion may give rise to a claim for damages for the loss caused by the delay, notwithstanding a clause in the contract providing for interest to be payable for the delay (*Raineri v Miles* (1981)), and even though time is not made of the essence in the contract.

An action for damages (or specific performance) may be brought after a reasonable time since contractual completion date has elapsed, despite the fact that no completion notice has been served (*Woods v Mackenzie Hill Ltd* (1975)).

## Standard Conditions 1.1.3, 6.8, 7.3, 7.5 and 7.6

**18.8**   The Standard Conditions of Sale provide for late completion in Conditions 6.8, 7.3, 7.5 and 7.6:

'1.1.3   A party is ready able and willing:

   (a) if he could be, but for the default of the other party, and

   (b) in the case of the seller, even though the property remains subject to a mortgage, if the amount to be paid on completion enables the property to be transferred freed of all mortgages (except those to which the sale is expressly subject).

6.8     *Notice to complete*

6.8.1   At any time on or after completion date, a party who is ready able and willing to complete may give the other a notice to complete.

6.8.2   The parties are to complete the contract within ten working days of giving a notice to complete, excluding the day on which the notice is given. For this purpose, time is of the essence of the contract.

6.8.3   On receipt of a notice to complete:

(a)     if the buyer paid no deposit, he is forthwith to pay a deposit of 10%

(b)     if the buyer paid a deposit of less than 10%, he is forthwith to pay a further deposit equal to the balance of that 10%.

7.3     *Late completion*

7.3.1   If there is default by either or both of the parties in performing their obligations under the contract and completion is delayed, the party whose total period of default is the greater is to pay compensation to the other party.

7.3.2   Compensation is calculated at the contract rate on an amount equal to the purchase price and the chattels price, less (where the buyer is the paying party) any deposit paid for the period by which the paying party's default exceeds that of the receiving party, or, if shorter, the period between completion date and actual completion.

7.3.3   Any claim for loss resulting from delayed completion is to be reduced by any compensation paid under this contract.

7.3.4   Where the buyer holds the property as tenant of the seller and completion is delayed, the seller may give notice to the buyer, before the date of actual completion that he intends to take the net income from the property until completion. If he does so, he cannot claim compensation under condition 7.3.1 as well.

7.5     *Buyer's failure to comply with notice to complete*

7.5.1   If the buyer fails to complete in accordance with a notice to complete, the following terms apply.

7.5.2   The seller may rescind the contract, and if he does so:

(a) he may

(i)   forfeit and keep any deposit and accrued interest

(ii)  resell the property and any chattels included in the contract

(iii) claim damages

(b) the buyer is to return any documents he received from the seller and is to cancel any registration of the contract.

7.5.3   The seller retains his other rights and remedies.

7.6     *Seller's failure to comply with notice to complete*

7.6.1   If the seller fails to complete in accordance with a notice to complete, the following terms apply.

7.6.2    The buyer may rescind the contract, and if he does so:

(a) the deposit is to be repaid to the buyer with accrued interest

(b) the buyer is to return any documents he received from the seller and is, at the seller's expense, to cancel any registration of the contract.

7.6.3    The buyer retains his other rights and remedies.'

## Time not of the essence

**18.9**    Time is not of the essence under the contract (Condition 6.1), but any delay in completion will potentially give rise to a claim for damages by the innocent party.

## Notice to complete

**18.10**    Provided a notice to complete is served in accordance with the requirements of Condition 6.8, the common law provisions relating to such a notice will be circumvented. In order to avoid any doubt over the application of the common law principles the notice should contain an express statement to the effect that it is served under the provisions of Condition 6.8 Standard Conditions of Sale. A notice which is invalid under Condition 6.8 may still take effect at common law, provided that the common law requirements are satisfied by the notice. Failing this, the innocent party would have to rely on his other remedies at common law (see Chapter 19).

The notice must be in writing and should be served in accordance with Condition 1.3 (see Chapter 4).

Condition 1.1.3 contains a definition of 'ready able and willing' in order to overcome the problems encountered in *Cole v Rose* (1978), see 18.6 above.

The service of the notice makes time of the essence of the contract and gives the defaulting party ten working days in which to comply with the notice. 'Working day' is defined by Condition 1.1.1(m) (see 2.1 above).

There is no provision within Condition 6.8 for time under the notice to be extended, nor for service of a second notice to complete following the expiry of the first notice. The parties could by special condition agree to do either of these things. If there were no contractual provision allowing time to be extended, the parties could still agree to an extension of time, but there is some doubt whether time would remain of the essence under an informal extension of the notice (*Buckland v Farmar & Moody* (1978)).

Where a deposit of less than 10% of the purchase price was paid on exchange of contracts, the balance of the 10% becomes immediately payable on service of a completion notice by the seller.

Conditions 7.5 and 7.6, which specify the remedies available on failure to comply with a notice to complete, are discussed in 19.22 below.

*Compensation for late completion*

**18.11**   By Condition 6.1.2 (see Chapter 17), if the money due on completion is received after 2.00 pm on the day of completion, compensation for late completion may (depending on the calculation of relative fault) be payable under Condition 7.3. If completion was due to take place on a Friday, the amount of the buyer's default will be calculated as three days, the money not being deemed to have arrived until the following Monday, and the weekend being included in the calculation because the provisions of Condition 7.3 are not subject to the definition of a 'working day'.

On the basis that pre-completion delays contribute towards the ultimate delay in completion, Condition 7.3 has been drafted to provide a concept of relative fault in relation to the payment of compensation for late completion. Thus, in assessing the entitlement to compensation, the solicitors for the parties must have regard not only to the length of time between contractual completion date and actual completion, but also to the timetable of procedural steps to be taken between contract and completion. If, for example, the seller had been two days late in delivering his evidence of title, but the buyer had been three days late in actually completing the purchase, the seller's two days' delay is set off against the three days' delay incurred by the buyer, with the result that in this example the buyer will have to pay one day's compensation to the seller. If the amount of delay incurred by the seller exceeds that incurred by the buyer, the result will be that the seller will have to allow compensation to the buyer on late completion rather than being entitled to receive it. A period of delay may be included in the computation of entitlement to compensation irrespective of whether it caused or contributed to the delay in completion. Delay means failure to perform or lateness in performing an obligation, thus where there is no obligation under the contract to perform a particular act, that act cannot be included in the computation of default. For example, Condition 4.3.1 makes time of the essence in relation to the delivery of requisitions on title. If requisitions on title are delivered late, there will be no obligation on the seller to answer them, but if he does answer them and delivers his replies outside the time limit specified in Condition 4.3.1, this lateness does not arise out of performing an 'obligation' under the contract and therefore cannot be counted against the seller in the assessment of liability for compensation. A table of the time limits applicable to the transaction is set out in Chapter 1.

The period of delay after contractual completion date is not calculated by reference to the definition of a 'working day' in Condition 1.1.1(m).

In calculating the compensation, credit is to be given for any deposit paid by the buyer, but not for any further instalments of the purchase price which have already been paid. Provided that money payable for chattels has been apportioned from the purchase price, compensation will not be payable on the price of the chattels.

'Contract rate' (Condition 7.3.2) is defined by Condition 1.1.1(e) and is discussed in Chapter 2.

*Damages*

**18.12**   Condition 7.3.3 takes account of the decision in *Raineri v Miles* (1981) by recognising the right of the innocent party to pursue a claim for damages for loss occasioned by the delay. Compensation received by the innocent party must be credited in the claim for damages. This latter provision reflects the common law rules relating to the assessment of damages which do not allow one party to profit from the other's breach of contract (see Chapter 19).

*Election to take net income*

**18.13**   Under Condition 7.3.4 a seller may elect by notice given before actual completion (not necessarily before contractual completion date) to take the net income of the property until actual completion. He is allowed to do this only where the buyer is in occupation of the property as a tenant. A buyer who goes into occupation under the terms of Condition 5.2 does so as licensee, not as tenant, and this provision does not therefore apply in that situation. Similarly, the condition does not apply if the buyer is not the direct tenant of the named seller.

Where the condition does apply, the election may be made even if the buyer is not in actual occupation at the time of the election. The seller cannot take both compensation and income from the property for the period of the delay. It seems that the seller could still make an election under this condition even in circumstances where the delay in completion was the seller's fault. This would be beneficial to the seller only where, for example, the buyer was in possession of part of the property, the remainder being let at a high commercial rent, the net income from which would exceed the seller's obligation to pay compensation for the delay in completion.

Where the buyer is the seller's tenant, apportionment of the rent normally takes place on the contractual completion date, so that, in the absence of a provision such as Condition 7.3.4, rent paid between contractual completion date and the date of actual completion is apportioned to the buyer under the provisions of Condition 6.3.2. If in these circumstances the amount of rent apportioned to the buyer exceeds the amount of compensation payable by him under Condition 7.3.1, the buyer would gain a financial advantage by deliberately delaying completion. In order to avoid this, Condition 7.3.4 allows the seller to elect to take the net income of the property until the date of actual completion, apportionments in this case being made on the day of actual completion.

*Buyer in possession before completion*

**18.14**   Where the buyer has gone into possession of the property under Condition 5.2 he will be paying interest on the balance of the purchase price from the date of his entry into possession. If completion is delayed, due to the buyer's default, he will then become liable to pay compensation under Condition 7.3. There is no double charge to interest in these circumstances since the buyer's licence to occupy automatically terminates on contractual completion date. A buyer who has taken possession but who delays in completing the transaction may be ordered by the court either to give up possession or to lodge the purchase money in court. However this order, known as a *Greenwood v Turner* order after the case of that name (1891), and see *Attfield v D J Plant Hire and General Contractors Co Ltd* (1986), is thought not to apply where the buyer takes possession under a contractual condition of this type.

## Suggested amendments

**18.15**    A buyer may seek to amend Condition 7.3 by including a provision allowing him to put the purchase money on deposit and to pay to the seller the interest actually earned by the money while on deposit, instead of the compensation assessed under the condition. This amendment will be worthwhile to a buyer who has the purchase price available to make the deposit (but not where the purchase price is being financed by a mortgage), and where current bank deposit interest rates are lower than the contract rate. This option is possibly available to the buyer under common law principles even in the absence of a special condition.

Compensation under Condition 7.3 is payable on the balance of the purchase price, taking account of the deposit but not other instalments of the purchase price. A buyer who is to pay the price by instalments will wish to amend this condition in order to avoid paying compensation on the instalments of the price which have already been paid. Where the property is in the course of construction or conversion by the seller, the buyer should ensure that no liability on his part to pay compensation arises until the construction of the property is complete.

In view of the difficulties which surround the service of a notice to complete at common law, most of which have been circumvented in the drafting of Condition 6.8, amendment of this condition is not recommended, except to alter the length of time for compliance with the notice if so desired.

## The Protocol

**18.16**    The aim of the Protocol for domestic conveyancing is to streamline and speed up the conveyancing process. The draftsman seems to have taken the view that if the Protocol procedures are adhered to, the transaction will be completed in accordance with the contract, rendering any reference to late completion in the Protocol unnecessary. Completion may of course be delayed for reasons beyond the immediate control of either party, for example if the mortgagee does not remit funds in time for completion to take place on the due date. In such circumstances the parties' rights and remedies are governed by the conditions discussed above, or, where these conditions do not apply to the contract, by the common law or other standard form contractual provisions.

# SCPC Condition 8.8

**18.17**    SCPC Condition 8.8 deals with the service of a notice to complete in identical terms to Standard Condition 6.8 which is discussed above.

# SCPC Conditions 9.5 and 9.6

**18.18**    SCPC Conditions 9.5 and 9.6 deal with failure to comply with a notice to complete in identical terms to Standard Conditions 7.5 and 7.6 discussed above.

# SCPC Condition 9.3

**18.19**    SCPC Condition 9.3 provides as follows:

'9.3.1    If the buyer defaults in performing its obligations under the contract and completion is delayed, the buyer is to pay compensation to the seller.

9.3.2    Compensation is calculated at the contract rate on the purchase price (less any deposit paid) for the period between completion date and actual completion, but ignoring any period during which the seller was in default.

9.3.3.    Any claim by the seller for loss resulting from delayed completion is to be reduced by any compensation paid under this contract.

9.3.4    Where the sale is not with vacant possession of the whole property and completion is delayed, the seller may give notice to the buyer, before the date of actual completion, that it will take the net income from the property until completion as well as compensation under condition 9.3.1.'

**18.20**    The way in which compensation for late completion is dealt with illustrates a striking difference between the Standard Conditions and the SCPC. The Standard Conditions deal with compensation by applying the concept of relative fault ie the party most at fault for the delay pays compensation. The SCPC have reverted to the traditional method of assessing such compensation so that the buyer has to pay where the delay is his fault but cannot claim compensation from the seller where the delay emanates from the seller. In these circumstances the buyer would have a claim against the seller in damages if he sustained loss as a result of the delay.

**18.21**    Where the property is tenanted and completion is delayed, the seller can, by giving notice to the buyer at any time before actual completion (ie not necessarily before contractual completion date) opt to take both the net income of the property and interest for the period of the delay. In so far as such sums overcompensate the seller for his actual loss sustained during this period it is arguable that the condition could be construed as a penalty.

# Chapter 19

# Remedies

## Introduction

**19.1**  The discussion of remedies in this chapter is confined mainly to situations where completion has not taken place. Once completion has taken place the contract merges with the purchase deed and generally the only remedy available after that time is an action for damages for breach of the implied covenants for title under the Law of Property (Miscellaneous Provisions) Act 1994. Actions on the covenants for title are not common. The effect of these covenants is sometimes limited by express contractual condition. Some contractual conditions do not merge with the purchase deed and remain extant despite completion having taken place. Arbitration clauses are a well known example of this type of condition.

### Definition of rescission

**19.2**  In conveyancing cases and texts the word 'rescission' is used both in the context of rescission *ab initio* (for example for fraud or misrepresentation) and to describe the situation where one party is entitled to treat himself as discharged from the contract by reason of the other party's breach. This latter situation is not strictly rescission at all, but a justified repudiation of the contract by the innocent party. In other chapters of this book the word 'rescission' has been used in the general sense to mean 'termination' but it was felt that in a chapter on remedies, a distinction between these shades of meaning should at least be attempted in order to avoid confusion; thus here, the word 'rescission' is used only in the context of rescission *ab initio*.

The distinction between the various interpretations of this word was discussed by Buckley LJ in *Buckland v Farmar & Moody* (1978).

## Damages

### Entitlement to damages

**19.3**  A breach of contract by one party will entitle the other party either to claim damages for the loss which he has sustained by reason of the breach, and/or to treat himself as being discharged from the contract, the latter course being available for a breach of condition only. Where the breach is of a warranty, only damages may be claimed. A condition is a major contractual term, a warranty a minor one. The fact that a clause in a contract is expressed to be a 'condition' does not necessarily mean that it is a condition in the strict sense of the word. Where there is doubt as to the status of a particular clause it may not be possible to classify it categorically until the effects of its breach are seen. If the consequences of breach of the clause are serious, breach of the clause will entitle the innocent party to repudiate and/or to claim damages. If not, damages only will be payable (*Cehave NV v Bremer Handelgesellschaft mbH* (1976)).

Where there has been unreasonable delay in completing the purchase the innocent party may treat himself as discharged from the contract without the need to serve a notice making time of the essence under the contract (*Howe v Smith* (1884); *Farrant v Oliver* (1922)).

*Assessment of damages*

**19.4**    The aim of contractual damages is to put the innocent party in the position in which he would have been had the contract been performed; that is, contractual damages are compensatory not punitive.

In furtherance of this aim the assessment of damages is usually made by quantifying the loss at the date of the breach, but the court may substitute a different date if it appears that an assessment at the date of breach would not provide proper compensation. For example, where the plaintiff has endeavoured after the breach to secure performance of the contract, the property may be valued (for the purpose of assessing the loss) at the date when negotiations between the parties finally broke down, rather than at the date of the breach (*Johnson v Agnew* (1980), applied in *GKN Distributors Ltd v Tyne Tees Fabrication Ltd* (1985)).

The starting point for the assessment of contractual damages is the case of *Hadley v Baxendale* (1854), which permits the innocent party to claim:

   (*a*)  losses arising naturally from the breach; and

   (*b*)  losses which ought reasonably to have been foreseen by the guilty party.

For a modern explanation of this principle see *H Parsons (Livestock) Ltd v Uttley Ingham & Co Ltd* (1978).

The scope of (b) is limited by the extent of the guilty party's knowledge at the date of the contract. Therefore if special circumstances pertain to the contract (for example, the buyer intends to develop the property after completion) the onus is on the buyer to impute knowledge of these facts to the seller before the date of the contract. In *Diamond v Campbell-Jones* (1961), damages for loss of development value of the property were not awarded to the buyer since the seller had not been aware of the buyer's intention to convert the property. In contrast to this, such damages were awarded in *Cottrill v Steyning and Littlehampton Building Society* (1966) where the seller was shown to have known of the buyer's intentions to redevelop the property. Damages for expenditure incurred before the making of the contract are not normally recoverable under general contractual principles but may sometimes be awarded (*Lloyd v Stanbury* (1971)).

*Remedies*

Although damages for mental distress under the principle established in *Jarvis v Swans Tours* (1973) can be awarded in an action for breach of contract, an award under this head is generally confined to 'leisure and pleasure' type contracts, and are unusual in the context of an action based on a contract for the sale of land (see *Bliss v South East Thames Regional Health Authority* (1987)).

*Buyer's breach*

**19.5**    Provided the seller can show that he was able and willing to give good title and had offered to convey the land, he is entitled to claim the full loss which he has sustained by the buyer's breach. Thus he will be entitled to claim the difference between the contract price and any lower resale price of the property plus the expenses of the resale, credit being given for any deposit paid by the buyer.

*Seller's breach*

**19.6**    In the absence of special circumstances known to the seller, damages will usually be assessed by reference to the difference between the contract price and the market price at the date of assessment of the loss. The loss is usually assessed at the date of the breach (but see 19.4 above).

The costs of investigating title are not normally awarded, but the costs incurred in the purchase of another property, and cost of accommodation pending the purchase of the new property may be claimed (*Beard v Porter* (1948)).

If there is no difference between the contract and market price of the property, so that no damages can be awarded under this head, the buyer may instead claim his abortive expenditure (*Wallington v Townsend* (1939)), but it is doubtful whether the amount awarded under this head would normally justify the costs of pursuing the action. Pre-contract expenditure may be claimed provided it can be shown that at the time of incurring the expense the parties were substantially in agreement over the terms of the contract. A survey fee might be recovered under this head. Damages for mental distress do not normally form part of the contractual assessment of damages.

Where the seller has, in breach of contract, resold the property at a profit, the buyer may as an alternative to an action for damages, claim from the seller the profit which he made on the resale (*Lake v Bayliss* (1974)).

This alternative course of action is useful to the buyer in a situation where the seller had gone bankrupt and was therefore unable to pay damages.

*Mitigation*

**19.7**    Any award of damages is subject to the principle that the innocent party must take reasonable steps to mitigate his loss (even if by so doing he increases his loss). See *Hoffberger v Ascot International Bloodstock Bureau Ltd* (1976) (not a conveyancing case, but the same principles apply). Failure to mitigate may reduce the award.

*Limitation of actions*

**19.8**    Claims for breach of contract must normally be brought within six years of the date of the breach (Limitation Act 1980) unless the contract is by deed when a twelve year limitation period applies. Time runs from the date of the breach, even where the breach has occurred before the date for performance of the contract, except where the cause of action has been concealed by mistake or fraud, when time starts running from the date when the innocent party should reasonably have become aware of the breach. Time does not run against an infant or person of unsound mind until cesser of the disability.

In certain cases a longstop limitation period of fifteen years may apply (Limitation Act 1980, ss 14 & 14A added by Latent Damage Act 1986). This would chiefly be of relevance to an action brought in negligence, such as one arising out of a design defect in the construction of a new building.

## Frustration

**19.9**    The doctrine of frustration will provide a total defence to an action for breach of contract where it can be shown by the guilty party that he was prevented by circumstances completely beyond his control from performing his contractual obligations. Although this doctrine has for many years been held not to apply to contracts for the sale of land, on the basis that such contracts confer on the buyer an estate in land and not merely the existence of proprietary rights, *National Carriers Ltd v Panalpina (Northern) Ltd* (1981) shows that the doctrine may in rare circumstances be applicable to such contracts.

Frustration was held not to have occurred on the facts of the *National Carriers* case itself, so no actual example exists to show the application of the doctrine. It is suggested, as a hypothetical example, that the doctrine might apply where land had been let on a long building lease and, subsequent to the grant of the lease, the whole site was destroyed by a landslide, to the extent that it would be impracticable to reinstate the site for the purpose for which it was let. The effect of frustration would be to terminate all future obligations under the lease from the date of the landslide but the parties would remain liable on obligations which had accrued up to that date. The parties' rights and remedies where frustration has occurred are governed by the Law Reform (Frustrated Contracts) Act 1943.

## Specific performance

**19.10**    The equitable decree of specific performance is available only where damages would not provide an adequate remedy for the breach. It is, however, an appropriate remedy in sale of land cases but its award is always in the discretion of the court, and a decree will not therefore be granted when it would cause exceptional hardship or where third party rights would be prejudiced by the decree. Lack of mutuality or an element of mistake (in the legal sense of the word) or fraud will also prevent the award of the decree. Although the Limitation Act 1980 does not apply to equitable remedies, the doctrine of laches may deprive the plaintiff of his decree where he has delayed in making application to the court. A decree may be applied for even before the contractual date for completion has passed and regardless of whether time of the completion date was of the essence.

Under the Supreme Court Act 1981 the court has power to award damages either in addition to or in substitution for a decree of specific performance. Damages awarded under this jurisdiction are assessed on the same principles as apply to common law damages.

# Deposit

*Forfeiture*

**19.11**  Even where the contract does not contain an express right for the seller to forfeit the deposit on the buyer's breach, this right is implied at common law (*Hall v Burnell* (1911)). The right to forfeit applies only to the deposit and not to other payments made by the buyer in part payment of the purchase price (*Mayson v Clouet* (1924)). Where the buyer is in breach and the seller forfeits the deposit, the buyer cannot recover his deposit if he later discovers a defect in the seller's title (*Soper v Arnold* (1889)).

It seems that the court may order a defaulting buyer to pay the whole of a 10% deposit to the seller, even in circumstances where the 10% payment would exceed the seller's actual loss. However there is the possibility that in these circumstances the buyer might be able to defend the seller's claim for the deposit by invoking the common law provisions relating to penalty clauses (*Damon Compania Naviera v Hapag-Lloyd International SA* (1983)).

A seller who sues for damages for the buyer's breach must give credit for the amount of the deposit paid.

*Return of deposit to buyer*

**19.12**  Under section 49(2) of the Law of Property Act 1925 the court has a wide discretion to order the return of his deposit to the buyer. In order to succeed in his action it is not necessary for the buyer to establish some fault on the part of the seller. In *Universal Corporation v Five Ways Properties* (1979), Buckley LJ said 'repayment must be ordered in any circumstances which make this the fairest course between the two parties'. The following factors may be relevant to the court in deciding whether or not to order the return of the buyer's deposit:

  (a)  the conduct of the parties, and of the applicant in particular;
  (b)  the gravity of the matters in question;
  (c)  the amount at stake; and
  (d)  the terms of the contract.

The court has power under section 49(2) to order the return of all the deposit or none of it, but there is no jurisdiction to order the return of part of the deposit. However in *Dimsdale Developments (South East) Ltd v De Haan* (1984), the court managed to circumvent this problem by ordering the return of the whole deposit to the defaulting buyer subject to the buyer's paying the seller's incidental expenses of the resale of the property.

## Failure to comply with notice to complete

**19.13**    The innocent party has a choice in that he may either:

(a) treat the guilty party as having repudiated the contract, accept the breach and proceed to sue for damages for the breach; or

(b) pursue an action for specific performance together with damages for loss caused by the delay.

If he elects to take the former course of action, the contract is brought to an end, and having chosen to sue for damages for breach, the innocent party cannot later change his mind and elect instead for specific performance.

If the latter course is chosen, but the decree does not assist the innocent party, it is possible for the innocent party to ask the court to discharge the decree of specific performance and to replace it with an order for damages (*Johnson v Agnew* (1980)).

## Liens

**19.14**    After the date of the contract the seller has an equitable lien over the property until the purchase price is paid in full. The lien continues to exist until payment is made despite the fact that completion has taken place or that possession of the property has been surrendered to the buyer. The buyer has a similar lien in respect of any money paid by him under the contract, including interest.

Unless supported by a deposit of the title deeds, such liens are enforceable against a subsequent buyer only if they are protected by notice in registered land or registered as a C(iii) land charge in unregistered land. A lien may be enforced by an order for sale of the property.

## Vendor and purchaser summons

**19.15**    A vendor and purchaser summons under section 49 of the Law of Property Act 1925 is a summary remedy which can be used to settle disputes arising between the parties between contract and completion. It is not a remedy for breach of contract and cannot be used to test the validity of the contract itself. It can be used to determine points such as the validity of a requisition raised by the buyer or the adequacy of a reply to a requisition given by the seller. The court has a discretion to make such order as it thinks fit, including an order for costs, but a decree of specific performance has never been awarded on an application made under the section. Although the remedy is supposedly both inexpensive and expeditious, in practice it may turn out to be neither. See *MEPC v Christian-Edwards* (1981), where an application under the section took three years to be resolved.

## Standard Condition 7

**19.16**    Condition 7 of the Standard Conditions of Sale provides in respect of remedies as follows:

'7.    REMEDIES

7.1    *Errors and omissions*

7.1.1    If any plan or statement in the contract, or in the negotiations leading to it, is or was misleading or inaccurate due to an error or omission, the remedies available are as follows.

7.1.2    When there is a material difference between the description or value of the property, or of any of the chattels included in the contract, as represented and as it is, the buyer is entitled to damages.

7.1.3    An error or omission only entitles the buyer to rescind the contract:

(a) where it results from fraud or recklessness, or

(b) where he would be obliged, to his prejudice, to accept property differing substantially (in quantity, quality, or tenure) from what the error or omission had led him to expect.

7.2    *Rescission*

If either party rescinds the contract:

(a) unless the rescission is a result of the buyer's breach of contract the deposit is to be repaid to the buyer with accrued interest

(b) the buyer is to return any documents he received from the seller and is to cancel any registration of the contract.

7.3    *Late completion*

7.3.1    If there is default by either or both of the parties in performing their obligations under the contract and completion is delayed, the party whose total period of default is the greater is to pay compensation to the other party.

7.3.2    Compensation is calculated at the contract rate on the purchase price and the chattels price, less (where the buyer is the paying party) any deposit paid, for the period by which the paying party's default exceeds that of the receiving party, or, if shorter, the period between completion date and actual completion.

7.3.3    Any claim for loss resulting from delayed completion is to be reduced by any compensation paid under this contract.

7.3.4    Where the buyer holds the property as tenant of the seller and completion is delayed, the seller may give notice to the buyer, before the date of actual completion that he intends to take the net income from the property until completion. If he does so, he cannot claim compensation under condition 7.3.1 as well.

7.4    *After completion*

7.4.1    Completion does not cancel liability to perform any outstanding obligation under this contract.

7.5    *Buyer's failure to comply with notice to complete*

7.5.1    If the buyer fails to complete in accordance with a notice to complete, the following terms apply.

7.5.2    The seller may rescind the contract, and if he does so:

(a) he may

   (i)   forfeit and keep any deposit and accrued interest

   (ii)  resell the property

   (iii) claim damages

(b) the buyer is to return any documents he received from the seller and is to cancel any registration of the contract.

7.5.3    The seller retains his other rights and remedies.

7.6    *Seller's failure to comply with notice to complete*

7.6.1    If the seller fails to complete in accordance with a notice to complete, the following terms apply.

7.6.2    The buyer may rescind the contract, and if he does so:

(a) the deposit is to be repaid to the buyer with accrued interest

(b) the buyer is to return any documents he received from the seller and is, at the seller's expense, to cancel any registration of the contract.

7.6.3    The buyer retains his other rights and remedies.'

*Errors and omissions*

**19.17**   Condition 7.1 (errors and omissions) defines the remedies available to the parties in the event of there being misdescription, misrepresentation, or non-disclosure. Misdescription is discussed in Chapter 7, misrepresentation in Chapter 8, and non-disclosure in Chapter 5.

Where the effect of the error or omission is not 'material' and is not caused by fraud or recklessness, Condition 7.1.2 attempts to deprive the innocent party of any remedy at all. The word 'material' is not defined by the condition. In such circumstances, at common law, compensation is available to the innocent party for misdescription or non-disclosure, and unless a misrepresentation was truly innocent (in that the defendant could establish the defence of grounds and belief under section 2 of the Misrepresentation Act 1967), damages are available for misrepresentation under section 2(1) of the Misrepresentation Act 1967.

If the error or omission was caused innocently or negligently and its effect is 'material', damages are available to the innocent party. No method of calculation or of payment of the compensation is specified by the condition. The method of calculation of compensation set out in Condition 7.3.2 is confined to the context of Condition 7.3 dealing with late completion and is not applicable here. Rescission for an innocent or negligent error or omission is available only where Condition 7.1.3(b) applies, the parties' rights on rescission being governed by Condition 7.2.

An error or omission caused by fraud or recklessness will lead to rescission under Condition 7.1.3, and provided the error or omission was material, compensation would be available under Condition 7.1.2. Since neither fraud nor recklessness is defined by the condition, these words must be construed in accordance with their ordinary dictionary meanings, recklessness involving a wanton disregard of the consequences of the statement or omission, amounting to more than mere carelessness. Fraud may be qualified by the definition of the word in *Derry v Peek* (1889) as a deliberately dishonest statement, made 'knowingly, or without belief in its truth, or recklessly, careless whether it be true or false'. At common law, rescission is available for a material fraudulent misdescription or non-disclosure, and both rescission and damages are available, either in tort for deceit or under the Misrepresentation Act 1967, for a fraudulent misrepresentation.

Difficulties may arise over the interpretation of the word 'material' and over the amount and method of payment of compensation.

### Exclusion of remedies

**19.18**   Conditions 7.1.2 and 7.1.3 are by their nature exclusion clauses which attempt to deprive the innocent party wholly or partly of his remedies. So far as the clauses apply to misrepresentation, their validity is subject to their satisfying the reasonableness test in section 11 of the Unfair Contract Terms Act 1977. This test is subjective, that is, the clause must be reasonable in the light of the circumstances of the particular transaction, and there is therefore no guarantee that the clauses will be upheld by the court.

### Rescission

**19.19**   The parties' rights on rescission are governed by Condition 7.2. This condition will apply in all situations where the right to rescind is validly exercised by one party under a right to do so given by one of the general conditions, and could by special condition be made to apply to a separate right to rescind given by a special condition in the contract.

Under the general conditions, rescission is available as a remedy in the following circumstances:

  (a) for misdescription, non-disclosure or misrepresentation (Condition 7.1.3);
  (b) where the property is rendered unusable between contract and completion (Condition 5.1.2); and

(c) where a licence to assign a leasehold property cannot be obtained (Condition 8.3.4).

Condition 7.2(a) allows the seller to keep the deposit if rescission is as a result of the buyer's breach of contract. Given the circumstances in which rescission is available, this situation is unlikely to occur. If the buyer were in breach of contract, the seller would be entitled to repudiate the contract and claim damages, his right to forfeit the deposit being dependent on the court's discretion to order its return to the buyer under section 49 of the Law of Property Act 1925 (see 19.12 above).

Except where the buyer is in breach of contract, he is entitled to the return of his deposit with accrued interest. 'Accrued interest' is defined in Condition 1.1.1(a) (see Chapter 2). The buyer is to return documents to the seller and to cancel any registration of the contract, both at his own expense. There is no provision for any other compensation to be paid to the buyer. In this respect the condition is less generous than the general law where, for example, in the event of rescission for misrepresentation, the buyer would be entitled to be compensated for his loss. Where rescission occurs as a result of a misrepresentation made by the seller, this clause would be subject to the reasonableness test in section 11 of the Unfair Contract Terms Act 1977.

## Damages

**19.20**   Condition 7.3 is discussed in Chapter 18. Any claim for damages arising out of a delayed completion is reduced by the amount of compensation paid under Condition 7.3 (Condition 7.3.3). This reflects the common law rules relating to the assessment of damages which aim to put the innocent party into the position in which he would have been had the contract been properly performed, and do not allow one party to make a profit out of the other's breach.

## Non-merger

**19.21**   The common law rule that the terms of the contract merge with the purchase deed on completion in so far as the two documents cover the same ground can cause problems since it effectively precludes any remedy stemming from the contract from being pursued after completion, leaving the buyer with the less than satisfactory remedy of an action based on the covenants for title under the Law of Property (Miscellaneous Provisions) Act 1994. For this reason it is common to find such a clause as Condition 7.4 included in the contract which prevents merger of the contract and conveyance, thus leaving open the option of pursuing contractual remedies for outstanding contractual obligations despite the fact that completion has taken place. The merger rule only affects actions stemming from the contract itself and does not prevent an action in another area of law, such as negligence or misrepresentation.

*Failure to comply with notice to complete*

**19.22**   Service of a notice to complete is governed by Condition 6.8 and is discussed in Chapter 18.

Where the buyer has failed to comply with a notice to complete the seller is, by Condition 7.5.2, entitled to all or any of the following remedies:

(a)  forfeit the deposit and accrued interest;

(b)  resell the property;

(c)  claim damages.

'Accrued interest' is defined in Condition 1.1.1(a) (see Chapter 2). The right to forfeit the deposit is dependent on the court's discretion to order its return to the buyer under section 49 of the Law of Property Act 1925 (see 19.12 above). If damages are claimed, credit must be given for the forfeited deposit. Similarly, if the property is resold by the seller, he would normally be able to claim damages from the buyer only where the resale resulted in financial loss to the seller. The costs of the resale would be claimable as a head of loss, but if this were the only damage suffered by the seller, the costs of bringing the action would probably exceed the damages payable. Any breach of contract gives rise to a potential claim for damages (*Raineri v Miles* (1981)), but the expense involved in bringing such an action precludes this remedy, except where the loss involved is substantial. Damages would be assessed under normal contractual principles (see 19.4 above). The seller is also entitled to the return of his documents from the buyer, and to the cancellation of any registration of the contract, both to be done at the buyer's expense.

The buyer's remedies on the seller's failure to comply with a notice to complete are dealt with by Condition 7.6 and are effectively a mirror image of the remedies available to the seller in the converse situation under Condition 7.5.

The phrase 'the [seller/buyer] retains his other rights and remedies' (Conditions 7.5.3 and 7.6.3) implies that the innocent party does not forfeit the right to use other common law remedies to recover his losses, including making an application for specific performance if that remedy is considered to be a feasible alternative or addition in the circumstances of the case.

The buyer's obligation to return documents to the seller and to cancel the registration of the contract (where appropriate) applies only where, on the expiry of the notice to complete, the option to rescind the contract is exercised.

The remedies given by Conditions 7.5 and 7.6 are available to the parties only where a valid notice to complete has been served, in the absence of which the rights and remedies of the parties are governed by the general law.

## Suggested amendments

**19.23**    Although the conditions discussed above make provision for the return of the buyer's deposit in certain circumstances, there is no reference to the return of any further instalments of the purchase price which may have been paid by the buyer before the contract was terminated. If the buyer is to pay the purchase price by instalments, he may consider amending these conditions to provide for the return of all money paid under the contract, with accrued interest. The rights given to the parties on rescission are limited and a buyer may feel that he should be entitled to some compensation in addition to the return of his deposit if the seller exercises his right to rescind in circumstances where the buyer is not in breach of contract. It may be reasonable for the seller to reimburse the buyer's solicitor's costs and an amendment of Condition 7.2 to this effect may be considered.

The remedies given by the conditions for misrepresentation would in some circumstances be less generous than those available under the Misrepresentation Act 1967, and it would be to the buyer's advantage to delete the exclusion clauses relating to misrepresentation and to rely instead on his statutory remedies. A seller who seeks to restrict the buyer's remedies for misrepresentation further than is already done by the conditions will have to draft his exclusion clause with extreme care to ensure that it will satisfy the reasonableness test under section 11 of the Unfair Contract Terms Act 1977 in the circumstances pertaining to the particular contract in which the clause is included. Previous editions of the Law Society and National Conditions of Sale included a clause allowing the seller to claim liquidated damages in lieu of compensation in certain circumstances. This clause could be used to the seller's advantage where the amount recoverable under the liquidated damages clause was greater than the actual loss occasioned to the seller by the buyer's breach. If it is sought to include such a clause it will need care in drafting to ensure that the clause is not void as a penalty.

## SCPC Conditions 9.1, 9.5 and 9.6

**19.24**    SCPC Conditions 9.1, 9.5 and 9.6 are identical in wording and effect to the equivalent Standard Conditions. The only matter to be noted in respect of SCPC 9.1 is that the exclusion clause relating to misrepresentation in these conditions will not normally be subject to the reasonableness test in the Unfair Contract Terms Act 1977, since the parties to a commercial contract will not be dealing as 'consumers'.

**19.25**    SCPC Condition 9.2 differs from its equivalent condition in Standard Condition 7.2 only in so far as sub-clause (c) represents an additional sub-clause dealing with insurance premiums. This sub-clause is discussed in Chapter 12.

**19.26**    SCPC Condition 9.3, dealing with compensation for late completion is substantially different from the equivalent condition found in Standard Condition 7.3. Both these conditions are discussed in Chapter 18.

# Chapter 20

# Tenanted Property

## The general law

**20.1** The general conditions discussed in other chapters of this book apply both to sales with vacant possession and to those which are sold subject to tenancies. The purpose of this chapter is to highlight some of the matters which apply only to the latter.

### Describing the property to be sold

**20.2** Under an open contract there is an implied condition that the sale will be with vacant possession. However, constructive notice of the existence of a tenancy may be imputed to the buyer; for example, if the buyer knows that a person is in occupation of the property, he is presumed to know the rights of the occupier, and where the occupier has a legal tenancy the buyer will take subject to that tenancy (*Hunt v Luck* (1902)). Where it is intended to sell the property subject to existing tenancies, this fact should be disclosed in the particulars of sale, and details of the tenancies given in the special conditions.

Care should be taken in drafting the particulars and special conditions so that the seller does not become liable for misdescription, non-disclosure, or misrepresentation.

The buyer should be given adequate opportunity to inspect the leases or tenancy agreements; for this purpose copies of such documents should be supplied to him with the draft contract. Although expired leases do not normally have to be abstracted it is suggested that this should be done where the tenant is still in occupation and the property is sold subject to the tenancy. This is of particular importance where the tenant has acquired the benefit of security of tenure under, for example, the Housing Act 1988.

### Enquiries to be made by the buyer

**20.3** Apart from the usual local authority search, enquiries and pre-contract enquiries, extra enquiries should be raised about the tenancy. Particular attention should be paid to the following:

(a) Ascertaining full details of any oral tenancies.
(b) Checking whether there is any breach of covenant on the part of either landlord or tenant and requiring these to be remedied prior to completion.

(c) Whether the rent reserved in the lease is the lawfully recoverable rent. Has it been increased under a rent review clause or decreased by the tenant's application to the Rent Assessment Committee (Housing Act properties)?

(d) Whether the tenant has any security of tenure.

(e) Copies of any notice to quit served by either landlord or tenant should be requested.

(f) Whether the landlord has consented to the making of any improvement by the tenant which might lead to a claim for compensation in the future (business premises or agricultural tenancies).

(g) Are there any outstanding claims for compensation by the tenant? (business premises and agricultural tenancies).

(h) Whether the tenant has the benefit of any option to purchase or to renew.

### Between contract and completion

**20.4**    The general rule that the seller holds the legal estate on trust for the buyer also applies to property which is sold subject to tenancies.

If the tenant vacates the property before completion the buyer becomes entitled to the consequent increase in value of the property without becoming liable to pay any additional price.

The seller's power as landlord to alter the terms of any tenancy seems to be suspended between contract and completion, in that if he terminates an existing tenancy without having consulted the buyer he is responsible for any resulting loss (*Rafferty v Schofield* (1897)), and he must not, without consulting the buyer, re-let vacant property on a lease which confers security of tenure on the tenant (*Abdullah v Shah* (1959)).

### Apportionment of rent

**20.5**    Where completion does not take place on a rent day and the rent is payable in arrear, the seller will be entitled to a proportion of the accrued rent from the last rent day until completion, but under the general law he cannot require the buyer to pay this apportioned part of the rent on completion. He must wait for the next rent day and then recover the sum from the buyer. This unsatisfactory common law provision is usually altered by the special conditions of the contract which will provide for an apportionment of the rent to be made on completion. See Condition 6.3.

### Completion and after

**20.6**    In addition to the normal requirements on completion (see Chapter 17), the counterpart leases or tenancy agreements should be handed over to the buyer together with an authority addressed to the tenant directing him in future to pay his rent to the buyer.

Where the tenancy or lease is of a dwelling-house the buyer must give written notice to the tenant informing him of the buyer's name, address and interest in the property (Landlord and Tenant Act 1985, s 3). The seller's liability as landlord continues until this information is given to the tenant by either the seller or buyer (Landlord and Tenant Act 1987, s 50).

# Standard Conditions 3.3, 4.5 and 6.3.1

**20.7**  The Standard Conditions of Sale provide for tenanted property as follows:

'3.3    *Leases affecting the property*

3.3.1    The following provisions apply if any part of the property is sold subject to a lease.

3.3.2    (a) The seller having provided the buyer with full details of each lease or copies of the documents embodying the lease terms, the buyer is treated as entering into the contract knowing and fully accepting those terms.

   (b) The seller is to inform the buyer without delay if the lease ends or if the seller learns of any application by the tenant in connection with the lease; the seller is then to act as the buyer reasonably directs, and the buyer is to indemnify him against all consequent loss and expense.

   (c) Except with the buyer's consent, the seller is not to agree to any proposal to change the lease terms nor to take any steps to end the lease.

   (d) The seller is to inform the buyer without delay of any change to the lease terms which may be proposed or agreed.

   (e) The buyer is to indemnify the seller against all claims arising from the lease after actual completion; this includes claims which are unenforceable against a buyer for want of registration.

   (f) The seller takes no responsibility for what rent is lawfully recoverable, nor for whether or how any legislation affects the lease.

   (g) If the let land is not wholly within the property, the seller may apportion the rent.

4.5    *Rents and rentcharges*

   The fact that a rent or rentcharge, whether payable or receivable by the owner of the property, has been or will on completion be, informally apportioned is not to be regarded as a defect in title.

6.3.1    Income and outgoings of the property are to be apportioned between the parties so far as the change of ownership on completion will affect entitlement to receive or liability to pay them.'

*Duty to disclose*

**20.8**    Where the property is sold subject to a tenancy this fact must be disclosed by special condition.

The seller is under a duty to make a full disclosure of the terms of any tenancy to which the property is subject (Condition 3.3.2(a)). Provided he does this, by supplying copies or full details of the tenancies, the buyer will be deemed to purchase with full knowledge of the tenancies and will not be able to complain if, say, the contract contains an inaccurate description of the tenancies. The buyer's right to query the tenancies is precluded, so any requisitions relating to their terms must be raised before exchange of contracts. It is suggested that whenever possible copies of the agreement should be supplied to the buyer rather than 'full details', the latter phrase being reserved for oral tenancies where a written agreement cannot be supplied. Where tenancies have not been disclosed in accordance with the condition the buyer may have a remedy in non-disclosure, misdescription or misrepresentation.

The word 'lease' includes a sublease, tenancy and an agreement for a lease or sublease (Condition 1.1.1(h)).

*Indemnity*

**20.9**    A reversioner (the seller) remains liable to his tenant in respect of breaches committed by the reversioner before completion. The buyer will normally require the seller to rectify such breaches before completion and will be unwilling to give an indemnity in respect of them. In relation to breaches of the landlord's covenants which occur after completion of the sale to the buyer, the outgoing landlord can, by giving notice to the tenant within four weeks of completion of the sale of the reversion, seek to be released from his future liability under the lease covenants under the Landlord and Tenant (Covenants) Act 1995. If the tenant does not object, the landlord is released; if the tenant does object, an application may be made to the court to decide the matter. Third party covenants (eg management company covenants) remain binding on both landlord and tenant. If a release from future obligations is obtained by the reversioner/seller, he will not need to take an indemnity covenant from his buyer. In other cases indemnity may be required. Provision for indemnity is contained in Condition 3.3.2(e). It should be noted that Condition 4.6.4 (see Chapter 16) requires the buyer to indemnify the seller against 'any obligation affecting the property'. This will include claims by tenants. The buyer should therefore ensure that he has made full enquiries relating to the extent of such claims before exchange of contracts, or should try to obtain an amendment to these conditions in relation to this type of liability.

Where the lease contains an option to renew or to purchase the reversion, Condition 3.3.2(e) imposes an obligation on the buyer to indemnify the seller against claims arising out of that option even though it cannot be enforced against him. Although it is unlikely that a buyer will often be troubled by such claims, he should ensure that he has received full details of the estate contract before agreeing to accept liability under this condition. A more satisfactory solution from the buyer's point of view would be to delete this requirement from the contract.

*Change in or determination of tenancy*

**20.10**   Condition 3.3.2(b) requires the seller to inform the buyer of any changes in the tenancy terms which occur after the contract is made, but places no sanction on the seller if he fails to do this. If the tenancy terms change before the contract is made, the seller would be in breach of his duty of disclosure and guilty of misrepresentation if he failed to inform the buyer of the change. The seller is also required under this condition to disclose to the buyer details of any application concerning the lease, for example an application to fix a fair rent or an application for a new tenancy made by a business tenant under the Landlord and Tenant Act 1954 as amended.

The provisions of Condition 3.3.2(b) reflect the decision in *Abdullah v Shah* (1959) and state expressly the seller's duty to inform the buyer if a tenancy terminates. The seller may then not re-let the property unless the buyer directs him to do so, the buyer being liable to indemnify the seller in respect of all losses and expenses incurred by the seller in the course of carrying out the buyer's instructions.

*Rent*

**20.11**   Condition 3.3.2(f) places on the buyer the onus of checking the lawfully recoverable rent from the tenanted property. Although the condition states that the seller 'takes no responsibility for this matter' the condition only provides limited protection for the seller who would still probably be liable in misrepresentation if he did not accurately disclose the actual rent which is currently being paid by the tenant. The buyer also bears the burden of checking the effect of any statutory provisions concerning for example, security of tenure, affecting the tenancy. Again the seller is not totally exonerated from liability by this condition since by Condition 3.1.3 the seller is under a duty to inform the buyer of anything in writing concerning an incumbrance. Tenancies will fall within the definition of 'incumbrance' in so far as they are 'mentioned in the agreement' (Condition 3.1.2(a)) ie specifically referred to in the special conditions. Certain matters relating to tenancies may fall within the definition irrespective of whether the tenancies are specifically referred to in the agreement, for example, where the tenancy is an overriding interest, or where there is an entry on a public register relating to the tenancy. The latter would include a summons issued by a tenant to obtain a new lease under Landlord and Tenant Act 1954 Part II as amended, or an application made by a residential tenant to the Rent Assessment Committee to determine the rent for the property.

Condition 3.3.2(g) applies where the property being sold is part only of the property subject to a lease and deals with the apportionment of rent between the part of the property now being sold and that which is to be retained by the seller. A legal apportionment of rent requires the consent of the owner of the rent. This condition allows the seller to make the apportionment. Similarly, Condition 4.5 permits the seller to make an informal apportionment of rent, to which the buyer may not object. Apportionment of rent on other cases is dealt with by Condition 6.3.1 (see Chapter 17).

## Suggested amendments

**20.12**  Except as discussed above no amendments are required to this condition.

## The Protocol

**20.13**  Although the Protocol is expressed to relate to all domestic transactions it contains no direct reference to tenanted property. An oblique reference to tenants is found in para 2.13 which requires the seller's solicitor to make enquiries about all persons who are in occupation of the property.

## SCPC Condition 4

**20.13**  SCPC Condition 4 provides as follows:

'4.1.1    This condition applies if any part of the property is sold subject to a lease.

4.1.2    The seller having provided the buyer with full details of each lease or copies of documents embodying the lease terms, the buyer is treated as entering into the contract knowing and fully accepting those terms.

4.1.3    The seller is not to serve a notice to end the lease nor to accept a surrender.

4.1.4    The seller is to inform the buyer without delay if the lease ends.

4.1.5    The buyer is to indemnify the seller against all claims arising from the lease after actual completion; this includes claims which are unenforceable against a buyer for want of registration.

4.1.6    If the property does not include all the land let, the seller may apportion the rent and, if the lease is a new tenancy, the buyer may require the seller to apply under section 10 of the Landlord and Tenant (Covenants) Act 1995 for the apportionment to bind the tenant.

4.2  **Property management**

4.2.1    The seller is promptly to give the buyer full particulars of:

(a) any court or arbitration proceedings in connection with the lease, and

(b) any application for a licence, consent or approval under the lease.

4.2.2    Conditions 4.2.3 to 4.2.8 do not apply to a rent review process to which condition 5 applies.

4.2.3　Subject to condition 4.2.4, the seller is to conduct any court or arbitration proceedings in accordance with written directions given by the buyer from time to time (for which the seller is to apply), unless to do so might place the seller in breach of an obligation to the tenant or a statutory duty.

4.2.4　If the seller applies for directions from the buyer in relation to a proposed step in the proceedings and the buyer does not give such directions within 10 working days, the seller may take or refrain from taking that step as it thinks fit.

4.2.5　The buyer is to indemnify the seller against all loss and expense resulting from the seller's following the buyer's directions.

4.2.6　Unless the buyer gives written consent, the seller is not to:

(a) grant or formally withhold any licence, consent or approval under the lease, or

(b) serve any notice or take any action (other than action in court or arbitration proceedings) as landlord under the lease.

4.2.7　When the seller applies for the buyer's consent under condition 4.2.6:

(a) the buyer is not to withhold its consent to attach conditions to the consent where to do so might place the seller in breach of an obligation to the tenant or a statutory duty

(b) the seller may proceed as if the buyer has consented when:

(i) in accordance with paragraph (a), the buyer is not entitled to withhold its consent, or

(ii) the buyer does not refuse its consent within 10 working days.

4.2.8　If the buyer withholds or attaches conditions to its consent, the buyer is to indemnify the seller against all loss and expense.

4.2.9　In all other respects, the seller is to manage the property in accordance with the principles of good estate management until completion.

4.3　**Continuing liability**

At the request and cost of the seller, the buyer is to support any application by the seller to be released from the landlord covenants in a lease to which the property is sold subject.

## 5　RENT REVIEWS

5.1　**Subject to condition 5.2, this condition applies if:**

(a) the rent reserved by a lease of all or part of the property is to be reviewed,

(b) the seller is either the landlord or the tenant,

(c) the rent review process started before actual completion, and

(d) no reviewed rent has been agreed or determined at the date of the contract.

5.2　The seller is to conduct the rent review process until actual completion, after which the buyer is to conduct it.

5.3     Condition 5.4 and 5.5 cease to apply on actual completion if the reviewed rent will only be payable in respect of a period after that date.

5.4     In the course of the rent review process, the seller and the buyer are each to:

(a) act promptly with a view to achieving the best result obtainable.

(b) consult with and have regard to the views of the other.

(c) provide the other with copies of all material correspondence and papers relating to the process.

(d) ensure that its representations take account of matters put forward by the other, and

(e) keep the other informed of the progress of the process.

5.5     Neither the seller nor the buyer is to agree a rent figure unless it has been approved in writing by the other (such approval not to be unreasonably withheld).

5.6     The seller and the buyer are each to bear their own costs of the rent review process.

5.7     Unless the rent review date precedes the apportionment day, the buyer is to pay the costs of a third party appointed to determine the rent.

5.8     Where the rent review date precedes the apportionment day, those costs are to be divided as follows:

(a) the seller is to pay the proportion that the number of days from the rent review date to the apportionment day bears to the number of days from that rent review date until either the following rent review date or, if none, the expiry of the term, and

(b) the buyer is to pay the balance.'

**20.14**   SCPC Condition 4 is similar in content to the equivalent Standard Condition but has been expanded and generally contains more detailed provisions suitable for the sale of a commercial tenanted property. The general scope of the condition is that the seller must inform the buyer of any changes or proposed changes to the tenancies. Since the buyer will at this stage be the beneficial owner of the property, it follows that the buyer is entitled to direct the seller to act as the buyer wishes in relation to the tenancies, subject to the buyer not requiring the seller to do anything which might put the seller into breach of his own obligations. SCPC Condition 4.2 requires the seller to manage the property in accordance with the principles of good estate management until completion. The seller holds the property on trust for the buyer between exchange and completion and arguably would be liable at common law to the buyer for loss sustained during this period, even in the absence of this condition.

**20.15**   SCPC Condition 8.3.1 is identical in wording to Standard Condition 6.3.1 and is discussed above.

**20.16**   SCPC Condition 5 contains provisions to cover the situation where a rent review commences prior to completion of the sale.

# Chapter 21

# Sales of Part

## Introduction

**21.1**    A sale of part of land is a more complex transaction than a sale of the whole of the seller's property. This chapter draws attention to some of the matters peculiar to sales of part with reference to those Standard Conditions which apply mainly or exclusively to such transactions. There is, of necessity, some overlap between the subject matter discussed in this chapter and elsewhere in the book, but repetition has been kept to a minimum by the use of cross-references.

## The particulars of sale

**21.2**    The description of the land contained in the seller's title deeds will not be appropriate for use in the present contract, since only part of the seller's land is now being sold. The new description must clearly identify the land which is to be sold and should preferably refer to an accurate plan annexed to the contract. The plan should be drawn to scale and should show the delineation of the land to be sold as well as of the land retained by the seller. Measurements must be shown in metric values (Units of Measurement Regulations 1986 (as amended)). Markings on the plan must conform to Land Registry requirements. The lines of boundary fences, pipe-lines and rights of way should also be clearly marked. As in all cases reference will also be made in the particulars of sale to existing easements and covenants to which the land will remain subject after completion. In addition there should be expressly set out easements to be granted to the buyer and reservations to be made in the seller's favour, the details of such matters being dealt with in the conditions of sale. New covenants to be imposed on either party should be stipulated.

## Grants and reservations

**21.3**    The buyer may want easements of way, drainage, light or air over the seller's retained land. Similarly, the seller may wish to reserve certain rights to himself over the land being sold.

Although section 62 of the Law of Property Act 1925 and the rule in *Wheeldon v Burrows* (1879) (see Chapter 6) may give the buyer limited rights over the seller's land the extent of these implied rights will often be insufficient and not sufficiently precise to meet the buyer's requirements so that a special condition should be included in the contract to deal with such matters. Since neither section 62 nor the rule in *Wheeldon v Burrows* operates in favour of the seller, express provision for reservations must always be included in the contract. Condition 3.4.2 deals with the grant and reservation of easements but the extent of the rights given under this condition is limited and it is usually considered necessary to expressly spell out the extent of the rights granted and reserved by special condition. A special condition relating to the grant or reservation of an easement should take into account the following matters:

(a) the exact passage of the easement, as shown on the plan annexed to the contract;

(b) the persons (or vehicles) who are entitled to benefit from the right given;

(c) the burden of maintenance;

(d) a right of entry to the land over which the easement passes in order to inspect and carry out repairs.

Rights of light and air may pass to the buyer automatically under section 62 of the Law of Property Act 1925 or under the rule in *Wheeldon v Burrows*. The seller should consider the exclusion of such rights in the contract in case he or his successors in title should at some future time wish to build on the retained land. Standard Condition 3.3 restricts the buyer's right to light and air but an express clause in favour of the seller preserving his right to build on the retained land may also be considered.

## Imposition of new restrictive covenants

**21.4**    The contract will often provide for the buyer to enter into new restrictive covenants with the seller in order to preserve the amenities of the seller's retained land. Covenants frequently deal with some or all of the following:

(a) the erection and maintenance of a boundary fence between the two plots;

(b) the restriction of the buyer's use of the land;

(c) the restriction of the buyer's right to build on the land.

The seller will wish to enjoy the benefit of the covenants given by the buyer and will usually wish to be able to pass that benefit on to his successors in title. He will also wish to ensure that the burden of the covenants runs with the buyer's land to ensure that the covenants will be enforceable against the buyer's successors in title. Provided that restrictive covenants are carefully drafted so that they are expressly taken for the benefit of the seller's retained land and are registered after completion on the charges register of a registered title, enforceability of the covenants should not prove to be problematical.

# The purchase deed

**21.5**     The purchase deed must be drafted to reflect the terms of the contract and will frequently be a complex document since it will contain clauses reserving rights to the seller and granting rights to the buyer. The buyer will often be entering into new restrictive covenants and so will need to execute the deed. A plan attached to the deed should also be signed by both parties but need not be witnessed. In registered land the seller's mortgagee will release his interest by using Form 53, rather than by being made a party to the transfer. The acknowledgement and undertaking procedure is not relevant to a registered title. (See also 16.7 above.)

# Completion and after

*Registered land*

**21.6**     In registered land transactions the seller's mortgagee will release the buyer's part of the property from the mortgage on receipt of a proportionate part of the purchase price. An undertaking relating to the discharge of the mortgage should be obtained on completion (see Chapter 17).

Restrictive covenants affecting registered land will be noted automatically when the buyer submits his application for registration of title.

*Unregistered land*

**21.7**     The Land Registry will need to check the examined abstract during the course of registration of the title. The seller will not hand over his title deeds on completion since they relate to land retained by him. It follows that the buyer must verify his abstract or epitome against the original deeds and mark up the abstract or epitome to show that it has been examined. Where the title is to be registered after completion, endorsement of these memoranda is strictly unnecessary since the new land or charge certificate will show the buyer's entitlement. However it is good practice to make the endorsements so that they are brought to the buyer's attention on a subsequent sale of the seller's retained land. A memorandum of the conveyance to the buyer should be indorsed on the most recent of the seller's retained deeds and a copy of the memorandum given to the buyer. If the seller enters into new covenants with the buyer burdening the retained land, a note of these covenants should also be indorsed on the seller's title deeds.

# Standard Conditions 3.4 and 4.6.5

**21.8**     The Standard Conditions of Sale contain the following provisions relating to sales of part:

'3.4    *Retained land*

Where after the transfer the seller will be retaining land near the property:

(a)  the buyer will have no right of light or air over the retained land, but

(b)  in other respects the seller and the buyer will each have the rights over the land of the other which they would have had if they were two separate buyers to whom the seller had made simultaneous transfers of the property and the retained land.

The transfer is to contain appropriate express terms.

4.6.5  The seller is to arrange at his expense that, in relation to every document of title which the buyer does not receive on completion, the buyer is to have the benefit of:

(a)  a written acknowledgement of his right to its production, and

(b)  a written undertaking for its safe custody (except while it is held by a mortgagee or by someone in a fiduciary capacity).'

*Effect of the condition*

**21.9**    The phrase 'retained land' in Condition 3.4 is inadequate to describe the property which is being retained by the seller and will have to be supplemented by a special condition which identifies the retained land clearly. The contract must be accompanied by a plan which shows the extent both of the land being sold and that retained.

One effect of Condition 3.4 is to provide for the grant of mutual easements and reservations in the purchase deed. The rights granted by this condition are inadequate to protect the parties' interests in most situations and will therefore generally be extended by special condition.

Condition 3.4 also precludes the buyer from the acquisition of rights of light and air over the seller's retained land. Such a condition is beneficial to the seller, and any move by the buyer to amend or delete it should be resisted.

Condition 4.5.5 extends slightly the general law contained in section 64 of the Law of Property Act 1925 relating to the giving of an acknowledgement and undertaking in respect of the custody of retained deeds. This condition is discussed at 16.11 above.

## Suggested amendments

**21.10**    The phrase 'retained land' in Condition 3.4 is not adequate to properly identify the land to which it refers and needs to be supplemented by special condition. Similarly the easements and reservations granted by the condition will not usually be sufficient to meet the needs of the parties on a sale of part; thus these matters too will need to be expressly dealt with in the contract.

If considered necessary, a provision may be included by a buyer to permit the indorsement of a memorandum by the seller on his retained title deeds and for the buyer to take a copy of it to keep with his own deeds. Such a provision is probably superfluous in a case where the land is to be registered after completion, and in other cases the buyer may choose to rely on his rights under section 200 of the Law of Property Act 1925 or section 36 of the Administration of Estates Act 1925 (see Chapter 17).

## The purchase deed

**21.11**   Easements, reservations and new covenants granted or created by the contract would normally be repeated in the purchase deed. HM Land Registry will still need to be made aware of them when an application for registration of the title is submitted, in order to note their effect on the register of the title. Although the contract for the purchase is one of the documents which has to be submitted to HM Land Registry with an application for first registration of land, it is suggested that the presence of these clauses in the contract and purchase deed is drawn specifically to the Registrar's notice when the application for registration is made in order to ensure that they are not overlooked when the register of the new title is prepared.

## The Protocol

**21.12**   Sales of part are not expressly mentioned in the Protocol. Paragraph 3.1 does however require the seller, when preparing the package for the buyer, to mark up as examined against the originals, any documents the original of which will not be handed to the buyer on completion.

## SCPC Conditions 3.3 and 6.6.5

**21.13**   SCPC Conditions 3.3 and 6.6.5 are identical in wording to their Standard Condition counterparts. Their effect is discussed above.

# Chapter 22

# Leaseholds

## Introduction

**22.1**  Most of the conditions discussed in other chapters of this book are relevant to the sale of leasehold property. This chapter attempts to draw together some of those conditions which are of particular importance in this context.

## Drafting the lease or assignment

**22.2**  Where the contract is for the grant of a lease it is usual for the landlord to draft the lease, the draft to be annexed to the contract. If the landlord requires the buyer to pay any part of the seller's costs of the preparation of the lease, he must include an express condition to this effect in the contract (Costs of Leases Act 1958, s 1). The assignment of an existing lease is usually prepared by and paid for by the buyer.

## The duty of disclosure

**22.3**  Apart from the general duty of disclosure discussed in Chapter 5, particular rules apply to leaseholds, although the precise extent of the seller's duty of disclosure is far from certain. It does seem, however, that the seller is under a duty to disclose any breach of repairing obligations in the lease.

There is also a duty to disclose any onerous or unusual covenants in the lease. What is 'unusual' is viewed subjectively having regard to the particular circumstances of the case.

If the contract describes the property as 'leasehold', the buyer may assume that the lease is a head lease.

## Enfranchisement and extended leases

*Leasehold Reform Act 1967*

**22.4**  Where the lease which is being sold was granted for a term exceeding twenty-one years, is of a house within the Leasehold Reform Act 1967 and there may be a right to claim either an extension of the term of the lease or enfranchisement under the Act. To exercise either of these rights certain qualifying provisions must first be satisfied. The rights are exercised by service of notice on the landlord. Once notice has been served, the rights emanating from such notice can be assigned with the lease. The buyer of a lease to which the Act applies should enquire of the seller whether he has served notice in accordance with the Act and if so, require the inclusion in the contract of a condition providing for the assignment to the buyer of the rights given by the notice.

If the seller is entitled to serve notice under the Act but has not done so, the buyer may consider the inclusion of a contractual clause requiring the seller first to serve such a notice, and then to assign his rights to the buyer with the lease. Such a clause will enable the buyer to benefit from the provisions of the Act without first having to establish a period of qualifying residence.

*Leasehold Reform (Housing and Urban Development) Act 1993*

**22.5**    The rights given by the Leasehold Reform Act 1967 (see 22.4 above) apply only to houses. Similar provisions relating to the enfranchisement of flats are contained in the Leasehold Reform (Housing and Urban Development) Act 1993. In relation to enfranchisement, the tenants' rights under the Act must be exercised collectively by a minimum number of tenants in the block, but the right to an extended lease can be exercised by individual tenants in relation to their own flats. A prospective buyer of a flat must make enquiries of the seller to ascertain whether any notice under the Act has been served and if so, what stage negotiations with the freeholder have reached. The right of an individual to extend his lease is subordinate to the collective right to purchase the freehold of the block so that a tenant's notice to extend his own lease is effectively held in abeyance pending the outcome of negotiations by the tenants' representative to purchase the freehold. Although a new tenant can, on completion of his purchase and if he wishes to do so, join in and take the benefit of an existing notice which has been served by the tenants relating to the purchase of the freehold, the existence of such a notice will cause temporary uncertainty over the management of the block and length and terms of the leases of the individual flats, since on an acquisition of the freehold, the tenants, as the new owners, may choose to surrender their existing leases and re-grant new leases on different terms. A new tenant who does choose to join in the enfranchisement will also be expected to pay his predecessor's share of the purchase price of the freehold and associated costs. The buyer's solicitor will need to raise pre-contract enquiries relating to the following matters:

(a)  whether the flat and the lease qualify under the 1993 Act;

(b)  how many qualifying flats and qualifying tenants there are in the block;

(c)  whether and when any initial notice has been served by the tenants and if so, how far negotiations have reached – a copy of the notice should be supplied by the seller's solicitor;

(d)  whether any steps have been taken by the seller to acquire an extension of his own lease and if so what and when.

Additional special conditions may need to be added to the contract to deal with a situation where a current valid notice is in operation relating either to the flat or to the block. The requirements of the buyer's lender in relation to enfranchisement and extended leases should also be ascertained before contracts are exchanged for the purchase. Notices served under the Act can be assigned with the benefit of the flat lease itself, so the fact that an initial notice has been served will not preclude the buyer from joining in the notice provided that the appropriate notice to this effect is served within the time limits prescribed by the Act. Some clients may however prefer not to proceed with their purchase until procedures under the Act have been finalised and there is certainty over the ownership of the freehold and terms of the leases under which the flats are held.

*Landlord and Tenant Act 1987*

**22.6**    This Act gives certain tenants of long leases of flats the right to purchase the landlord's reversionary interest. Although similar to the collective enfranchisement provisions of the 1993 Act, see 22.5 above, the 1987 Act only gives the tenants the right to purchase the landlord's 'reversionary interest' which may be a head lease and not the freehold itself. Unlike the 1993 Act, here the tenants can generally only exercise their rights if and when the landlord decides to sell. A service of notices similar to but less complex than those required under the 1993 Act, have to be served to initiate the procedures under the Act. A buyer of a landlord's reversionary interest will need to make enquiries of the seller to ascertain whether the property falls within the provisions of the Act, and if so, whether the seller has served the appropriate notice on the qualifying tenants offering them the right to buy the reversion. The buyer's purchase can only proceed in these circumstances if the tenants' rights to buy have been extinguished. The Act also contains provisions allowing the court to appoint a manager to exercise the landlord's management functions and in certain circumstances to order the transfer of the reversion to a nominee (usually one or more of the tenants). The variation of a lease can also be ordered by the court where the lease contains inadequate provisions for (*inter alia*) maintenance, repair or insurance. A buyer, whether of the lease or of the reversionary interest, will need to make enquiries of the seller in relation to these matters.

# Deducing title

**22.7**    On the grant of a lease by a freeholder the tenant is not entitled to require the landlord to deduce his title (Law of Property Act 1925, s 44(2)). This open contract rule is clearly unsatisfactory where the lease is to be for a long term of years and/or a premium is to be paid for the grant of the lease. In either of these situations the tenant will want to ensure that the landlord's title is sound, otherwise the purported lease may prove to be worthless. It is therefore usual in such situations for the contract to provide expressly that the landlord will deduce his title to the tenant in the same way that he would do to a purchaser of the freehold, regardless of whether or not the reversion is registered land.

On the grant of a head lease out of a registered title the freehold reversion will often be deduced to the tenant by the usual method of producing office copy entries in accordance with section 110 of the Land Registration Act 1925. A special condition will have to be inserted in the contract to deal with this matter since there is no common law or statutory entitlement to the deduction of the title to the reversion of the grant of a lease out of registered land.

Where a sublease is to be granted out of a registered lease it is common practice for office copy entries to be supplied, together with a copy of the superior lease. On the assignment of a registered lease or sublease office copy entries of the title, and a copy of the lease or sublease should be supplied. Where the lease is registered with less than an absolute title there is no guarantee that the lease was validly granted and further investigation of the title as appropriate to unregistered land should be considered.

On the grant of a sublease of unregistered land under an open contract, the superior lease, out of which the sublease is to be derived, and where appropriate, all dispositions under which the superior lease has been held for the period of fifteen years preceding the date of the contract, must be shown. On the assignment of an unregistered lease or sublease, the lease or sublease which is being sold, together with all dispositions under which it has been held for a period of fifteen years preceding the date of the contract must be shown under an open contract.

Section 45(2) of the Law of Property Act 1925 reinforces the provisions of section 44(2) of the Law of Property Act 1925 by requiring the buyer to assume, unless the contrary appears, that the lease which he has contracted to buy was validly granted. Further, on production of the receipt for the last payment of rent due before actual completion, he must assume, unless the contrary appears, that the rent has been paid and all the covenants in the lease have been performed up to the date of completion.

## Insurance

**22.8**    The risk attaching to the property passes to the buyer of a lease on exchange of contracts (see Chapter 12), but before taking out a policy over the property the buyer should first check the insurance obligations in the lease; some leases will impose the insurance obligations on the landlord; others will specify not only the type of risk to be insured against, but also that the policy must be taken out with a named insurance company. Where the buyer is financing his purchase with the assistance of a mortgage from a building society, the society should be informed of the insurance requirements contained in the lease so that any policy effected by the society over the property complies with such requirements.

# Covenants for title

*Grant of lease*

**22.9**   The provisions of the Law of Property (Miscellaneous Provisions) Act 1994 which, by the use of the key phrase 'the seller sells with [full/limited] title guarantee', imports certain covenants for title into the purchase deed for the benefit of the buyer, are capable of applying on the grant of a new lease. Although it is unlikely that a landlord who is granting a short lease (particularly of residential property) would consider it appropriate to give any covenants at all in this situation, the buyer/tenant who is taking a long lease or who is paying a premium for its grant will probably want to insist on the landlord giving at least some covenants in the lease. The nature and extent of these covenants is discussed in Chapter 3. Consideration must be given by both parties to the question of what covenants, if any, are to be given by the landlord, and appropriate clauses inserted in the contract and purchase deed to reflect their decisions. Where no covenants at all are to be given, this fact should be stated in the contract in order to override Standard Condition 4.6.2 which would otherwise give the buyer the benefit of an unamended full title guarantee.

*Assignment*

**22.10**   The buyer of an existing lease should check to see which covenants, if any, were given on the grant of the lease. Similarly the buyer of a reversion will need to check which covenants, if any, have been given to the tenants under existing leases.

On the assignment of a lease and irrespective of whether value is given for the assignment, if either a full or limited title guarantee is given by the seller, in addition to the normal freehold covenants, the buyer will take the benefit of covenants for title to the effect that:

(a)   the lease is valid and subsisting; and

(b)   the rent has been paid and other obligations under the lease performed up to the time of the conveyance (assignment/transfer).

Repairing obligations under a lease will frequently not have been strictly observed by the seller, and since liability under the covenants is strict, even technical breaches of covenant could in theory give rise to liability under (b) above if the operation of this implied covenant is not modified in the transaction between seller and buyer. For this reason, a modification of (b) above is usual in practice and must be done by express clause to this effect contained in the contract and reflected in the purchase deed. Standard Condition 3.2 effectively provides this modification, but it is good practice to bring this point to the buyer's attention by the inclusion of an appropriate special condition.

*Variation of the covenants*

**22.11**  Any variation of exclusion of the covenants must, in the case of registered land, be set out in the purchase deed by reference to the sections of the Law of Property (Miscellaneous Provisions) Act 1994 which have been altered. Although the register of title will state that the covenants have been modified, the nature and extent of that modification is not shown on the register, and evidence of the precise modification (the lease itself, or on an assignment a copy of the contract or purchase deed) will need to be retained in order to provide details of these modifications. The requirement to show the express modification of the covenants in the purchase deed is not obligatory in unregistered land, but it is good practice to do so.

# Indemnity covenants

*Sale of reversion of lease granted after 1 January 1996*

**22.12**  On a sale of his reversionary interest, the outgoing landlord can apply to the tenant(s) before or within four weeks of completion of the sale, to be released from his future liability under the covenants (Landlord and Tenant (Covenants) Act 1995). Where such consent is granted the seller does not need to take an indemnity covenant from the buyer. If such consent is not forthcoming an express indemnity covenant will be required from the buyer in the purchase deed and appropriate provision for this must therefore be included in the contract (see Standard Condition 4.6.4). The general law does not imply an indemnity covenant in this situation. Liability for breaches which occurred before completion remains with the outgoing landlord and the buyer should insist that such breaches are remedied before completion takes place, or, if this is not possible, the contract should make express provision dealing with this situation. An indemnity covenant given by the seller to the buyer will not always be an appropriate solution to this problem.

*Sale of reversion of lease granted before 1 January 1996*

**22.13**  The Landlord and Tenant (Covenants) Act 1995 does not apply to such leases. The outgoing landlord will therefore remain liable on his covenants despite the assignment of the reversion. Unless he can obtain an express release of future liability from his tenant(s) he needs to take an indemnity covenant from his buyer. Section 77 of the Law of Property Act 1925 implies a covenant in this situation provided value is given for the transaction. A similar effect is achieved in registered land by section 24 of the Land Registration Act 1925 irrespective of whether value is given for the transaction. Where neither of these statutory provisions apply the seller is entitled to ask the buyer to enter an indemnity covenant under Standard Condition 4.6.4. The position in relation to pre-existing breaches of landlord's covenants is as set out in 22.12 above.

*Sale of lease granted after 1 January 1996*

**22.14**   On the assignment of a lease the outgoing tenant is automatically released from future liability under his lease covenants, subject to the landlord's right to call for an 'authorised guarantee agreement' under the Landlord and Tenant (Covenants) Act 1995. Such an agreement will require the outgoing tenant (and his guarantor) to guarantee the performance by his immediate assignee of the lease obligations, but the tenant's liability under this agreement automatically comes to an end when his immediate assignee transfers the property to a new tenant. The outgoing tenant is only liable under the authorised guarantee agreement if the land-lord serves notice on him within six months of the liability occurring, and, in general, is not liable for breaches arising out of variations to the lease which occurred after the tenant assigned the property. Where the outgoing tenant is being released from liability on completion, he will not need to take an indemnity covenant from his buyer. Where he is being required to enter into an authorised guarantee agreement he should take indemnity from the buyer. It is probably not necessary to expressly restrict the duration of the covenant to the period of the assignee's own tenure, since once the assignee has himself assigned the property to a third party, the original seller's liability, which is the obligation which is being indemnified, ceases. Liability for breaches which were committed by the outgoing tenant before completion of the assignment are not released by the 1995 Act and the assignee/buyer should ensure that all such breaches are remedied before completion, or that appropriate contractual clauses are included to deal with these matters.

*Sale of lease granted before 1 January 1996*

**22.15**   Unless the outgoing original tenant can obtain an express release of future liability from his landlord, he will remain liable on the lease covenants throughout the remainder of the term of the lease, and so needs to take an express indemnity covenant from his buyer. Indemnity covenants are implied by section 77 of the Law of Property Act 1925 (unregistered land) or section 24 of the Land Registration Act 1925 (registered land). If these sections do not apply Standard Condition 4.6.4 provides for indemnity to be given by the buyer. For his own protection, the buyer should insist that existing breaches of covenant are remedied by the seller before completion, or that appropriate contractual clauses are included to deal with the situation. If the seller is an assignee from the original tenant, his liability will usually cease when he ceases to be the owner of the property. However a continuing liability, in respect of which an indemnity from the buyer will be needed, may exist if the assignee has entered into a direct covenant with the landlord eg in a licence to assign.

## Consent to assignment

**22.16**   A lease which contains a qualified covenant against alienation, that is, a covenant not to assign etc. without licence or without consent, is subject to the provisions of section 19 of the Landlord and Tenant Act 1927 (as amended) (which cannot be excluded) whereby the landlord may not unreasonably with-hold his consent to an assignment.

In relation to leases granted before 1 January 1996 and new leases of noncommercial property granted after that date, clauses which attempt to pre-empt the operation of section 19 by providing that a tenant who wishes to assign must first offer a surrender of his lease to the landlord must be protected by notice (or registered against the tenant as a C(iv) land charge in unregistered land) in order to bind a buyer of the lease. Further, a landlord's agreement to accept a surrender of business premises within Part II of the Landlord and Tenant Act 1954 has been held to be void as contravening section 38 of that Act (*Adler v Upper Grosvenor Street Investments* (1957), *Greene v Church Commissioners for England* (1974), *Allnatt (London) Properties Ltd v Newton* (1981)).

In relation to leases of commercial property granted on or after 1 January 1996 section 22 of the Landlord and Tenant (Covenants) Act 1995, allows the parties to a lease to agree in the lease itself the terms or conditions on which the land-lord would be prepared to grant an assignment. In such a situation the comments contained in the preceding paragraph relating to section 19 of the Landlord and Tenant Act 1927 have no application.

Covenants against assignment are also subject to the provisions of the Race Relations Act 1976 and the Sex Discrimination Act 1975 which prohibit the withholding of consent to an assignment on the grounds of colour, race, nation-ality, ethnic or national origins or on the grounds of sex or marital status.

Where the landlord's consent to an assignment is necessary the proposed assignee may expect to be asked to supply suitable references for the landlord's approval. Contracts should not be exchanged until it is certain that the land-lord's consent will be forthcoming. The landlord may often ask the assignee to join as a party to the licence to assign so that the assignee enters a direct covenant with the landlord to observe and perform the covenants in the lease. It is uncertain whether, in the absence of a covenant to this effect in the lease which is being assigned, the landlord could insist on this as a condition of his giving consent to the assignment.

Where the lease contains a qualified covenant against assignment the landlord must, within a reasonable time, either grant written consent to the assignment or serve written notice on the tenant giving the reasons for his refusal of consent (Landlord and Tenant Act 1988).

## Options

**22.17**  Although covenants contained in leases are not generally capable of registration as land charges, options to renew and options to purchase the reversion must (in the case of an unregistered reversion) be registered as C(iv) land charges if they are to be enforceable against a purchaser of the reversion.

An option to renew is within the doctrine of privity of estate, and assuming due compliance with the terms of the option it may be enforced by an assignee of the lease against the original landlord or against a purchaser of the reversion in unregistered land if duly registered. An option to purchase the reversion is not within the doctrine of privity of estate but, unless the lease restricts its assignability, the benefit of such an option may be expressly assigned or may pass impliedly with the assignment of the lease.

If the reversionary title is registered, such options will be overriding interests if the tenant is in occupation of the land, but it will avoid subsequent contention if they are protected by notice against the reversionary title.

An option to renew should be drafted to provide for renewal on terms which will not necessarily include a further option to renew since otherwise a perpetually renewable lease may be created (*Northchurch Estates Ltd v Daniels* (1947)).

Options to purchase (save as between the original parties) are subject to the perpetuity rule, but an option to purchase the reversion contained in a lease granted after 15 July 1964 will not be subject to the rule at all provided that:

(a) the option is exercisable only by the tenant and his successors in title; and

(b) the option ceases to be exercisable not later than one year after the end of the term granted by the lease.

## Apportionments and service charges

**22.18**    The apportionment of rent on the property will be dealt with in the usual way on completion (see Chapter 17). Service charges, which are usually regarded as outgoings on the property, are also subject to apportionment but may be difficult to apportion accurately on completion since the rate of the charge will vary depending on the landlord's expenditure on the property, and the exact figures for the period during which completion takes place may not be known until after completion. There are several methods of dealing with this matter. One solution is that the service charge will not be apportioned at all, but that undertakings are given on completion that the buyer will pay (or the seller will reimburse, as the case may be) an appropriate proportion of the service charge as soon as the amount is ascertained. Another solution would be to apportion the service charge on completion by reference to the last payment of the charge, and to undertake to adjust that apportionment after completion when the amount for the current period is ascertained. The Law Society's Standard Formula for apportionment of rent provides another acceptable method of dealing with this problem (set out in full in the Law Society's Conveyancing Handbook). Statutory restrictions, imposed by sections 13–18 of the Landlord and Tenant Act 1985, as amended by the Landlord and Tenant Act 1987, apply to the recovery of service charges for dwellings and give the tenant the right to demand certain information from his landlord in relation to the amount of the service charge. A buyer of a dwelling should enquire of the seller whether he has requested any information from the landlord under these provisions. The buyer of any lease imposing a service charge should make full enquiries about the service provided by the landlord and the amount of the charge since such charges can sometimes impose a heavy financial obligation on the tenant.

# Completion and post-completion

**22.19**   In addition to the normal requirements on completion (see Chapter 17) it may be necessary to obtain an undertaking relating to the payment of a service charge. On the grant of a lease, the tenant will receive the lease executed by the landlord and will hand to the landlord a counterpart lease executed by the tenant. On the assignment of an existing lease, the transfer (or assignment in the case of unregistered land) will be handed to the buyer and in appropriate cases he should also receive the licence to assign executed by the landlord.

A completed stock transfer form and the seller's share certificate may also be handed over in cases where the lease requires the tenant to become a shareholder in a management company or residents' association.

After completion of an assignment, in addition to the requirements outlined in Chapter 17, it may be necessary to give notice of the assignment (and also of the buyer's mortgage, depending on the wording of the covenant in the lease) to the landlord. Where the assignment is of the landlord's reversionary interests the outgoing landlord must give notice to the tenant(s) within four weeks of completion if he wants to be released for future liability under the landlord's covenants (Landlord and Tenant (Covenants) Act 1995). Stamp duty on leases is assessed in relation to the rent reserved by the lease, its term and the amount of any service charge. Additional duty may be payable where a premium is taken on the grant of a lease. Stamp duty on an assignment is payable by reference to the usual *ad valorem* rates applicable to conveyances.

Options to renew or to purchase the reversion which are contained in a lease should be registered (see 22.17 above).

A lease for a term of more than seven years, or the assignment on sale of a subsisting lease which still has more than seven years to run at the date of the assignment, must be registered at the Land Registry within two months of the grant or assignment irrespective of whether or not the reversion is registered. Where the reversion is registered, a lease granted out of that reversion for a term exceeding seven years must itself be registered with separate title in order that the tenant acquires a legal estate. Unless title to the freehold reversion is available to the registry on the application for registration of the lease it cannot be registered with an absolute title and may not therefore be acceptable as security to a mortgagee.

# Standard Conditions

**22.20**   The Standard Conditions of Sale deal with leaseholds in Conditions 8, 6.6, 6.3.1, 6.3.5, 4.6.4, and 4.5:

'8.   LEASEHOLD PROPERTY

8.1   *Existing leases*

8.1.1   The following provisions apply to a sale of leasehold land.

8.1.2   The seller having provided the buyer with copies of the documents embodying the lease terms, the buyer is treated as entering into the contract knowing and fully accepting those terms.

8.1.3   The seller is to comply with any lease obligations requiring the tenant to insure the property.

8.2   *New leases*

8.2.1   The following provisions apply to a contract to grant a new lease.

8.2.2   The conditions apply so that:

'seller' means the proposed landlord

'buyer' means the proposed tenant

'purchase price' means the premium to be paid on the grant of a lease.

8.2.3   The lease is to be in the form of the draft attached to the contract.

8.2.4   If the term of the new lease will exceed 7 years, the seller is to deduce a title which will enable the buyer to register the lease at the Land Registry with an absolute title.

8.2.5   The seller is to engross the lease and a counterpart of it and is to send the counterpart to the buyer at least five working days before completion date.

8.2.6   The buyer is to execute the counterpart and deliver it to the seller on completion.

8.3   *Consent*

8.3.1   (a) The following provisions apply if a consent to let, assign or sub-let is required to complete the contract.

(b) In this condition "consent" means consent in the form which satisfies the requirements to obtain it.

8.3.2   (a) The seller is to apply for the consent at his expense, and to use all reasonable efforts to obtain it.

(b) The buyer is to provide all information and references reasonably required.

8.3.3   Unless he is in breach of his obligation under condition 8.3.2, either party may rescind the contract by notice to the other party if three working days before completion date (or before a later date on which the parties have agreed to complete the contract):

(a) the consent has not been given, or

(b) the consent has been given subject to a condition to which a party reasonably objects.

In that case, neither party is to be treated as in breach of contract and condition 7.2 applies.

6.6   *Rent receipts*

The buyer is to assume that whoever gave any receipt for a payment of rent or service charge which the seller produces was the person or the agent of the person then entitled to that rent, or service charge.

6.3.1   Income and outgoings of the property are to be apportioned between the parties so far as the change of ownership on completion will affect entitlement to receive or liability to pay them.

6.3.5   When a sum to be apportioned is not known or easily ascertainable at completion, a provisional apportionment is to be made according to the best estimate available. As soon as the amount is known, a final apportionment is to be made and notified to the other party. Any resulting balance is to be paid no more than ten working days later, and if not then paid the balance is to bear interest at the contract rate from then until payment.

4.6.4   If after completion the seller will remain bound by any obligation affecting the property which was disclosed to the buyer before the contract was made, but the law does not imply any covenant by the buyer to indemnify the seller against liability for future breaches of it:

(a) the buyer is to covenant in the transfer to indemnify the seller against liability for any future breach of the obligation and to perform it from then on, and

(b) if required by the seller, the buyer is to execute and deliver to the seller on completion a duplicate transfer prepared by the buyer.

4.5   *Rent and rentcharges*

The fact that a rent or rentcharge, whether payable or receivable by the owner of the property, has been or will on completion be, informally apportioned is not to be regarded as a defect in title.'

## Deducing title

**22.21**   Condition 8 deals separately with existing leases (Condition 8.1) and contracts for the grant of a new lease (Condition 8.2). Where the sale is of an existing lease, there is no requirement in the condition for the seller to deduce title to the buyer. This means that the open contract rules under section 44 of the Law of Property Act 1925 will apply to the transaction (see 22.7 above) and under the condition as drafted the buyer will never have the right to call for deduction of the reversionary title. Although this situation may be satisfactory in the case of a short lease where no premium is being paid for its transfer, it may provide less than adequate protection for the buyer in other cases. If the interest being sold is itself registered with an absolute title at HM Land Registry, the buyer has no need to call for deduction of the reversionary title and in this situation the condition is perfectly satisfactory.

If, however, the interest being sold is registered with less than an absolute title (for example, good leasehold), or is currently unregistered but will need to be registered on completion of the present transaction, the buyer should consider whether he and/or his mortgagee need to investigate the superior title to the lease. A lease which is registered with a title other than absolute is regarded by some mortgagees as inadequate security and may therefore be difficult to mortgage or to sell. If the lease being sold was created more than, say, fifteen years ago, and is currently registered with good leasehold title, it should be possible to apply to have the title upgraded to absolute on registration of the dealing, thus resolving the problem. If the lease was created less than, say, fifteen years ago and/or is unregistered at the present time, an Index Map search should be undertaken at the Land Registry to ascertain whether the title to the reversion is registered, and, if so, office copies of the reversionary title should be obtained. Where the freehold reversion is registered, the leasehold interest will normally be awarded an absolute title, and again in this situation this condition does not create a problem. Where, however, the freehold reversion is not registered, the assignee will not be able to obtain registration of his own interest with an absolute title unless he can show satisfactory deduction of the reversionary freehold title when he applies for registration. In this situation, therefore, the assignee should not generally proceed with his purchase of a registrable lease unless the assignor agrees by special condition in the contract to deduce the freehold title to the assignee. The length and nature of the title required will be the same as if the assignee himself were purchasing the freehold interest in the land.

Condition 8.2, dealing with the grant of a new lease, requires the seller to deduce the reversionary title to the buyer only where the lease is to be granted for a term which will exceed seven years. This length of lease is registrable in its own right and unless reversionary title is produced to the Land Registry on the application for first registration, an absolute title will not be awarded. Since good leasehold titles are regarded by some mortgagees as being inferior security, the buyer should insist on his rights under this condition and resist any attempt by the seller to exclude or modify its provisions. Although the issue of reversionary title is less vital in cases where a short lease only is being granted, if a premium is being paid for that lease, or the lease attracts security of tenure, so that in either case the tenant regards the lease as a capital asset, consideration should be given to the desirability of requiring modification of this clause to require deduction of the reversionary title to the tenant. The open register at the Land Registry provides the tenant with a means of checking the landlord's reversionary title in cases where the seller refuses to amend this condition in favour of the tenant, provided that the landlord's title is itself registered.

### Existing lease

**22.22** Full details of an existing lease must be supplied to the buyer under Condition 8.1.2. This will normally be done by giving the buyer a copy of the lease at the pre-contract stage. The buyer is by this condition barred from raising requisitions about the terms of the lease. This means that any queries about the lease terms must be dealt with before exchange of contracts. This condition modifies the seller's duty of disclosure in relation to onerous or unusual covenants (*Re Haedicke & Lipski's Contract* (1901)).

### Insurance

**22.23** Condition 8.1.3 requires the seller to comply with any lease obligation relating to insurance. Where the seller is by the terms of his lease required to insure the property he will have to maintain his policy until completion. In these circumstances this condition will override Condition 5.1.3 (see Chapter 12).

*Implied covenants*

**22.24**   Condition 3.2 (see Chapter 5) also contains a statement requiring the buyer to accept the property in the physical state it is in when the contract is made and makes the sale of the property subject to any subsisting breach of a condition or tenant's obligation, but it is doubtful whether the existence of this Condition alone would give the seller the right to insist on the modification of the covenants for title in the transfer. Accordingly, the contract and subsequent purchase deed should, for the seller's protection, contain a clause which modifies the effect of the covenants for title (see Chapter 3 and 22.9–22.11 above).

*Preparing the deeds*

**22.25**   Where the contract is for the grant of a new lease, the seller is to draft the lease and supply a copy of it to the buyer with the draft contract (Condition 8.2.3). The seller will also engross the lease and counterpart and send the counterpart to the buyer at least five working days before completion date (Condition 8.2.5). This latter provision replaces Condition 4.3.2 which applies to the preparation of the transfer in other types of transactions (see Chapter 16).

*Licence to assign or sublet*

**22.26**   By Condition 8.3.2, where a licence to assign or sublet is required, it is the seller's duty to apply for, obtain and pay for the licence, the buyer being under a duty to co-operate by providing all information and references reasonably required. Provided that a party has complied with his obligations under Condition 8.3.2, he has the right to rescind the contract if the consent has not been given by three working days before completion date, or if by that time consent has been given but is subject to a condition to which the buyer reasonably objects. Either party thus has the option of rescinding in these circumstances. The effect of inclusion of this right to rescind is to make the contract conditional on the landlord's consent. The removal of this right to rescind excludes the uncertainties of a conditional contract from the transaction and may be considered to be a necessary amendment where the seller is involved in a chain of transactions.

The wording of the condition leaves room for argument about what type of condition the buyer may 'reasonably' object to. If the licence cannot be obtained, the seller can exercise his right to rescind irrespective of whether the landlord's refusal of consent was reasonable (*Bickel v Courtenay Investments (Nominees) Ltd* (1984)). The seller can also choose to rescind under the condition even where the buyer would be content to proceed without the licence being obtained. If a licence to assign or sublet could not be obtained, the seller would not be able to make good title, and so the buyer would be able to rescind the contract even in the absence of this condition. The notice to rescind must be in writing and be served under Condition 1.3 (see Chapter 4). No length of notice is specified. The parties' rights on rescission are governed by Condition 7.2 (see Chapter 19).

## Informal apportionment

**22.27** Condition 4.5 prevents the buyer from asserting that an informal apportionment of a rent or rentcharge is to be regarded as a defect in title. Where only a part of property comprised in the lease is being sold the buyer would, in the absence of this condition, be entitled to insist on a legal apportionment of the rent, that is, an apportionment made with the consent of the owner of the rent.

## Covenant for indemnity

**22.28** Condition 4.6.4 provides for the buyer to give the seller a covenant for indemnity in the assignment or transfer, except where such a covenant is implied by law. No such covenant is implied by law and should therefore be given expressly by the buyer where necessary. Where the outgoing tenure has been released for future liability no covenant is required. In other cases eg where an authorised guarantee agreement has been entered into or no express release has been obtained for the landlord, the seller may require the buyer to provide indemnity.

## Apportionment of outgoings

**22.29** The apportionment of outgoings, which will include rent, service charge and insurance premiums, is dealt with by Condition 6.3.1 (see Chapter 17). Where a service charge is payable on the property it is often not possible to ascertain the precise amount due on completion date, since the accounting period for the service charge will rarely coincide with actual completion. It is therefore common to make a provisional apportionment of this item on completion, according to the figures available at that time, the final amount being adjusted after completion when the true figures are known. A provisional apportionment is permitted under Condition 6.3.5 with the adjustment (if any) to be notified to the other party as soon as the figures are known, the resulting balance to be paid no later than ten working days after notification and, if not paid within this time, bears interest at the contract rate. The provisional apportionment is to be made on the 'best estimate' available, but this phrase is not defined.

Condition 6.6 requires the buyer to assume that a rent or service charge receipt produced by the seller is valid. This condition reflects and extends the provisions of section 45(2) of the Law of Property Act 1925. There is also authority to suggest that the buyer must make this assumption under common law principles (*Pegler v White* (1864)).

*Sublease*

**22.30**   The conditions contain no provision precluding the buyer from raising objections where the covenants in a sublease do not correspond with the covenants in a head lease. If such discrepancies do occur, the buyer should note them carefully since he may be bound by the covenants in the head lease through the doctrine of notice.

The word 'lease' is defined by Condition 1.1.1(h) to include a sublease, and an agreement for a sublease.

## Suggested amendments

**22.31**   The question of the right to deduction of the reversionary title is always critical in leasehold transactions. Although Condition 8 as drafted will now be satisfactory in most situations, the buyer should always consider carefully whether the general contractual provisions are sufficient to protect his own interests and those of his mortgagee and, if not, seek an appropriate amendment to the contract to permit deduction of the reversionary title.

Under Condition 8.3.3 the seller may choose to limit the buyer's right to rescind by specifying the grounds which would form the basis of the buyer's 'reasonable objection' to a condition imposed on a licence to assign or sublet. The existence of this right to rescind, which is likely only to be used very close to actual completion day, does pose problems for the seller, since it has the effect of making the contract conditional on the licence being satisfactorily obtained. If the landlord's consent and agreement to the terms of the licence cannot be obtained or agreed before exchange of contracts, it may be preferable for the seller to exclude totally the buyer's right to rescind under this condition. The seller needs to keep his own right to rescind in case the landlord does not grant the licence, but permitting the buyer to rescind, in a situation where the seller is involved in a chain of transactions, could have disastrous consequences.

As drafted, Condition 8 does not require the buyer to pay for or contribute towards the cost of an engrossment of the new lease prepared by the seller. Many sellers would wish to pass on the cost of the engrossment to the buyer.

The condition provides for a new lease to be executed with a counterpart. If the seller prefers to have the new lease executed in duplicate, rather than by lease and counterpart, an amendment to Conditions 8.2.5 and 8.2.6 will be needed.

Where Condition 6.3.5 is relevant, the words 'best estimate' might be replaced by a provision stating that the provisional apportionment is to be made on the basis of the amount payable under the last demand for the service charge plus a fixed percentage to account for inflation.

## The Protocol

**22.32**   When the seller's solicitor prepares the package for the buyer he is, by para 2.14, to ask the seller to produce the last receipt for payment of rent, or evidence of that payment, together with the maintenance accounts for the last three years, with evidence of payment, and details of the buildings insurance policy. If any of the above are not available but are necessary to the transaction, the seller's solicitor should obtain them from the landlord. The seller's solicitor must also investigate whether the landlord's consent to the assignment is needed, and if so, ask the landlord what references are required and (if relevant) whether the landlord requires the seller to enter into an authorised guarantee agreement or is prepared to release the seller from future liability under the lease covenants. In the case of retirement schemes he should also enquire whether a charge is payable to the management company in respect of the change of ownership. A copy of the lease together with the information outlined above is to be supplied to the buyer's solicitor with the draft contract (para 4.4).

All the above procedures relate to the assignment of an existing lease. The Protocol contains no specific reference to the grant of a new lease.

## SCPC Condition 10

**22.33**   SCPC Condition 10 provides as follows:

'10   **LEASEHOLD PROPERTY**

10.1   *Existing leases*

10.1.1   The following provisions apply to a sale of leasehold land.

10.1.2   The seller having provided the buyer with copies of the documents embodying the lease terms, the buyer is treated as entering into the contract knowing and fully accepting those terms.

10.1.3   The seller is to comply with any lease obligations requiring the tenant to insure the property.

10.2   *New leases*

10.2.1   The following provisions apply to a contract to grant a new lease.

10.2.2   The conditions apply so that:
"seller" means the proposed landlord
"buyer" means the proposed tenant
"purchase price" means the premium to be paid on the grant of a lease.

10.2.3   The lease is to be in the form of the draft attached to the contract.

10.2.4   If the term of the new lease will exceed seven years, the seller is to deduce a title which will enable the buyer to register the lease at the Land Registry with an absolute title.

10.2.5   The seller is to engross the lease and a counterpart of it and is to send the counterpart to the buyer at least five working days before completion date.

10.2.6   The buyer is to execute the counterpart and deliver it to the seller on completion.

10.3    *Consents*

10.3.1  (a)  The following provisions apply if a consent to let, assign or sub-let is required to complete the contract.

   (b)  In this condiiton "consent" means consent in a form which satisfies requirements to obtain it.

10.3.2  (a)  The seller is to:

   (i)  apply for the consent at its expense, and to use all reasonable efforts to obtain it.

   (ii)  give the buyer notice forthwith on obtaining the consent.

   (b)  The buyer is to comply with all reasonable requirements, including requirements for the provision of information and references.

10.3.3  Where the consent of a reversioner (whether or not immediate) is required to an assignment the sub-letting, then so far as the reversioner lawfully imposes such a condition:

   (a)  the buyer is to:

   (i)  covenant directly with the reversioner to observe the tenant's covenants and the conditions in the seller's lease.

   (ii)  use reasonable endeavours to provide guarantees of the performance and observance of the tenant's covenants and the conditions in the seller's lease.

   (iii) execute or procure the execution of the licence.

   (b)  the seller, in the case of an assignment, is to enter into an authorised guarantee agreement.

10.3.4  Neither party may object to a reversioner's consent given subject to a condition:

   (a)  which under section 19(1A) of the Landlord and Tenant Act 1927 is not regarded as unreasonable, and

   (b)  which is lawfully imposed under an express term of the lease.

10.3.5  If any required consent has not been obtained by the original completion date:

   (a)  the time for completion is to be postposed until five working days after the seller gives written notice to the buyer that the consent has been obtained or four months from the original completion date whichever is the earlier.

   (b)  the postposed date is to be treated as the completion date.

10.3.6  At any time after four months from the original completion date, either part may rescind the contract by notice to the other, if:

   (a)  consent has still not been given, and

   (b)  no declaration has been obtained from the court that consent has been unreasonably withheld.

10.3.7  If the contract is rescinded under condition 10.3.6 the seller is to remain liable for any breach of condition 10.3.2(a) or 10.3.3(b) and the buyer is to remain liable for any breach of condition 10.3.2(b) or 10.3.3(a). In all other respects neither party is to be treated as in breach of contract and condition 9.2 applies.

10.3.8 A party in breach of its obligations under condition 10.3.2 or 10.3.3 cannot rescind under condition 10.3.6 for so long as its breach is a cause of the consent's being withheld.'

**22.34** SCPC Condition 10.1 relating to existing leases is identical in wording to Standard Condition 8.1 and suffers from the same deficiencies. This condition is discussed above.

**22.35** SCPC Condition 10.2 has minor variations in wording from Standard Condition 8.2 but the effect of the condition is identical. This condition is discussed above.

**22.36** SCPC Condition 10.3 differs in its wording and effect from Standard Condition 8.3, although both conditions deal with the same area, namely, grant of a licence from a reversioner. Under SCPC 10.3 the seller is to apply for the licence at its own expense and to make all reasonable efforts to obtain it. There is a reciprocal clause requiring the buyer to co-operate in this process by eg supplying references (and see Standard Condition 8.3.2 (a)). The seller is to enter an authorised guarantee agreement. This last provision is absent from the Standard Conditions. The buyer is also obliged by the condition (if the landlord so requires) to enter into a direct covenant with the landlord, to use reasonable endeavours to procure guarantors and to execute the licence.

**22.37** A buyer would normally be reluctant to enter into an unconditional contract to purchase the lease without knowing that the landlord's consent will be forthcoming. However if this should occur, condition 10.3.5 provides fall back provisions if for some reason the landlord's consent has not been obtained by contractual completion date. Completion date is postponed until five working days after the seller has informed the buyer that the licence has been obtained with a long stop completion date of four months from the original contractual completion date, after which time either party may exercise the right to rescind under Condition 10.3.6. Condition 10.3.7 refers to the rescission rights contained in Condition 10.3.6 subject to the parties remaining separately liable to each other for any outstanding breach of Conditions 10.3.2 and 10.3.3 (failure to co-operate in attempts to obtain a licence). A party who is in breach of either Condition cannot use its own breach as an excuse to rescind (Condition 10.3.8). It is suggested that the landlord's willingness or otherwise to grant a licence will become apparent well before the four month period speicified in Conditions 10.3.4 and 10.3.5 have expired and this period may be too long for the parties to wait to resolve the issue. An amendment to reduce the four month long stop completion date contained in these clauses may therefore be appropriate.

**22.38** SCPC Condition 10.3.4 provides that neither party may object to a condition attached to a licence which would not be regarded as unreasonable under s 19 (1A) Landlord and Tenant Act 1927 or which is lawfully imposed under the terms of the lease. This clause probably does not add much to the rights of the parties under the general law but is useful in order to provide clarity in the contract.

## SCPC Condition C

**22.39**

### 'C  REVERSIONARY INTERESTS IN FLATS

C1      *No tenants' rights*

C1.1    In this condition, sections refer to sections of the Landlord and Tenant Act 1987 and expressions have the special meanings given to them in that Act.

C1.2    The seller warrants that:

(a) it gave the notice required by section 5.

(b) no acceptance notice was served on the landlord or no person was nominated for the purposes of section 6 during the protected period, and

(c) that period ended less than 12 months before the date of the contract.

C2      *Tenants' right of first refusal*

C2.1    In this condition, sections refer to sections of the Landlord and Tenant Act 1987 and expressions have the special meanings given to them in that Act.

C2.2    The seller warrants that:

(a) it gave the notice required by section 5, and

(b) it has given the buyer a copy of:

(i) any acceptance notice served on the landlord and

(ii) any nomination of a person duly nominated for the purposes of section 6.

C2.3    If the sale is by auction:

(a) the seller warrants that it has given the buyer a copy of any notice served on the landlord electing that section 8B shall apply,

(b) condition 8.1.1 applies as if "thirty working days" were substituted for "twenty working days",

(c) the seller is to send a copy of the contract to the nominated person as required by section 8B(3), and

(d) if the nominated person serves notice under section 8B(4):

(i)  the seller is to give the buyer a copy of the notice, and

(ii) condition 9.2 is to apply as if the contract had been rescinded.'

**22.40**    Standard Commercial Property Condition C (an optional condition in Part II of the conditions) deals with the situation where the sale comprises a reversionary interest in a block of flats to which the Landlord and Tenant Act 1987 applies (see 22.6 above).

Condition C1 should be used where the seller has given the appropriate notice to the tenants and the tenants have chosen not to exercise their right to purchase the landlord's interest.

Condition C2 applies where the tenants have served a counter-notice on the landlord. The sale to the buyer is unlikely to proceed during the validity of such a counter-notice and the inclusion of additional clauses making the contract conditional on the tenants' right of first refusal being defeated would need to be considered by the buyer.

Condition C3 applies where the sale is by auction. Note the extension of the fall back completion date to thirty working days in this context.

# Chapter 23

# Auctions

## The general law

**23.1**    Where land is to be sold by auction the contract for sale is often prepared jointly by the seller's solicitor and his estate agent, the former being responsible for drafting the terms on which the property is to be sold, the latter for a description of the property. The contract usually incorporates standard conditions of sale and is frequently annexed to the estate agent's brochure which gives a detailed description of the land.

A prospective buyer may not have had time before the auction to complete his normal pre-contract searches and enquiries, but he will be expected to sign the contract at the auction itself, and should appreciate that this contract will not normally incorporate a condition allowing him to rescind if later searches reveal an undesirable incumbrance. For this reason, it is not uncommon for the seller to have made a local land charges search and enquiries before the auction and for the results of such enquiries to be available at the auction for inspection. Title deeds should also be available for inspection, and the seller's solicitor should attend the auction in order to answer any enquiries relating to the property made by prospective buyers.

The seller will normally wish to reserve the right to withdraw the property from the auction if the bidding does not reach a figure which is acceptable to him. This figure will have been agreed between the seller and his estate agent before the auction and need not be revealed to the buyer, but in order to comply with section 5 of the Sale of Land by Auction Act 1867, the contract must make it clear that the sale is subject to a reserve price. A condition in the contract which merely gives the seller the right to reserve a price if he so wishes is probably not sufficient to comply with section 5. If a reserve is placed on the property and the auctioneer accepts a bid which is lower than the reserve, no binding contract arises (*McManus v Fortescue* (1907)).

The seller should always be advised to place a reserve on the property, otherwise the auctioneer can sell the property to the highest bidder, however low that bid may be. Whether the auctioneer is in these circumstances bound to accept the highest bid is uncertain. The Scottish case of *Fenwick v Macdonald, Frazer & Co* (1904) suggests that the auctioneer may refuse to accept a bid and thus is not bound; *obiter dicta* in *Warlow v Harrison* (1859) suggest otherwise.

Where the property is subject to a reserve price (but not otherwise) the seller may also reserve the right to bid at the auction and so boost the bidding up to or beyond the reserve price. The right to bid must be expressly reserved in the contract. It will not exist by implication simply because the contract states that the property is subject to a reserve price (Sale of Land by Auction Act 1867, ss 5 and 6; *Gilliat v Gilliat* (1869)). The right to bid may be exercised by the seller or one person acting as his agent.

The auctioneer is not 'offering' the property for sale but making an invitation to treat. Offers to buy are made by the bidders, and in accordance with general contractual principles, the auctioneer is free to accept or reject any bid (*Payne v Cave* (1789)). The fall of the auctioneer's hammer usually signifies acceptance of the offer or bid and thus a contract exists from that moment. This method of acceptance specified by section 57(2) of the Sale of Goods Act 1979 only applies to the sale of goods, but is customarily acknowledged as being the moment of conclusion of an auction contract. It is suggested that the court would probably adopt a common law implication similar to section 57(2) if the question were to arise in connection with a contract for the sale of land.

An agreement between prospective buyers that they will not bid against one another does not invalidate a subsequent contract. The Auctions (Bidding Agreements) Act 1927 does not apply to land. See also *Harrop v Thompson* (1975).

The contract will normally be signed immediately the auction is concluded. The auctioneer has implied authority to sign on the seller's behalf both at the time of the sale and for a short time afterwards. A signature on behalf of the seller which was not inserted into the contract until after the auctioneer had left the sale room and returned to his office would be binding but not a signature made a week later (*Chaney v Maclow* (1929)). The auctioneer's authority to sign in this situation may be expressly laid down by standing instructions from his employer. Authority to bind the buyer is also implied, but this authority only exists at the time of the sale itself and not afterwards (*Bell v Balls* (1897)). This implied authority is personal to the auctioneer himself and will not extend to the auctioneer's clerk, although express authority may be given to the clerk (*Sims v Landray* (1894)).

The deposit is payable on signature of the contract. The auctioneer is entitled to insist on payment in cash. He may accept a cheque or banker's draft but not other types of bills of exchange (*Johnson v Boyes* (1899)).

In the absence of contrary provisions he receives the deposit as stakeholder, even though he signs the contract as the seller's agent.

After the auction the contract proceeds to completion in the normal way.

Although it is customary for a memorandum of the sale to be signed by or on behalf of both parties at the auction itself, auction contracts are specifically excluded from section 2 of the Law of Property (Miscellaneous Provisions) Act 1989. Thus a contract which is made at auction is binding on both parties on the fall of the hammer, irrespective of whether a signed contract has or will come into existence.

# Standard Condition 2.3

**23.2**    The Standard Conditions of Sale provide as follows:

'2.3    *Auctions*

2.3.1    On a sale by auction the following conditions apply to the property and, if it is sold in lots, to each lot.

2.3.2    The sale is subject to a reserve price.

2.3.3    The seller, or a person on his behalf, may bid up to the reserve price.

2.3.4    The auctioneer may refuse any bid.

2.3.5    If there is a dispute about a bid, the auctioneer may determine the dispute or restart the auction at the last undisputed bid.

2.3.6    The deposit is to be paid to the auctioneer as agent for the seller.'

Conditions 2.3.2 and 2.3.3 reserve the seller's right to bid and state that the property is subject to a reserve price. Both of these clauses are necessary in order to comply with sections 5 and 6 of the Sale of Land by Auction Act 1867.

The auctioneer's power in Condition 2.3.4 to refuse any bid is probably implied under the general law, but is repeated here for the sake of clarity. The right to fix the amount of each bid is implicit from the power to refuse a bid. The seller's right to withdraw the property from the sale is also implied by virtue of the auctioneer's right (acting as the agent of the seller) to refuse to accept any bid.

Condition 2.3.5 gives the auctioneer authority to determine a dispute which arises over the bidding. (For an example of the application of this principle see *Richards v Phillips* (1969).)

The date of the contract will be governed by Condition 2.1, and subject to contrary agreement will be the date of the auction.

By Condition 2.2.1, a deposit of 10 per cent of the purchase price is payable by the buyer 'no later than the date of the contract'. At auction the deposit may be paid by banker's draft or cheque. Condition 2.2.2, giving the seller the right to discharge the contract if the deposit cheque is not honoured, will apply to auction contracts. (Deposits are discussed fully in Chapter 11.) The deposit is to be held by the auctioneer as agent for the seller and so could be handed over to the seller before completion.

# Suggested amendments

**23.3**    No amendments to this condition are required in normal circumstances unless the seller wishes to make expressly clear to the buyer that he reserves the right (through his auctioneer) to fix the amount of each bid, and to withdraw the property from the sale. Some safeguard over the deposit is given to the seller by the application of Condition 2.2.2, but he may prefer to include a condition stating that the deposit must be paid either by cash, banker's draft, solicitors' or building society cheque.

## The Protocol

**23.4**    The Protocol deals with the sale of domestic property by private treaty and contains no reference to auctions.

## SCPC Condition 2.3

**23.5**    SCPC Condition 2.3 provides as follows:

'2.3.1    On a sale by auction the following conditions apply to the property and, if it is sold in lots, to each lot.

2.3.2    The sale is subject to a reserve price.

2.3.3.    The seller, or a person on its behalf, may bid up to the reserve price.

2.3.4    The auctioneer may refuse any bid.

2.3.5    If there is a dispute about a bid, the auctioneer may resolve the dispute or restart the auction at the last undisputed bid.

2.3.6    The auctioneer is to hold the deposit as agent for the seller.

2.3.7    If any cheque tendered in payment of all or part of the deposit is dishonoured when first presented, the seller may, within seven working days of being notified that the cheque has been dishonoured, give notice to the buyer that the contract is discharged by the buyer's breach.'

**23.6**    Most of SCPC Condition 2.3 repeats verbatim the content of Standard Condition 2.3 which is discussed above. The main difference between the two conditions lies in SCPC 2.3.6, which does appear in the Standard conditions but under the heading of 'deposit' (Standard Condition 2.2). Condition 2.3.6 of the SCPC relates to dishonoured deposit cheques and appears in the auction section of the contract (and not under the deposit condition) because the only time when a cheque will normally be tendered for a deposit under the SCPC is under an auction contract. In all other cases money is to be paid by direct credit only, there is thus no danger of there being a referred deposit cheque except in the context of an auction. The effect of SCPC 2.3.6 is identical to Standard Condition 2.2 and is discussed in Chapter 11. Note that SCPC Condition C.2.3 (Part II) may need to be considered where the sale is of a reversionary interest in a block of flats (see 22.39).

## The Common Auction Conditions

**23.7**    The Common Auction Conditions (CAC) are designed specifically for use in property auctions and are published by the Royal Institute of Chartered Surveyors. The full text of the CAC (second edition) is set out in Appendix 3 and a summary of their contents appears below. The second edition came into effect on 1 October 2005.

**23.8**    The CAC occupy some 20 pages of text, including introductory notes and a memorandum of sale. They are drafted in plain English and are designed to be used by property professionals and the general public. A warning note advises that legal advice should be taken as to the suitability of the conditions for use. The CAC must either be reproduced in full or the document in which they are incorporated must show clearly any amendments which have been made to them.

**23.9** The CAC are divided into three main sections (not including the memorandum of sale or any special conditions which may be annexed). Section 1 contains an extensive glossary defining words used in the CAC, Section 2 deals with the conduct of the auction, and Section 3 sets out the general conditions of sale.

**23.10** The CAC bear a bold print note in the following terms: 'The Conditions assume that the buyer has acted like a prudent buyer. If you choose to buy a lot without taking these normal precautions you do so at your own risk'. A 'prudent buyer' is defined as one who will:

'• Take professional advice from a conveyancer and, in appropriate cases, a chartered surveyor and an accountant.
- Read the conditions.
- Inspect the lot.
- Carry out usual searches and make usual enquiries.
- Check the content of all available leases and other documents relating to the lot.
- Check that what is said about the lot in the catalogue is accurate.
- Have finance available for the deposit and the purchase price.
- Check whether VAT registration and election is advisable.'

The phrase 'usual searches' is not defined and would probably be interpreted by reference to *Cooper v Stephenson* (1852) which encompasses a local search with additional enquiries of the local authority and pre-contract enquiries of the seller. It seems that the buyer would not therefore be required to undertake any of the less usual searches prior to auction.

# Glossary

**23.11.1** The Glossary contains an extensive (but unnumbered) definitions section. Most of the definitions are either self explanatory or identical in effect to those contained in the Standard Conditions of Sale and/or the Standard Commercial Property Conditions. The following should however be noted.

*Business day*

**23.11.2** The definition of 'business day' equates with the definition of 'working day' under the Standard Conditions of Sale and Standard Commercial Property Conditions except that under the CAC 'bank holiday' is not defined by reference to a statutory bank holiday. Extra or special bank holidays would under these conditions (but not under the Standard Conditions of Sale or Standard

Commercial Property Conditions ) be excluded from the computation of business days.

### Agreed completion date

**23.11.3** The agreed completion date is either the date agreed in the contract or 20 business days after the contract date or the next following business day if the 20th day is not itself a business day.

### Documents

**23.11.4** Documents of title relating to registered land refer to copies (but not to 'official copies') of the register of title. Unless this condition is amended, the buyer should therefore check the date of the copies offered and if necessary obtain his own up to date official copies.

### Interest rate

**23.11.5** The default interest rate is set at 4% above the base rate from time to time of Barclays Bank plc. The Standard Conditions of Sale and Standard Commercial Property Conditions both set their interest rate by reference to the Law Society's interest rate. In practice there will be little difference between these two rates.

### Practitioner

**23.11.6** Practitioner is defined as a receiver, administrative receiver or liquidator or a trustee in bankruptcy. The Standard Conditions of Sale and Standard Commercial Property Conditions have no equivalent definition.

### Ready to complete

**23.11.7** This definition differs from the Standard Conditions of Sale and Standard Commercial Property Conditions in that it is expressed in simpler language but does not make allowance for a situation where the buyer is in default.

### TUPE

**23.11.8** TUPE refers to the Transfer of Undertakings (Protection of Employment) Regulations 1981 which has the effect of preserving continuity of employment of employees where a business is sold as a going concern. There is no equivalent definition under the Standard Conditions of Sale or the Standard Commercial Property Conditions.

## Bidding and reserve price

**23.12** The CAC contain statements which allow the auctioneers to place a reserve price on a lot, refuse to accept a bid, resolve disputed bids, or withdraw a lot which fails to meet its reserve. The right for the seller or his agent to bid is also reserved. These statements are needed to satisfy the requirements of the Sale of Land by Auction Act 1867 (see 23.1 above) but, unlike the Standard Conditions of Sale and Standard Commercial Property Conditions, the statements in the CAC do not form part of the general conditions but are set out as preliminary statements.

## Agent for the seller

**23.13** The auctioneers are stated to be agents for the seller and as such have the right to sign the sale memorandum on the seller's behalf.

## Exclusion clauses

**23.14** The auctioneers expressly exclude any duty of care towards the buyer 'to the extent permitted by the law' and give no warranty as to the accuracy of information contained in the particulars of sale. Both of these exclusions form part of the preliminary statements and do not form part of the auction contract itself. The clauses are very brief and general and their effectiveness to protect the auctioneer against negligence is doubtful.

## The contract

**23.15** A further preliminary page sets out the buyer's responsibilities when a successful bid is accepted and points out in unambiguous terms that the buyer is personally responsible for completing the purchase, even if acting as agent for a third party at the auction.

## General conditions

**23.16** The CAC contain 28 general conditions most of which are similar in effect to those contained in the Standard Conditions of Sale or Standard Commercial Property Conditions. A brief summary of their contents is set out below.

*The lot (Condition 1)*

**23.16.1** This condition defines the property which is being sold (other than its physical extent) and is similar in effect to Standard Conditions of Sale Condition 3. The CAC condition also includes an exclusion clause to the effect that the buyer is not relying on the information contained in the particulars or replies to preliminary enquiries. The effect of the exclusion clause may be limited by the Unfair Contract Terms Act 1977 (see 8.4).

### Deposit (Condition 2)

**23.16.2** The deposit is to be either the minimum deposit specified in the contract or 10% of the purchase price exclusive of VAT. It is payable either by cheque or banker's draft drawn on a UK clearing bank or building society or such other means of payment as may be specified by the auctioneers (eg credit card). The deposit is payable to the auctioneers who hold it as stakeholders. Interest on the deposit is payable to the seller. Condition 2.4 contains provision for the seller to treat the contract as being as at an end if the buyer's cheque is dishonoured.

### Transfer of risk and insurance (Condition 3)

**23.16.3** The general proposition in this condition is that the buyer takes the risk in the property from the date of the contract and so must insure from that time. Section 47 of the Law of Property Act 1925 is excluded (see 12.2). The seller must insure if either he is required to do so by a special condition or the lot is sold subject to a tenancy which requires the seller to insure.

### Possession before completion (Condition 3.5)

**23.16.4** The buyer is not allowed to take possession before completion unless the buyer is already in lawful occupation of the property.

### Title (Condition 4)

**23.16.5** The buyer is precluded from raising requisitions in relation to any matters arising out of documents which were made available to him before the auction or to any superior title. Subject to the preceding sentence, the seller is to deduce title within five business days of the date of the contract, and in the case of registered land copies supplied must be official copies of the register entries. The buyer then has a further seven business days in which to raise requisitions on that title. The seller is to sell with full title guarantee.

### Transfer (Condition 5)

**23.16.6** Condition 5 sets the timetable for the preparation of the purchase deed, calculated backwards from completion date and provides for an indemnity covenant to be given in appropriate circumstances.

### Sub-sales (Conditions 5.3 and 26)

**23.16.7** Conditions 5.3 and 23 both preclude the buyer from contracting a sub-sale or assigning the benefit of the contract. This condition could give rise to difficulties where a third party attends the auction on behalf of the actual buyer.

*Completion (Condition 6)*

**23.16.8** The fallback date of completion is specified in the glossary which does not form part of the contract. Completion must take place between 09.00 and 17.00 on a business day and at the offices of the seller's conveyancer or where the seller may reasonably require. Payment is to be made by direct credit in pounds sterling. Completion is deemed to be late if it occurs (other than by the seller's default) after 14.00.

*Non-merger (Condition 6.6)*

**23.16.9** The terms of the contract and purchase deed do not merge on completion. Several of the conditions contain provisions which are designed to continue in effect after completion, or which only come into effect after completion.

*Notice to complete (Condition 7)*

**23.16.10** The time allowed by a notice to complete is 10 business days. The person giving the notice must be 'ready to complete'. The definition of this phrase is contained in the glossary and not in the Conditions themselves. Rights and remedies upon service of a notice to complete are similar to those under the Standard Conditions of Sale and Standard Commercial Property Conditions. Remedies when the contract is brought to an end are dealt with by Condition 8.

*Landlord's licence (Condition 9)*

**23.16.11** Where a formal licence is required the contract is conditional on that licence being obtained. A three-month long stop completion date is set by Condition 9.6 after which if the licence is not forthcoming either party may rescind. The Standard Conditions of Sale and Standard Commercial Property Conditions provide for a four-month time limit in these circumstances. Where the licence is obtained completion is to take place not earlier than five business days after the seller had given notice to the buyer that the licence has been obtained. The service of notices is dealt with in Condition 27.

*Interest and apportionments (Condition 10)*

**23.16.12** For the purpose of apportionments the day of completion belongs to the seller. Income and expenditure is deemed to accrue at an equal daily rate assuming 365 days in the year. A provisional apportionment made on a 'best estimate' basis is permitted where actual amounts are not known at completion with the adjusted amounts to be payable within five business days of the date when the amount is known. This provision should be amended to allow the buyer to pay within five business days of receipt of notification of the adjusted amount. As drafted the buyer does not seem to be entitled to be notified of the adjusted figures and the amount therefore becomes due within five business days of the seller becoming aware of the sum due.

197

Interest for late completion is payable only by the buyer (as is the case under the Standard Commercial Property Conditions).

### Arrears (Condition 11)

**23.16.13** Condition 11 reserves to the seller the right to receive and recover 'old arrears' (defined in the glossary as arrears due under any tenancy which is not a 'new' tenancy under the Landlord and Tenant (Covenants) Act 1995 (see Chapter 22)). The buyer is under an obligation to try to collect those arrears and then remit them to the seller, but need not take legal proceedings or distrain or forfeit the tenancy. Arrears so collected must be handed over to the seller within five business days of receipt. Late payment attracts interest calculated on a daily basis. No equivalent condition exists in the Standard Conditions of Sale or Standard Commercial Property Conditions.

### Management (Condition 12)

**23.16.14** Condition 12 applies where the lot is sold subject to tenancies and contains similar provisions to Standard Commercial Property Conditions Condition 4.2.

### Rent deposits (Condition 13)

**23.16.15** Condition 13 applies where the seller is holding or is entitled to a rent deposit under a tenancy and makes provision for transfer of that deposit to the buyer. There is no equivalent provision in the Standard Conditions of Sale or Standard Commercial Property Conditions.

### VAT (Condition 14)

**23.16.16** VAT is only payable by the buyer where a valid VAT invoice is supplied by the seller. Where the special conditions state that no VAT election has been made, the seller gives a warranty to this effect and further that none will be made before completion.

### Transfer as a going concern (Condition 15)

**23.16.17** Condition 15 only applies where the special conditions state that the sale is to be treated as a transfer as a going concern and assumes that the buyer is registered for VAT. The Condition is concerned broadly with the VAT position on the transfer of the business and is similar in effect to Condition A2 in Part II of the Standard Commercial Property Conditions.

### Capital allowances (Condition 16)

**23.16.18** Condition 16 only applies where a special condition states that there are capital allowances available in respect of the lot. The Condition is similar in effect to Condition B in Part II of the Standard Commercial Property Conditions.

*Maintenance agreements (Condition 17)*

**23.16.19** If the property has the benefit of maintenance agreements which are specified in the special conditions as being transferable to the buyer this condition imposes on the seller an obligation to use reasonable endeavours to transfer the benefit of those agreements to the buyer. The buyer is to pay the cost of the transfer and must both assume liability for them and provide indemnity to the seller in respect of them as from the actual completion date. Unless a separate written indemnity is given by the buyer on completion, this provision would remain extant after completion under the provisions of Condition 6.6. Neither the Standard Conditions of Sale nor the Standard Commercial Property Conditions contain an equivalent general condition.

*Landlord and Tenant Act 1987 (Condition 18)*

**23.16.20** This condition applies where the sale is of the reversion of a block of flats to which the Landlord and Tenant Act 1987 applies, giving the tenants a right of first refusal to acquire the reversion. Unless the special conditions otherwise provide the seller is warranting that he has served the requisite notices under the Act and that the tenants are not proceeding with a purchase of the reversion. The buyer should ensure that he inspects the relevant notices and satisfies himself as to the position, preferably before the auction takes place. Standard Commercial Property Condition C (Part II) deals with this topic in more detail.

*Sale by practitioner (Condition 19)*

**23.16.21** This condition applies where the seller is a 'practitioner' acting on behalf of the legal owner. The word practitioner is defined in the glossary as a receiver, administrative receiver, liquidator or a trustee in bankruptcy. Since a practitioner will not generally have had any personal dealings with the property he is not in a position to give any warranties as to its condition, or title. The condition therefore requires the buyer to take the property as it is with no warranties being given by the practitioner seller and no title guarantee included in the transfer deed. There are no equivalent general conditions in either the Standard Conditions of Sale or Standard Commercial Property Conditions.

*TUPE (Condition 20)*

**23.16.22** Where a business is transferred as a going concern the employment contracts of personnel employed by the business will normally be transferred to the new owner on completion. Dismissal of employees whether before or after the transfer may result in claims for unfair dismissal from the staff whose contracts have been terminated. This condition contains two alternative warranties depending on whether the special conditions state that TUPE applies. If TUPE does apply, the seller must inform the buyer which employees are subject to TUPE. The wording of the condition says 'has informed the buyer', suggesting that this must be done prior to the auction. The buyer must then make offers of employment to the affected employees on the same or on better terms than their existing contracts and must confirm to the seller that he has done this no less than five business days before the agreed completion date. The buyer must also indemnify the seller against future liability under TUPE for those employees. The exact names of every employee affected should be given to the buyer, together with copies of the employees' contracts of employment or statements of terms. The indemnity given to the seller should be in writing. Despite the fact that this condition will remain extant after completion, it is couched in very general terms and the seller would be advised to include a more specific condition (including the exact wording of any indemnity required) as a special condition in the contract. The application of TUPE is complex and specialist advice from an employment lawyer is recommended. There is no equivalent condition under either the Standard Conditions of Sale or Standard Commercial Property Conditions.

### Environmental (Condition 21)

**23.16.23** Condition 21 only applies if the special conditions so provide. The liability to remediate land which is contaminated can be onerous. The buyer should be wary of accepting this condition without a full investigation since its inclusion may indicate that the land has or is suspected to have a potential liability under the Environmental Protection Act 1990. The general indemnity which the buyer is required to give under Condition 21.3 is open ended in terms of both time and money and as such is undesirable from the buyer's point of view.

### Service charge (Condition 22)

**23.16.24** Service charges are not to be apportioned on completion. Instead the seller is to provide the buyer with a detailed statement of service charges within two months of completion showing the expenditure attributable to each tenancy, the payments received from each tenant, the amounts due but unpaid from each tenant and details of any amounts which are irrecoverable. Apportionments are then to be made in respect of each separate tenancy with excesses of receipts over expenditure being paid to the buyer; but where there are excesses of expenditure over receipts the buyer is merely under a duty to use all reasonable endeavours to recover the sums due at the next 'service charge reconciliation date' (not defined) and then pay over amounts so recovered within five business days of being in receipt of cleared funds. This is a cumbersome method of dealing with service charges which provides no certainty over payment to either party. This part of the condition would be better dealt with by a special condition dealing with apportionment on completion on a best estimate basis (see Standard Conditions of Sale Condition 6.3.5). Where there is expenditure which is not attributable to the tenancy, and thus not recoverable, Condition 22.5 says that the seller bears any expense related to this which was incurred before actual completion date and the buyer must pay in respect of expenditure incurred after that time. This condition is curious since if the service charge provisions in the lease are properly drafted there should not be any items of properly incurred service charge which are not recoverable. Further, expenditure after the date of actual completion is within the control of the buyer and is thus of no concern to the seller. Condition 22.6 provides for the seller to assign any reserve or sinking fund to the buyer on completion with the buyer covenanting to maintain the fund in accordance with the terms of the tenancies and to provide indemnity to the seller if he does not do so. It is unlikely in most cases that the seller could be sued after completion of the sale of the reversion by a tenant for failure to maintain the sinking fund and this indemnity provision may not be strictly necessary. The condition does not specify how in practice the money is to be transferred to the buyer nor does it give a time limit for this to be done.

*Rent reviews (Condition 23)*

**23.16.25** Condition 23 applies where a property is sold subject to a tenancy under which a rent review due on or before actual completion date has not been agreed or determined. The seller is entitled to continue negotiations or proceedings with the tenants up to the actual completion date but, broadly, must consult with the buyer and cannot agree a revised rent without the buyer's written consent. However, Condition 23.3 says that where the review is not completed before completion the buyer must complete the rent review but may not agree the new rent without the seller's written consent. Between contract and completion the seller holds the legal estate on trust for the buyer, therefore it is reasonable to expect him to consult with the buyer about the rent review and to respect the buyer's wishes. It is not however useful for the buyer to have to consult the seller about the level of rent after completion when the seller had parted with his legal interest in the property, unless the review is to take effect retrospectively, in which case the seller had a vested interest in the outcome of the negotiations. If the review is retrospective (ie applies to rent which fell due before actual completion) the buyer must account to the seller for any increased back rent due to him within five business days of receipt of cleared funds. Standard Commercial Property Condition 5 contains similar provisions.

*Tenancy renewals (Condition 24)*

**23.16.26** Condition 24 applies where the sale includes tenanted property where the tenant is protected by the Landlord and Tenant Act 1954 (as amended) and requires the seller not, without the buyer's written consent, to serve or respond to any notice or begin or continue any proceedings to terminate or renew the tenancy. If the seller does receive a notice from the tenant he must send the buyer a copy of it within five business days and must then act as the buyer reasonably directs. Once completion has taken place the buyer is required to substitute himself as the landlord in any negotiations or proceedings and use all reasonable endeavours to conclude the tenancy renewal. Any increased rent recovered from the tenant which is attributable to the period of the seller's ownership must be paid to him within five business days of the receipt of cleared funds. This latter provision is only really of relevance to an interim rent (which is normally backdated to the date of the court application) since any increased rent under the new lease will not commence until the term of the new lease starts, and as this provision (Condition 24.4) relates to the post-completion period, that rent would belong to the buyer in its entirety. Where this provision applies, it remains in effect after completion by virtue of Condition 6.6.

## Warranties (Condition 25)

**23.16.27** This condition applies to any warranties which are set out as special conditions in the contract. Where the warranties are assignable to the buyer the seller must so assign on completion and give notice of assignment to the give of the warranty. There is no provision for such assignment to be given in writing, although clearly written assignment and notice is desirable in these circumstances. Further, the buyer would be advised to obtain a copy of the notice of assignment given by the seller as proof that this step has been taken. The condition as drafted does not provide for this. Where consent to assign is needed the seller must apply for the consent but both parties must use all reasonable endeavours to obtain that consent. The condition does not specify who is to bear the costs of obtaining the consent. Where the warranty is not assignable the seller holds it on trust for the buyer and must act on it as the buyer lawfully instructs and at the buyer's cost.

## Notices (Condition 27)

**23.16.28** Condition 27 requires all communications, including notices, to be in writing. The glossary does not define 'communications' but ordinary usage would imply that it includes all dealings between the parties and their agents. The requirement for writing seemingly precludes oral communications by phone or face to face. Where a communication is delivered by hand or is 'otherwise proved to have been received' it is delivered when received, subject to the proviso that delivery after 17.00 on a business day is deemed to be delivery on the next following business day. There is no explanation of the phrase 'proved to have been received' but it is suggested that if communications are sent by fax, a print out of the transmission verification is kept by the sender and if email is used, the email is sent with a receipt acknowledgement tag and a print-out of the acknowledgement is kept as proof of its arrival at its destination. Communications sent by first class post are deemed to have been received on the second business day after posting. Again, some proof of the date of posting is advisable. No express provision is made for delivery by second class post, private mail company or DX. Standard Conditions of Sale Condition 1.3 and Standard Commercial Property Conditions Condition 1.3 are more detailed and specific in their definitions of when and how documents and other communications are to be served and deemed to be received.

## Third parties (Condition 28)

**23.16.29** In limited circumstances a third person may take the benefit of a contract to which he is not named as a party ( Contracts (Rights of Third

Parties) Act 1999). Condition 28, which has no equivalent condition under either the Standard Conditions of Sale or Standard Commercial Property Conditions, explicitly precludes the possibility of a third party acquiring rights under a contract made using the CAC. This may be viewed as a back-up provision reinforcing condition 26 and 5.3.

## General comments

**23.17.1** Following the general conditions, the CAC contain several pages on which it is intended that special conditions applicable to the particular lot being sold. The pages contain a number of headings which act as reminders of the matters which may need to be addressed in relation to the sale. The amount of space given on the printed form is not large and in some cases it may be more practical to deal with the special conditions by referring to a schedule attached to the document.

**23.17.2** The final page of the CAC comprises the memorandum of sale which contains details of the buyer's conveyancer but not of the seller's conveyancer. This latter information is contained on one of the special conditions pages.

**23.17.3** The CAC have been drafted in plain English and their content should therefore be readily understood by a non-lawyer attending an auction. However, in places the desire to simplify has led to a lack of clarity (eg service of documents). The conditions attempt to deal with a wide variety of circumstances and include matters which are not dealt with by either the Standard Conditions of Sale or the Standard Commercial Property Conditions (eg warranties, TUPE). The commendable brevity also means that in places the conditions are less detailed than the Standard Condition or Standard Commercial Property Condition counterparts. There is no specific condition relating to chattels or fixtures and fittings, both of which might be needed,for example in the sale of tenanted property. Similarly there is no condition which deals with commonhold land (see Chapter 24).

**23.17.4** In some cases the conditions are more onerous on the buyer than would be the case in an openly negotiated contract (eg environmental liabilities). Since the buyer at auction has to accept the contract as drafted and has no opportunity to seek amendments prior to signing, he must be advised to study the contract terms, including the general conditions very carefully before deciding to bid at the auction. He must also bear in mind that he is required by the CAC to undertake the searches and enquiries which a prudent buyer would do prior to the auction.

# Chapter 24

# Commonhold

**24.1**    The Commonhold and Leasehold Reform Act 2002 introduced a new way of holding freehold land designed to overcome the difficulties encountered with traditional leaseholds, eg in dealing with shared facilities and obligations.

**24.2**    A commonhold can be created out of freehold land held with an absolute title and may be for the purposes of residential, commercial or mixed use developments. Agricultural land is excluded from the provisions of the Act.

**24.3**    It is also possible to create a commonhold from an existing leasehold title.

**24.4**    The creation of a commonhold is effected by the registration of the freehold title as commonhold, together with the formation of a commonhold association (like a management company). A commonhold community statement sets out the rights and obligations of individual unit holders. The contents of commonhold documents are prescribed by the Act and Regulations made under it. Use of the prescribed forms is mandatory.

**24.5**    Once set up, the commonhold association will own the freehold and common parts of the building and the unit holders (like leaseholders) will each own their respective units. Unit holders will be members of the commonhold association and are mutually bound by the commonhold community statement. The association acts like a management company with the right to manage the commonhold and to enforce obligations (eg service charge). Unit holders may be required to become members of the commonhold association.

**24.6**    The sale or purchase of a commonhold unit will proceed in a similar way to the sale or purchase of an existing leasehold. The buyer's solicitor should require the seller's solicitor to provide a commonhold information certificate which will show details of the assessment (service charge) for the unit and of any other claims against the unit. Additionally the buyer's solicitor should make a company search against the commonhold association to ensure it exists and is active. The annual accounts, budget and estimates of the association should be checked.

**24.7**    Dealings with part only of a unit require the prior consent of the commonhold association. Consent may be expensive to obtain because it will involve changes to the commonhold community statement, eg to redefine the extent of the unit and to adjust voting rights.

**24.8**   The commonhold association must be notified after completion of the change of ownership.

**24.9**   Land Registry Practice Guide 60 explains the practical issues involved with setting up and dealing with commonholds.

**24.10**   Although at the present time very few commonholds exist both the Standard Conditions of Sale and Standard Commercial Property Conditions contain a condition which deals with the sale of an existing commonhold unit.

**24.11**   Standard Condition 9 provides as follows:

'9   *Commonhold land*

9.1   Terms used in this condition have the special meanings given to them in Part I of the Commonhold and Leasehold Reform Act 2002.

9.2   This condition applies to a disposition of commonhold land.

9.3   The seller having provided the buyer with copies of the current versions of the memorandum and articles of the commonhold association and of the commonhold community statement, the buyer is treated as entering the contract knowing and fully accepting their terms.

9.4   If the contract is for the sale of property which is or includes part only of a commonhold unit:

(a)   the seller is, at his expense, to apply for the written consent of the commonhold association and is to use all reasonable efforts to obtain it;

(b)   either the seller, unless it is in breach of its obligations under para-graph (a), or the buyer may rescind the contract by notice to the other party if three working days before completion date (or before a later date on which the parties have agreed to complete the contract ) the consent has not been given. In that case, neither party is to be treated as in breach of contract and condition 7 applies'.

**24.12**   Standard Commercial Property Condition 11 is identical in wording except that the reference to rescission is to Condition 9.2.

**24.13**   Sub-clause 3 requires the seller to provide copies of the commonhold association's memorandum and articles and of the community statement so that the buyer can check these documents. The buyer will also need to ask for the supply of a commonhold information certificate in order to ascertain the finan-cial liability (if any) attaching to the unit and should also require the supply of the association's accounts and budget. The information certificate will bind the commonhold association and so provides some certainty for the buyer as to financial liability.

**24.14**   Apportionments between seller and buyer will be made on completion in the normal way, although in many cases completion will take place part-way through a financial year and a provisional assessment of charges may need to be made under the terms of Standard Condition 6.3.5 or Standard Commercial Condition 8.3.5.

**24.15**   Sub-condition 4 deals with the sale of part only of a unit and recognises that consent to the sale may be difficult to obtain by providing a right to either party to rescind if consent has not been obtained by three working days before completion date.

**24.16**   This condition as drafted contains only the bare outlines of the matters which may be required on the sale of a commonhold unit and other matters may have to be dealt with by special condition. Since no commonholds have yet changed hands it is not possible at present to speculate on the precise contents of additional special conditions.

# Chapter 25

# Special Circumstances

## Introduction

**25.1**    Various matters, other than those referred to in previous chapters, may need to be dealt with by special condition, depending on the nature of the transaction. In particular, special clauses will be needed to deal with contracts for the sale of a farm or of a business, the complexity of which is beyond the scope of this book. Some of the matters not dealt with in the Standard Conditions of Sale, but which may need to be considered when drafting the contract, are listed below. The selection of topics within this chapter is necessarily subjective and does not pretend to be comprehensive. Any suggested clauses which appear below are the author's own form of wording and should therefore be carefully analysed by the reader before use to ensure that the wording meets the reader's requirements. A full treatment of special conditions of sale to fit most circumstances is to be found in *Encyclopaedia of Forms and Precedents* (5th ed) Vol. 35 (Butterworths).

## Fixtures

**25.2**    Fixtures, as opposed to fittings, will pass with the property. If the seller intends to remove any fixtures a special condition should be inserted which specifically excludes named items from the contract.

## Occupiers' rights

**25.3**    Where the matrimonial home of a married couple is held in the name of one spouse alone, the other spouse may be able to claim a beneficial interest in the house. (See *Caunce v Caunce* (1969); *Williams & Glyn's Bank Ltd v Boland* (1979).) In such a situation it may be necessary to include a provision in the contract so that the spouse who claims an interest in the property agrees with the buyer that he or she has no claim against the property in relation to such interest. In this case the non-owning spouse should be joined as a party to the contract and should sign it. This is of most relevance to registered land, but may also be applicable to unregistered estates. (*Midland Bank Ltd v Farmpride Hatcheries Ltd and Willey* (1980); *City of London Building Society v Flegg* (1988)).

The problem is not confined solely to married couples; it may equally affect an unmarried couple who are living together, a couple who are in a civil partnership, or a brother and sister who are sharing a house, where both have made contributions to the purchase price, but the legal estate is held in one name alone.

A problem caused by a spouse's rights of occupation under the Family Law Act 1996 does not fit into this category, since such rights can affect a buyer only if they are protected by registration (Class F land charge in unregistered land, or notice in registered land).

By the Family Law Act 1996, where such rights are protected by registration, it is an implied term of a contract to sell with vacant possession that the seller will procure the cancellation of the registration before completion at his own expense. Thus no express contractual condition is necessary to deal with this matter.

Following *City of London Building Society v Flegg* (1988), it seems that the appointment of a second trustee to the legal estate will overreach an overriding interest in registered land, and this is one way of dealing with a purported beneficial interest in the land asserted by a non-owning occupier. A similar result is achieved in unregistered land by the appointment of a second trustee. The best solution to this problem is undoubtedly to make the non-owning occupier a party to the contract, but an alternative approach is merely to require the non-owner to sign a release of his or her rights. Such release should be obtained before exchange of contracts after the nature of the occupier's interest has been fully investigated, and any disclaimer must be carefully worded by the buyer to cover precisely the situation in hand, ensuring that all existing and potential rights in the property, whether arising by statute, common law or otherwise and whether affecting the legal or equitable interest in the property, are released. In *Aspin v Appleton* (1988) a disclaimer signed by a non-owning occupier was held not to be valid on the grounds that the interest which the occupier had in the property was a Rent Act tenancy; since the Rent Act 1977 prohibited any form of contracting out, it was not possible, simply by signing a disclaimer, to erode rights which came into existence through the Act. A similar reasoning would apply to an assured tenancy under the Housing Act 1988. It is, however, interesting to note that the general validity of such disclaimers was not challenged by the court in this case. Despite this, the protection afforded to the buyer by the disclaimer should not be regarded as impregnable. The problems which the disclaimer seeks to overcome will not, for practical purposes, be solved if the occupier simply refuses to vacate the property; or if he or she decides to challenge the validity of the disclaimer by saying that it was obtained under duress, or that the consequences of signing had not been properly explained to the occupier before signature.

The following form of wording could be used either as a contractual clause or as a separate form of release, in either case to be addressed to the buyer(s) and signed by the non-owning spouse:

'In consideration of your today entering into a contract with (*name of seller*) for the purchase of the property known as (*address of property*), I agree to release any equitable interest which I may have in the property. I also agree to procure the cancellation of any registration which may have been made in respect of rights of occupation which I may have under the Family Law Act 1996.'

The above wording is not wholly appropriate for a non-spouse cohabitee, since only a spouse can take the benefit of Matrimonial Homes Act rights. In the case of a non-spouse cohabitee the following form of consent could be incorporated into the contract:

'In consideration of the buyer entering into a contract to purchase (*address of property*) from (*name of seller*) I (*name of cohabitee*) agree to the sale of the property on the terms of this agreement, that I will not seek to enforce against the buyer any rights, whether legal equitable or otherwise which I may purport to have in the property, and that I will vacate the property by the date of completion as stated in the contract'.

## Assignment of guarantees etc

**25.4**    Although not strictly necessary, in appropriate cases it may be useful to include a special condition to provide for all or any of the following:

(a)  assignment of subsisting NHBC (or similar) Agreement;
(b)  assignment of a guarantee in respect of structural repairs to the property (for example, dry rot treatment);
(c)  assignment of a notice served under the Leasehold Reform Act 1967 or the Leasehold Reform (Housing and Urban Development) Act 1993.

## Disclosure

**25.5**    The seller is under a duty to disclose incumbrances and latent defects in title (see Chapter 5). It is customary for the seller to disclose such matters in the contract, and then to add a special condition which limits the buyer's right to raise requisitions or enquiries relating to the matters disclosed. Such a clause will not protect the seller unless he has made a full and frank disclosure of the relevant matters (*Faruqi v English Real Estates Ltd* (1979)).

## Sales to sitting tenants

**25.6**    The Standard Conditions do not deal with sales to sitting tenants and some additional clauses may be necessary to protect the seller, for example:

'The lease between the seller and the buyer shall continue in full force and effect until the buyer has paid the purchase price in full under this agreement'; or

*Special Circumstances*

'The buyer will remain liable on the tenant's covenants contained in the lease until actual completion'.

Either of these clauses prevents the relationship of landlord and tenant from being brought to an end inadvertently, for example by the existence of the contract for sale. If this happened problems could arise if the buyer failed to complete.

# Unrepresented parties

**25.7**    The Law Society recommends the insertion of special clauses where either the seller or buyer is not represented by a solicitor or licensed conveyancer. (See Guidelines, *Law Society's Conveyancing Handbook Appendix II.5.*)

*Buyer not represented*

**25.8**    To protect the seller's solicitor a clause needs to be inserted in the contract to ensure that the title deeds are handed to the proper person at completion and that there is no possibility of the buyer bringing an action against the seller's solicitor if, for instance, the buyer's representative absconds with the deeds. Wording similar to that set out below may be used for this purpose:

'The buyer shall attend personally at completion'; or

'The buyer shall on or before completion supply the seller with a written authority authorising the seller to hand the [*deeds of the property etc.*] to [*name of buyer's representative*] whose written receipt for such items shall be a full discharge of the seller's obligations in this respect.'

*Seller not represented*

**25.9**    Where the seller is not represented, the deposit should be paid to the *buyer's* solicitors as stakeholder; or to an estate agent as stakeholder; or placed in a joint deposit account in the names of both parties. The seller should be required to attend personally at completion or to give written authority for payment to be made to his representative. Similar clauses to those set out in 24.8 above for the buyer could be adapted for this purpose. An undertaking given by an unqualified person to discharge the seller's mortgage should not be accepted. A clause will have to be included to require the seller to obtain the discharge of his mortgage(s) on or before completion, for example:

'On or before completion the seller will discharge all existing mortgages over the property and at completion will hand to the buyer the [sealed Form 53] in respect of each discharged mortgage'.

In an attempt to avoid problems arising out of incorrect replies given pre-contract enquiries and similar documents, a clause may be included to require the seller personally to sign the answers to such documents, rather than to accept answers which have been prepared and signed by the seller's unqualified agent, thus:

'The answers given by the seller to any pre-contract enquiries, requisitions on title, or other queries raised by the buyer shall be signed by the seller personally.'

## Restraint of trade

**25.10** On the sale of a business the buyer may need to include a clause restraining the seller from competing with the buyer after completion, thus preserving the goodwill which will form part of the business being acquired. The clause will satisfy UK and EEC anti-trust law if only one person (the seller) gives the covenant and the covenant only lasts for a reasonable period not exceeding four years (in respect of technical know-how) or two years (in respect of a transfer of goodwill only), and the covenant is otherwise reasonable both as to business scope and the geographical area of the restraint. A clause similar to that set out below may be included in addition to the actual terms of the restraint in an attempt to avoid the whole of the clause from being struck out if part of it is found to be unreasonable. Restraint clauses should also be drafted by way of separate sub-clauses, each dealing with one aspect of the restriction. This device assists the court to 'sever' a void sub-clause from the remainder, leaving the remainder of the clause valid and unaffected.

'The sellers agree that they consider the restrictions contained in this clause are no greater than is reasonable and necessary for the protection of the interest of the buyer but if any such restriction shall be held to be void but would be valid if deleted in part or reduced in application such restriction shall apply with such deletion or modification as may be necessary to make it valid and enforceable.'

## Completion notice

**25.11** A clause similar to that set out below, entitling the seller to recover his expenses incurred in relation to the service of a notice to complete is sometimes included in the contract. There is a danger that such a clause might be construed as a penalty if the sums required to be paid under it exceed the costs incurred by the seller:

'If due to the default of the buyer completion does not take place on the contractual completion date the buyer shall pay the costs of the seller's solicitors in the sum of £... plus VAT for re-calculating the completion figures and preparing and serving a notice to complete and the costs shall be a part of the balance due on completion.'

## Application for registration pending

**25.12** Special conditions will need to be inserted in the contract where the seller is unable to deduce title to the buyer because the seller's own application for registration of title is still being processed by the Land Registry. For example:

'The seller has made application to the Land Registry for the registration of himself as proprietor. If the seller's title to the property is not registered before completion then title shall consist of copy Land Register entries and a copy of the transfer from the registered proprietor to the seller. If the buyer requires the seller's title to be registered before completion then the buyer shall pay interest to the seller on the balance of the purchase price at the prescribed rate from the contractual completion date until actual completion.'

## Declaration of no title for right of way

**25.13** Where the property being sold purports to enjoy a right of way to which the seller is unable to prove title, a clause similar to the following may be included in the contract to preclude the buyer's objections to the defect in title. This wording could be adapted to fit other situations where there is a defect in the seller's documentary title to the property:

'The property is sold with the benefit of a right of way [on foot only (*or as the case may be*)] between the points marked [A] and [B] on the plan. The seller [and his predecessors] have used the right of way without interruption or complaint from the owner of the land for a continuous period of [twelve] years prior to the date of this contract. The buyer shall not call for the production of any documentary evidence of the seller's title to the right of way and shall accept such title as the seller has without raising any objection or requisition with regard thereto. [At the buyer's request and expense the seller will on completion supply the buyer with a statutory declaration of these facts.]'

## Abstract to be open to inspection

**25.14** The following clause, giving the buyer the right to inspect the seller's title deeds may be required in an auction contract:

'Title shall commence with a conveyance on sale dated the ... day of (*unregistered land*) or Title will be deduced by the supply of office copies (*registered land*) ... Evidence of the title will be produced [in the saleroom] at the time of the sale or by appointment with the seller's solicitors at any time within [seven] working days before [or after] the sale. The evidence may be inspected by any [intending] buyer but no buyer shall be entitled to the delivery of copies unless he applies in writing to the [auctioneer *or* seller's solicitor] within [nine] working days after the date of the sale. The cost of supplying copies is to be borne by the buyer and is payable on delivery of the copies to him. Unless the buyer delivers his requisitions on the title in writing to the seller's solicitor within [fourteen] working days after the date of the sale he will be deemed to have accepted the title.'

## Sale by attorney

**25.15** Where an attorney is selling the property on behalf of the owner, special clauses may be required in the contract. The nature of such clauses will differ, depending whether the attorney holds an ordinary power of attorney or an enduring power.

### *Ordinary power*

**25.16** A clause for an ordinary power of attorney would be as follows:

'The seller is selling the property under a power of attorney granted on the (*date*) by (*name of donor*). The power is valid and subsisting and has not been revoked. [A certified copy of] the power will be handed over on completion. The buyer having been supplied with a copy of the power shall raise no objection or requisition relating to it.'

### *Enduring power*

**25.17** A clause for an enduring power of attorney would be as follows:

'The seller is selling the property under an enduring power of attorney granted by (*name of donor*) on (*date*). The donor is of full mental capacity and has not revoked the power which has not been registered at the Court of Protection [or an application to register the power was made to the Court of Protection on (*date*) and this transaction is one which the attorney is entitled to make pending the registration of the power] [or the power was registered by the Court of Protection on (*date*)]. The buyer having been supplied with a copy of the power [and of the registration order] shall make no objection or requisition relating to the seller's capacity to sell the property. A certified copy of the power [and registration order] will be handed over on completion.'

## Interest on stakeholder deposits

**25.18** If the conditions of sale do not provide for interest to be payable on a deposit which is held by a stakeholder (Standard Condition 2 does so provide, see Chapter 11), the form of wording recommended by the Law Society for inclusion in the contract is as follows:

'The stakeholder shall pay to the seller/buyer a sum equal to the interest the deposit would have earned if placed on deposit (less costs of acting as stakeholder).'

## Restrictive covenants

**25.19** Where the transfer is to impose new restrictive covenants on the buyer this matter must be dealt with in the contract. From the seller's point of view it is important to ensure that the wording of the covenants to be contained in the transfer will ensure that the covenants are properly annexed to the seller's retained land, failing which the covenants may be unenforceable. Annexation of the covenants may be implied (see *Federated Homes Ltd v Mill Lodge Properties Ltd* (1980)), but the application of this principle is sporadic (see *J Sainsbury plc v Enfield London Borough Council* (1989) and *Jamaica Mutual Life Assurance Society v Hillsborough* (1989) (Privy Council)). Where the criteria for a building scheme, as laid down in *Re Dolphin's Conveyance* (1970) are satisfied, there is no problem, but in other cases care should still be taken to ensure that express words of annexation are used when imposing restrictive covenants. The safest way to do this is for the seller to specify in the contract the actual wording which he requires the buyer to use in the transfer, for example:

'The transfer to the buyer shall contain a covenant by the buyer in the following terms:

The buyer covenants with the seller, to the intent that the burden of the covenant will run with and bind the property and every part of it and that the benefit of the covenant will be annexed to and run with the retained land and every part of it, to observe and perform the following stipulations [If *the covenants are to be limited to seisin add the words* "but not so as to impose any personal liability on the buyer or any successor in title of the buyer after he has parted with all his interest in the property"]:

(a) [*insert wording of restrictions*].'

A restrictive covenant relating to use as a private dwelling house might be as follows:

'The buyer shall not use the property or any part of it except as a private dwelling house [in the occupation of one family].'

And a general nuisance covenant:

'The buyer shall not do or allow to be done on the property anything which may be or grow to be a nuisance or annoyance to the seller or his successors in title who are the owners for the time being of the retained land.'

# Conditional contracts

**25.20** Conditional contracts carry with them some risks and uncertainties which make them inappropriate for everyday use, but they may be considered for use in the following circumstances:

(a) where the buyer has not had the opportunity before exchange of contracts to make searches and enquiries or to conduct a survey, or where his mortgage arrangements have not been finalised;

(b) where the contract is dependent on planning permission being obtained for the property;

(c) where the sale requires the consent of the Charity Commissioners under the Charities Act 1992;

(d) where the sale is dependent on permission being obtained from a third party, for example ministerial consent, landlord's consent;

(e) where the parties wish to be bound to a contract but there is some other unresolved matter which prevents commitment to an unconditional contract for the time being, for example where the seller has to get in part of the legal estate.

Conditional contracts are generally not desirable since they leave an element of doubt as to the very existence and validity of the contractual obligations between the parties. Most of the situations in which conditional contracts are proposed for use benefit the buyer more than the seller, for example 'subject to satisfactory searches', and the seller should resist the suggestion of entering a conditional contract if at all possible. A conditional contract may, however, be inevitable where the seller needs the consent of the Charity Commissioners to the sale under the Charities Act 1992, since an unconditional contract which is entered into without such consent is illegal (see below).

Conditional contracts should not be used where one or both of the parties has an unconditional sale or purchase contract which is dependent on the conditional contract. In this situation, if the conditional contract were to be rescinded for non-fulfilment of the condition, this would give rise to great difficulties in the fulfilment of the linked unconditional contract and may result in a breach of that contract.

Before agreeing to enter a conditional contract the seller should consider whether there are any viable alternative solutions which could be used in preference to the conditional contract. Where the buyer has suggested that the sale is made 'subject to satisfactory searches', it may be preferable to delay exchange until the results of searches have been received by the buyer, rather than enter into a hastily drafted conditional contract. An alternative solution may be to grant the buyer, for a nominal consideration, an option to purchase the property, to be exercised within a stated period.

It was held in *Aberfoyle Plantations Ltd v Cheng* (1960), that the time for performance of the condition is of the essence and cannot be extended either by agreement between the parties or by the court. The same case also laid down the rules relating to the time for performance of the condition, which are summarised as follows:

(a) where the contract contains a completion date, the condition must be fulfilled by that date, irrespective of whether time was of the essence of the contractual completion date;

(b) if a time is stated for the fulfilment of the condition, that time limit must be complied with or the contract will fail;

(c) if no time limit is specified the condition must be fulfilled within a reasonable time. (This provision is patently unsatisfactory since it leaves room for argument about what is a reasonable time.)

The drafting of a condition requires extreme care to ensure that the requirements outlined above have been satisfied. The following considerations should be borne in mind:

(a) the precise event(s) on which the contract is to be made conditional;

(b) the time by which the condition must be fulfilled (bear in mind that the specified time limit cannot be extended);

(c) the precise terms on which the party with the benefit of the condition may rescind;

(d) there should be no loopholes which would enable one party to escape from the contract other than for the non-fulfilment of the event(s) contemplated in (*a*) above;

(e) an established precedent, tailored to fit the exact requirements of the case should be used;

(f) a hastily drafted condition may contain unforeseen errors.

National Condition 3 (an optional condition which, if desired, can be incorporated into the contract by special condition) has the effect of making the contract conditional by giving the buyer the right to rescind in a wide variety of circumstances. This condition is not to the seller's advantage, and he should resist any attempt to include it in the contract.

# Charities

**25.21** Where a charity is registered as the proprietor of land, any restriction contained in the proprietorship register of the title must be observed. If the charity is an 'exempt' charity, no problems arise in relation to sale of land transactions. Most charities do not have exempt status and the following paragraphs will therefore be relevant.

All non-exempt charities must comply with sections 32–37 of the Charities Act 1992 which provide that no disposition of an interest in land by a charity (the word 'disposition' includes contract as well as conveyance/transfer/lease etc.) can be made without an order of the court or the Charity Commissioners unless the following conditions are all satisfied:

(a) the trustees must obtain a written report about the proposed disposition from a qualified surveyor;

(b) the property is advertised for the period and in the manner advised by the surveyor;

(c) the trustees decide that in the light of the surveyor's report they are satisfied that the terms of the disposition are the best that can be obtained;

(d) prescribed words are inserted in both contract and purchase deed.

*Prescribed words:*

    (i)     the land is held by or on trust for the charity;

    (ii)    the charity is/is not an exempt charity; *and if not exempt*

    (iii)   the land is subject to section 32 of the Charities Act 1992;

    (iv)   the trustees certify that section 32 has been complied with.

## Licensed premises

**25.22**    The premises are being bought on the basis that the licence is current, valid and transferable to the buyer – if not the transaction cannot proceed. Thus certain checks need to be carried out in the conveyancing procedure to ensure the smooth passage of the transaction. It is suggested that the contract is drafted to include warranties given by the seller to the effect that the licence is valid and subsisting and that there are no proceedings in existence or threatened which might result in revocation of the licence or its non-renewal. Similarly the seller should be asked to give a warranty that he will not oppose the grant of a protection order to the buyer or his nominee (in the case of a liquor licence). The contract should be made conditional upon the protection order being obtained or licence being transferred to the buyer, since without it the premises are worthless to the buyer.

## Proper law

**25.23**    Where the contract is dealing with property which is outside the jurisdiction or with obligations which may need to be performed outside the jurisdiction, consideration may be given to the inclusion of a clause stating that the proper law applying to the contract is the law of England and Wales (or as appropriate).

## Seller's right to rescind

**25.24**    Most standard forms of contract used to contain a clause permitting the seller to rescind the contract if he could not make good title to the property (eg National Condition 10). Such clauses are rarely relied on in practice; where in extreme circumstances a seller does seek to rely on such a clause, the inevitable outcome will be litigation to resolve the problem, with the court taking a very restrictive view of the interpretation of such clauses. It may be considered that the inclusion of such a clause in a modern contract is anachronistic and outmoded, particularly in view of the fact that the rule in *Bain v Fothergill* (restricting the buyer's damages where the seller could not make good title), which was based on a concept similar to the type of clause under discussion, was abolished by the Law of Property (Miscellaneous Provisions) Act 1989. This certainly is the view taken by the draftsmen of the Standard Conditions who have omitted such a clause from the third edition. If such a clause is required to protect a seller client, the form of clause from the first edition of the Standard Conditions is reproduced in para 24.31. National Condition 10 contains similar provisions.

The following paragraphs deal only with the situation where the seller cannot make good title to the land which he has agreed to sell and wants to withdraw from the contract.

*Grounds for rescission*

**25.25**   In the absence of an express provision in the contract the seller has no right to withdraw from the contract after exchange unless the buyer wrongfully repudiates the contract.

The grounds on which the seller can rescind, and the buyer's rights in the event of such rescission, depend on the wording of the particular condition, but the following general principles are relevant.

A condition which allows the seller to rescind where the buyer *makes* an unwelcome requisition will allow the seller to withdraw without giving notice of his intention to the buyer and without attempting to negotiate to resolve the dispute. Attempted negotiations by the seller under such a clause will probably act as a waiver of the right to rescind. The seller must make his decision to rescind immediately on receiving the requisition without asking the buyer whether he will withdraw the requisition and without giving the buyer the opportunity of withdrawing the requisition voluntarily and thus keeping the contract alive.

This type of condition is not commonly met in practice since its operation is too arbitrary and benefits neither party.

In place of the type of condition described above it is more usual to find that the condition allows the seller to rescind only where the buyer persists or insists on making a requisition with which the seller is unable or unwilling to comply. This slightly wider wording allows the seller to attempt to negotiate a solution with the buyer before exercising his right to rescind. It also gives the buyer the opportunity to withdraw his objection to the title.

A clause permitting negotiation will still deprive the seller of his right to rescind if he merely refutes the buyer's allegation, because disputing the existence of the defect is outside the ambit of the word 'negotiation'.

Where such a clause is included in the contract, four conditions must be fulfilled before the seller is entitled to exercise his right to rescind:

(a)  the buyer has made his requisition;

(b)  the seller is unwilling to comply with that requisition;

(c) the seller has notified the buyer of his unwillingness to comply with the requisition;

(d) the buyer has not withdrawn his requisition.

The application of rescission clauses was discussed fully in *Selkirk v Romar Investments Ltd* (1963) from which case it appears that the seller cannot use such a clause to escape from the contract unless:

(a) he can show some title. If he can show no title at all his withdrawal from the contract will be a breach and full damages are payable to the buyer;

(b) the seller was unaware of the defect of which the buyer complains at the time when the contract was made.

The seller's lack of knowledge must not have been due to lack of care. It is unclear whether the lack of care must be attributable to the seller personally or whether a lack of care attributable to the seller's having relied on inaccurate or inadequate professional advice will also preclude rescission;

(c) the defect is either irremovable, or only removable at disproportionate expense;

(d) the seller relies on the condition both definitely and within a reasonable time. 'Definitely' indicates that the seller cannot choose to negotiate to resolve the problem unless the condition specifically allows this. 'Within a reasonable time' need not necessarily be before contractual completion date provided that time was not of the essence of the contract;

(e) the seller shows that he was reasonable in exercising his right to withdraw. In assessing reasonableness the seller 'does not have to be beyond criticism before he can exercise his right to rescind' ([1963] 1 WLR at 1425). No distinction seems to be drawn between a seller who is unable to comply with the buyer's requisition and one who is unwilling so to comply. The concept of reasonableness applies equally to both.

## General limitations on the use of rescission clauses

**25.26** The clauses are restricted to requisitions on title only. Requisitions on conveyance are precluded unless the contractual condition states otherwise. (See 14.2 above for the distinction between title and conveyance.)

If the seller withdraws after declining to answer a requisition on conveyance he puts himself in breach of contract and full damages are payable to the buyer (*Day v Singleton* (1899)).

If the seller cannot show any title at all his withdrawal from the contract constitutes a breach and full damages are payable.

The seller will not be allowed to rely on a rescission clause if he was reckless in entering the contract or where he knew or ought to have known of the defect before entering the contract.

Reliance on the clause will not be permitted unless the seller acted reasonably and promptly in exercising his rights under the clause.

An irremovable defect in title caused by a Class F land charge (or equivalent notice in registered land) does not give the seller the protection of the clause. Full damages for breach will be payable to the buyer (*Wroth v Tyler* (1974)).

Unless the condition expressly allows negotiation, the right to rescind will be lost if the seller negotiates with the buyer in an attempt to resolve the dispute.

The seller will also lose his right to rescind if:

(a)  he expressly elects to keep the contract alive; or

(b)  he commences an action for specific performance against the buyer; or

(c)  an action (other than (b) proceeds to judgment (*Re Arbib & Class's Contracts* (1891)). The seller may rescind, or the buyer may elect to withdraw his requisition at any time up to judgment.

## Statutory limitations on the application of rescission clauses

**25.27**   Under sections 42, 45 and 125 of the Law of Property Act 1925, the buyer has a non-excludable right to raise objections to the seller's title in relation to certain matters. The seller is not able to use his contractual right to rescind in order to avoid correcting a defect covered by one of these provisions. His inability or unwillingness to correct such a defect will amount to a breach of contract in respect of which full damages will be payable.

## Buyer's rights where the seller rescinds

**25.28**   The buyer's rights and/or remedies where the seller rescinds, other than under a contractual condition, are governed by the general law and would include an action for damages against the seller. The quantum of damages would include compensation for loss of bargain.

Until the deposit is returned, the buyer has an equitable lien over the seller's property which may be enforced by an order for sale of the property. To be enforceable against another buyer the lien must be registered as a notice or caution in registered land (C(iii) land charge in unregistered land), unless supported by a deposit of title deeds.

Where there is conflict in the contract between a clause allowing rescission and a clause allowing the buyer to claim compensation for a misdescription, the former clause prevails. Thus in exercising his right to rescind the seller can defeat the buyer's contractual rights to compensation.

## Effect of rescission on estate agent's commission

**25.29**   A seller may still find himself liable to pay commission to his estate agent despite the fact that he has validly exercised his right to rescind the contract for sale. The agent's right to commission in these circumstances will depend on the terms of the contract between the agent and the seller. The terms of the agent's contract should be ascertained and the seller advised as to the position before the decision to rescind is effected.

*Example clause from the Standard Conditions (1st ed)*

'Where the seller is unable or, on reasonable grounds, unwilling to satisfy any requisition, he may give the buyer notice of that fact and of his reasons and require the buyer within seven working days to withdraw the requisition. Unless the buyer withdraws it, he may rescind the contract notwithstanding any intermediate negotiation or litigation.'

# Appendix 1

# The Standard Conditions of Sale
# (4th edition)

© The Law Society. Reproduced with kind permission of The Law Society and Solicitors' Law Stationery Society.

1      GENERAL

1.1    *Definitions*

1.1.1  In these conditions:

(a) "accrued interest" means:

  (i) if money has been placed on deposit or in a building society share account, the interest actually earned

  (ii) otherwise, the interest which might reasonably have been earned by depositing the money at interest on sevens days' notice of withdrawal with a clearing bank

  less, in either case, any proper charges for handling the money

(b) "chattels price" means any separate amount payable for chattels included in the contract

(c) "clearing bank" means a bank which is a shareholder in CHAPS Clearing Co. Limited

(d) "completion date" has the meaning given in condition 6.1.1

(e) "contract rate" means the Law Society's interest rate from time to time in force

(f) "conveyancer" means a solicitor, barrister, duly certified notary public, licensed conveyancer or recognised body under sections 9 or 23 of the Administration of Justice Act 1985

(g) "direct credit" means a direct transfer of cleared funds to an account nominated by the seller's conveyancer and maintained by a clearing bank

(h) "lease" includes sub-lease, tenancy and agreement for a lease or sub-lease

(i) "notice to complete" means a notice requiring completion of the contract in accordance with condition 6

(j) "public requirement" means any notice, order or proposal given or made (whether before or after the date of the contract) by a body acting on statutory authority

(k) "requisition" includes objection

(l) "transfer" includes conveyance and assignment

(m)"working day" means any day from Monday to Friday (inclusive) which is not Christmas Day, Good Friday or a statutory Bank Holiday.

1.1.2 In these conditions the terms "absolute title" and "official copies" have the special meanings given to them by the Land Registration Act 2002.

1.1.3 A party is ready, able and willing to complete:

(a) if he could be, but for the default of the other party, and

(b) in the case of the seller, even though the property remains subject to a mortgage, if the amount to be paid on completion enables the property to be transferred freed of all mortages (except any to which the sale is expressly subject).

1.1.4 These conditions apply except as varied or excluded by the contract.

1.2 *Joint parties*

If there is more than one seller or more than one buyer, the obligations which they undertake can be enforced against them all jointly or against each individually.

1.3 *Notices and documents*

1.3.1 A notice required or authorised by the contract must be in writing.

1.3.2 Giving a notice or delivering a document to a party's conveyancer has the same effect as giving or delivering it to that party.

1.3.3 Where delivery of the original document is not essential, a notice or document is validly given or sent if it is sent:

(a) by fax, or

(b) by e-mail to an e-mail address for the intended recipient given in the contract.

1.3.4 Subject to conditions 1.3.5 to 1.3.7, a notice is given and a document is delivered when it is received.

1.3.5 (a) A notice or document sent through a document exchange is received when it is available for collection

(b) A notice or document which is received after 4.00 pm on a working day, or on a day which is not a working day, is to be treated as having been received on the next working day

(c) An automated response to a notice or document sent by e-mail that the intended recipient is out of the office is to be treated as proof that the notice or document was not received.

1.3.6 Condition 1.3.7 applies unless there is proof:

(a) that a notice or document has not been received, or

(b) of when it was received.

1.3.7  A notice or document sent by the following means is treated as having been received as follows:

(a) by first-class post: before 4.00 pm on the second working day after posting

(b) by second-class post: before 4.00 pm on the third working day after posting

(c) through a document exchange: before 4.00 pm on the first working day after the day on which it would normally be available for collection by the addressee

(d) by fax: one hour after despatch

(e) by e-mail: before 4.00 pm on the first working day after despatch.

1.4    *VAT*

1.4.1  An obligation to pay money includes an obligation to pay any value added tax chargeable in respect of that payment.

1.4.2  All sums made payable by the contract are exclusive of value added tax.

1.5    *Assignment*

The buyer is not entitled to transfer the benefit of the contract.

2      FORMATION

2.1    *Date*

2.1.1  If the parties intend to make a contract by exchanging duplicate copies by post or through a document exchange, the contract is made when the last copy is posted or deposited at the document exchange.

2.1.2  If the parties' conveyancers agree to treat exchange as taking place before dupicate copies are actually exchanged, the contract is made as so agreed.

2.2.   *Deposit*

2.2.1  The buyer is to pay or send a deposit of 10 per cent of the total of the purchase price and the chattels price not later than the date of the contract.

2.2.2  If a cheque tendered in payment of all or part of the deposit is dishonoured when first presented, the seller may, within seven working days of being notified that the cheque has been dishonoured, give notice to the buyer that the contract is discharged by the buyer's breach.

2.2.3  Conditions 2.2.4 to 2.2.6 do not apply on a sale by auction.

2.2.4  The deposit is to be paid by direct credit or to the seller's conveyancer by a cheque drawn on a solicitor's or licensed conveyancer's client account.

2.2.5  If before completion date the seller agrees to buy another property in England and Wales for his residence, he may use all or any part of the deposit as a deposit in that transaction to be held on terms to the same effect as this condition and condition 2.2.6.

2.2.6  Any deposit or part of a deposit not being used in accordance with condition 2.2.5 is to be held by the seller's conveyancer as stakeholder on terms that on completion it is paid to the seller with accrued interest.

2.3  *Auctions*

2.3.1  On a sale by auction the following conditions apply to the property and, if it is sold in lots, to each lot.

2.3.2  The sale is subject to a reserve price.

2.3.3  The seller, or a person on his behalf, may bid up to the reserve price.

2.3.4  The auctioneer may refuse any bid.

2.3.5  If there is a dispute about a bid, the auctioneer may resolve the dispute or restart the auction at the last undisputed bid.

2.3.6  The deposit is to be paid to the auctioneer as agent for the seller.

3  MATTERS AFFECTING THE PROPERTY

3.1  *Freedom from incumbrances*

3.1.1  The seller is selling the property free from incumbrances, other than those mentioned in condition 3.1.2.

3.1.2  The incumbrances subject to which the property is sold are:

(a) those specified in the contract

(b) those discoverable by inspection of the property before the contract

(c) those the seller does not and could not reasonably know about

(d) entries made before the date of the contract in any public register except those maintained by the Land Registry or its Land Charges Department or by Companies House

(e) public requirements.

3.1.3  After the contract is made, the seller is to give the buyer written details without delay of any new public requirement and of anything in writing which he learns about concerning a matter covered by condition 3.1.2.

3.1.4  The buyer is to bear the cost of complying with any outstanding public requirement and is to indemnify the seller against any liability resulting from a public requirement.

3.2  *Physical state*

3.2.1  The buyer accepts the property in the physical state it is in at the date of the contract unless the seller is building or converting it.

3.2.2.  A leasehold property is sold subject to any subsisting breach of a condition or tenant's obligation relating to the physical state of the property which renders the lease liable to forfeiture.

3.2.3  A sub-lease is granted subject to any subsisting breach of a condition or tenant's obligation relating to the physical state of the property which renders the seller's own lease liable to forfeiture.

3.3.  *Leases affecting the property*

3.3.1  The following provisions apply if any part of the property is sold subject to a lease.

3.3.2  (a) The seller having provided the buyer with full details of each lease or copies of the documents embodying the lease terms, the buyer is treated as entering into the contract knowing and fully accepting those terms.

(b) The seller is to inform the buyer without delay if the lease ends or if the seller learns of any application by the tenant in connection with the lease; the seller is then to act as the buyer reasonably directs, and the buyer is to indemnify him against all consequent loss and expense.

(c) Except with the buyer's consent, the seller is not to agree to any proposal to change the lease terms nor to take any step to end the lease.

(d) The seller is to inform the buyer without delay of any change to the lease terms which may be proposed or agreed.

(e) The buyer is to indemnify the seller against all claims arising from the lease after actual completion; this includes claims which are unenforceable against a buyer for want of registration.

(f) The seller takes no responsibility for what rent is lawfully recoverable, nor for whether or how any legislation affects the lease.

(g) If the let land is not wholly within the property, the seller may apportion the rent.

3.4   *Retained land*

Where after the transfer the seller will be retaining land near the property:

(a) the buyer will have no right of light or air over the retained land, but

(b) in other respects the seller and the buyer will each have the rights over the land of the other which they would have had if they were two separate buyers to whom the seller had made simultaneous transfers of the property and the retained land.

The transfer is to contain appropriate express terms.

4.    TITLE AND TRANSFER

4.1   *Proof of title*

4.1.1 Without cost to the buyer, the seller is to provide the buyer with proof of the title to the property and of his ability to transfer it, or to procure its transfer.

4.1.2 Where the property has a registered title the proof is to include official copies of the items referred to in rules 134(1)(a) and (b) and 135(1)(a) of the Land Registration Rules 2003, so far as they are not to be discharged or overridden at or before completion.

4.1.3 Where the property has an unnregistered title, the proof is to include:

(a) an abstract of title or an epitome of title with photocopies of the documents, and

(b) production of every document or an abstract, epitome or copy of it with an original marketing by a conveyancer either against the original or an examined abstract or an examined copy.

4.2    *Requisitions*

4.2.1  The buyer may not raise requisitions:

(a) on the title shown by the seller taking the steps described in condition 4.1.1 before the contract was made

(b) in relation to the matter covered by condition 3.1.2.

4.2.2  Notwithstanding conditon 4.2.1, the buyer may, within six working days of a matter coming to his attention after the contract was made, raise written requisitions on that matter. In that event, steps 3 and 4 in condition 4.3.1 apply.

4.2.3  On the expiry of the relevant time limit under condition 4.2.2 or condition 4.3.1, the buyer loses his right to raise requisitions or to make observations.

4.3    *Timetable*

4.3.1  Subject to condition 4.2 and to the extent that the seller did not take the steps described in condition 4.1.1 before the contract was made, the following are the steps for deducing and investigating the title to the property to be taken within the following time limits:

| Step | Time limit |
| --- | --- |
| 1. The seller is to comply with condition 4.1.1 | Immediately after making the contract |
| 2. The buyer may raise written requisitions | Six working days after either the date of the seller's evidence of title on which the contract or the date of delivery of the requisitions are raised whichever is the later |
| 3. The seller is to reply in writing to any requisitions raised | Four working days after receiving the requisitions |
| 4. The buyer may make written observations on the seller's replies | Three working days afer receiving the replies |

The time limit on the buyer's right to raise requisitions applies even where the seller supplies incomplete evidence of his title, but the buyer may, within six working days from delivery of any further evidence, raise further requisitions resulting from that evidence.

4.3.2  The parties are to take the following steps to prepare and agree the transer of the property within the following time limits:

| Step | Time limit |
| --- | --- |
| A. The buyer is to send the seller a draft transfer | At least twelve working days before completion date |
| B. The seller is to approve or revise that draft and either return it or retain it for use as the actual transfer | Four working days after delivery of the draft transfer |
| C. If the draft is returned the buyer is to send an engrossment to the seller | At least five working days before completion date |

4.3.3  Periods of time under conditions 4.3.1 and 4.3.2 may run concurrently.

4.3.4 If the period between the date of the contract and completion date is less than 15 working days, the time limits in conditions 4.2.2, 4.3.1 and 4.3.2 are to be reduced by the same proportion as that period bears to the period of 15 working days. Fractions of a working day are to be rounded down except that the time limit to perform any step is not to be less than one working day.

4.4 *Defining the property*

4.4.1 The seller need not:

(a) prove the exact boundaries of the property

(b) prove who owns fences, ditches, hedges or walls

(c) separately identify parts of the property with different titles further than he may be able to do from information in his possession.

4.4.2 The buyer may, if it is reasonable, require the seller to make or obtain, pay for and hand over a statutory declaration about facts relevant to the matters mentioned in condition 4.4.1. The form of the declaration is to be agreed by the buyer, who must not unreasonably withhold his agreements.

4.5 *Rents and rentcharges*

The fact that a rent or rentcharge, whether payable or receivable by the owner of the property, has been, or will on completion be, informally apportioned is not to be regarded as a defect in title.

4.6 *Transfer*

4.6.1 The buyer does not prejudice his right to raise requisitions, or to require replies to any raised, by taking any steps in relation to preparing or agreeing the transfer.

4.6.2 Subject to condition 4.6.3, the seller is to transfer the property with full title guarantee.

4.6.3 The transfer is to have effect as if the disposition is expressly made subject to all matters covered by condition 3.1.2.

4.6.4 If after completion the seller will remain bound by any obligation affecting the property which was disclosed to the buyer before the contract was made, but the law does not imply any covenant by the buyer to indemnify the seller against liability for future breaches of it:

(a) the buyer is to covenant in the transfer to indemnify the seller against liability for any future breach of the obligation and to perform it from then on, and

(b) if required by the seller, the buyer is to execute and deliver to the seller on completion a duplicate transfer prepared by the buyer.

4.6.5 The seller is to arrange at his expense that, in relation to every document of title which the buyer does not receive on completion, the buyer is to have the benefit of:

(a) a written acknowledgement of his right to its production, and

(b) a written undertaking for its safe custody (except while it is held by a mortgagee or by someone in a fiduciary capacity).

5    PENDING COMPLETION

5.1    *Responsibility for property*

5.1.1    The seller will transfer the property in the same physical state as it was at the date of the contract (except for fair wear and tear), which means that the seller retains the risk until completion.

5.1.2    If at any time before completion the physical state of the property makes it unusable for its purpose at the date of the contract:

(a) the buyer may rescind the contract

(b) the seller may rescind the contract where the property has become unusable for that purpose as a result of damage against which the seller could not reasonably have insured, or which it is not legally possible for the seller to make good.

5.1.3    The seller is under no obligation to the buyer to insure the property.

5.1.4    Section 47 of the Law of Property Act 1925 does not apply.

5.2    *Occuation by buyer*

5.2.1    If the buyer is not already lawfully in the property, and the seller agees to let him into occupation, the buyer occupies on the following terms.

5.2.2    The buyer is a licensee and not a tenant. The terms of the licence are that the buyer:

(a) cannot transfer it

(b) may permit members of his household to occupy the property

(c) is to pay or indemnify the seller against all outgoings and other expenses in respect of the property

(d) is to pay the seller a fee calculated at the contract rate on a sum equal to the purchase price and the chattels price (less any deposit paid) for the period of the licence

(e) is entitled to any rents and profits from any part of the property which he does not occupy

(f) is to keep the property in as good a state of repair as it was in when he went into occupation (except for fair wear and tear) and is not to alter it

(g) is to insure the property in a sum which is not less than the purchase price against all risks in respect of which comparable premises are normally insured

(h) is to quit the property when the licence ends.

5.2.3    On the creation of the buyer's licence, condition 5.1 ceases to apply, which means that the buyer then assumes the risk until completion.

5.2.4    The buyer is not in occupation for the purposes of this condition if he merely exercises rights of access given solely to do work agreed by the seller.

5.2.5    The buyer's licence ends on the earliest of: completion date, rescission of the contract or when five working days' notice given by one party to the other takes effect.

5.2.6 If the buyer is in occupation of the property after his licence has come to an end and the contract is subsequently completed he is to pay the seller compensation for his continued occupation calculated at the same rate as the fee mentioned in condition 5.2.2(d).

5.2.7 The buyer's right to raise requisitions is unaffected.

6 COMPLETION

6.1 *Date*

6.1.1 Completion date is twenty working days after the date of the contract but time is not of the essence of the contract unless a notice to complete has been served.

6.1.2 If the money due on completion is received after 2.00 pm, completion is to be treated, for the purposes only of conditions 6.3 and 7.3, as taking place on the next working day as a result of the buyer's default.

6.1.3 Condition 6.1.2 does not apply and the seller is treated as in default if:

(i) the sale is with vacant possession of the property or any part of it, and

(ii) the buyer is ready, able and willing to complete but does not pay the money due on completion until after 2.00 pm because the seller has not vacated the property or that part by that time.

6.2 *Arrangements and place*

6.2.1 The buyer's conveyancer and the seller's conveyancer are to co-operate in agreeing arrangements for completing the contract.

6.2.2 Completion is to take place in England and Wales, either at the seller's conveyancer's office or at some other place which the seller reasonably specifies.

6.3 *Apportionments*

6.3.1 Income and outgoings of the property are to be apportioned between the parties so far as the change of ownership on completion will affect entitlement to receive or liability to pay them.

6.3.2 If the whole property is sold with vacant possession or the seller exercises his option in condition 7.3.4, apportionment is to be made with effect from the date of actual completion; otherwise, it is to be made from completion date.

6.3.3 In apportioning any sum, it is to be assumed that the seller owns the property until the end of the day from which apportionment is made and that the sum accrues from day to day at the rate at which it is payable on that day.

6.3.4 For the purpose of apportioning income and outgoings, it is to be assumed that they accrue at an equal daily rate throughout the year.

6.3.5 When a sum to be apportioned is not known or easily ascertainable at completion, a provisional apportionment is to be made according to the best estimate available. As soon as the amount is known, a final apportionment is to be made and notified to the other party. Any resulting balance is to be paid no more than ten working days later, and if not then paid the balance is to bear interest at the contract rate from then until payment.

6.3.6 Compensation payable under condition 5.2.6 is not to be apportioned.

6.4    *Amount payable*

The amount payable by the buyer on completion is the purchase price and the chattels price (less any deposit already paid to the seller or his agent) adjusted to take account of:

(a) apportionments made under condition 6.3

(b) any compensation to be paid or allowed under condition 7.3.

6.5    *Title deeds*

6.5.1  As soon as the buyer has complied with all his obligations on completion the seller must hand over the documents of title.

6.5.2  Condition 6.5.1 does not apply to any documents of title relating to land being retained by the seller after completion.

6.6    *Rent receipts*

The buyer is to assume that whoever gave receipt for a payment of rent or service charge which the seller produces was the person or the agent of the person then entitled to that rent or service charge.

6.7    *Means of payment*

The buyer is to pay the money due on completion by direct credit and, if appropriate, an unconditional release of a deposit held by a stakeholder.

6.8    *Notice to complete*

6.8.1  At any time on or after completion date, a party who is ready, able and willing to complete may give the other a notice to complete.

6.8.2  The parties are to complete the contract within ten working days of giving a notice to complete, excluding the day on which the notice is given. For this purpose, time is of the essence of the contract.

6.8.3  On receipt of a notice to complete:

(a) if the buyer paid no deposit, he is forthwith to pay a deposit of 10 per cent

(b) if the buyer paid a deposit of less than 10 per cent, he is forthwith to pay a further deposit equal to the balance of that 10 per cent.

7.     REMEDIES

7.1    *Errors and omissions*

7.1.1  If any plan or statement in the contract, or in the negotiations leading to it, is or was misleading or inaccurate due to an error or omission, the remedies available are as follows.

7.1.2  When there is a material difference between the description or value of the property, or of any of the chattels included in the contract, as represented and as it is, the buyer is entitled to damages.

7.1.3  An error or omission only entitles the buyer to rescind the contract:

(a) where it results from fraud or recklessness, or

(b) where he would be obliged, to his prejudice, to accept property differing substantially (in quantity, quality or tenure) from what the error or omission had led him to expect.

7.2    *Rescission*

If either part rescinds the contract:

(a) unless the rescission is a result of the buyer's breach of contract the deposit is to be repaid to the buyer with accrued interest

(b) the buyer is to return any documents he received from the seller and is to cancel any registration of the contract.

7.3    *Late completion*

7.3.1  If there is default by either or both of the parties in performing their obligations under the contract and completion is delayed, the party whose total period of default is the greater is to pay compensation to the other party.

7.3.2  Compensation is calculated at the contract rate on an amount equal to the purchase price and the chattels price, less (where the buyer is the paying party) any deposit paid, for the period by which the paying party's default exceeds that of the receiving party, or, if shorter, the period between completion date and actual completion.

7.3.3  Any claim for loss resulting from delayed completion is to be reduced by any compensation paid under this contract.

7.3.4  Where the buyer holds the property as tenant of the seller and completion is delayed, the seller may give notice to the buyer, before the date of actual completion, that he intends to take the net income from the property until completion. If he does so, he cannot claim compensation under condition 7.3.1 as well.

7.4    *After completion*

Completion does not cancel liability to perform any outstanding obligation under this contract.

7.5    *Buyer's failure to comply with notice to complete*

7.5.1  If the buyer fails to complete in accordance with a notice to complete, the following terms apply.

7.5.2  The seller may rescind the contract, and if he does so:

(a) he may

    (i)    forfeit and keep any deposit and accrued interest

    (ii)   resell the property and any chattels included in the contract

    (iii)  claim damages

(b) the buyer is to return any documents he received from the seller and is to cancel any registration of the contract.

7.5.3  The seller retains his other rights and remedies.

7.6    *Seller's failure to comply with notice to complete*

7.6.1  If the seller fails to complete in accordance with a notice to complete, the following terms apply.

7.6.2  The buyer may rescind the contract, and if he does so:

(a) the deposit is to be repaid to the buyer with accrued interest

(b) the buyer is to return any documents he received from the seller and is, at the seller's expense, to cancel any registration of the contract.

7.6.3 The buyer retains his other rights and remedies.

8     LEASEHOLD PROPERTY

8.1    *Existing leases*

8.1.1 The following provisions apply to a sale of leasehold land.

8.1.2 The seller having provided the buyer with copies of the documents embodying the lease terms, the buyer is treated as entering into the contract knowing and fully accepting those terms.

8.1.3 The seller is to comply with any lease obligations requiring the tenant to insure the property.

8.2    *New leases*

8.2.1 The following provisions apply to a contract to grant a new lease.

8.2.2 The conditions apply so that:

"seller" means the proposed landlord

"buyer" means the proposed tenant

"purchase price" means the premium to be paid on the grant of a lease.

8.2.3 The lease is to be in the form of the draft attached to the contract.

8.2.4 If the term of the new lease will exceed seven years, the seller is to deduce a title which will enable the buyer to register the lease at the Land Registry with an absolute title.

8.2.5 The seller is to engross the lease and a counterpart of it and is to send the counterpart to the buyer at least five working days before completion date.

8.2.6 The buyer is to execute the counterpart and deliver it to the seller on completion.

8.3    *Consent*

8.3.1 (a) The following provisions apply if a consent to let, assign or sub-let is required to complete the contract.

(b) In this condition "consent" means consent in the form which satisfies the requirement to obtain it.

8.3.2 (a) The seller is to apply for the consent at his expense, and to use all reasonable efforts to obtain it.

(b) The buyer is to provide all information and references reasonably required.

8.3.3 Unless he is in breach of his obligation under condition 8.3.2, either party may rescind the contract by notice to the other party if three working days before comletion date (or before a later date on which the parties have agreed to complete the contract):

(a) the consent has not been given, or

(b) the consent has been given subject to a condition to which a party reasonably objects.

In that case, neither party is to be treated as in breach of contract and condition 7.2 applies.

9.    COMMONHOLD LAND

9.1    Terms used in this condition have the special meanings given to them in Part 1 of the Commonhold and Leasehold Reform Act 2002.

9.2    This condition applies to a disposition of commonhold land.

9.3    The seller having provided the buyer with copies of the current versions of the memorandum and articles of the commonhold association and of the commonhold community statement, the buyer is treated as entering into the contract knowing and fully accepting their terms.

9.4    If the contract is for the sale of property which is or includes part only of a commonhold unit:

(a) the seller is to apply for the written consent of the commonhold association at his expense and is to use all reasonable efforts to obtain it

(b) either the seller, unless he is in breach of his obligation under paragraph (a), or the buyer may rescind the contract by notice to the other party if three working days before completion date (or before a later date on which the parties have agreed to complete the contract) the consent has not been given. In that case, neither party is to be treated as in breach of contract and condition 7.2 applies.

10.    CHATTELS

10.1    The following provisions apply to any chattels which are included in the contract, whether or not a separate price is to be paid for them.

10.2    The contract takes effect as a contract for sale of goods.

10.3    The buyer takes the chattels in the physical state they are in at the date of the contract.

10.4    Ownership of the chattels passes to the buyer on actual completion.

SPECIAL CONDITIONS

1    (a) This contract incorporates the Standard Conditions of Sale (Fourth Edition).

(b) The terms used in this contract have the same meaning when used in the Conditions.

2    Subject to the terms of this contract and to the Standard Conditions of Sale, the seller is to transfer the property with either full title guarantee or limited title guarantee, as specified on the front page.

3    The chattels which are on the property and are set out on any attached list are included in the sale and the buyer is to pay the chattels price for them.

4    The property is sold with vacant posession.

(or)

4     The property is sold subject to the following leases or tenancies:

**Seller's conveyancers\*:**

**Buyer's conveyancers\*:**

\* Adding an e-mail address authorises service by e-mail: see condition 1.3.3(b).

## Explanatory notes on the Standard Conditions of Sale (fourth edition)

*General*

The fourth edition of the Standard Conditions of Sale (the SCS) takes effect on 13 October 2003, being the date on which the main provisions of the Land Registration Act 2002 come into force. The fourth edition takes account of the changes made by that Act, and also anticipates the coming into force in early 2004 of the rovisions relating to commonhold in Part I of the Commonhold and Leasehold Reform Act 2002.

The SCS are intended primarily for use in residential sales and in the sale of small business premises. For more complex commercial transactions, conveyancers are likely to find the Standard Commercial Property Conditions (the SCPC) better suited to their needs. A second edition of the SCPC is planned for later in 2003.

The fourth edition of the SCS represents the 24th Edition of the National Conditions of Sale and the Law Society's Conditions of Sale 2003.

*'Contract'*

Previous editions of the SCS have distinguished between 'the agreement' (meaning the contractual document which contains the individually negotiated terms and incorporates the SCS) and 'the contract' (meaning the whole bargain, including the SCS). Some users of the SCS have found this distinction confusing, and it has been abandoned in the present edition, which refers only to 'the contract'.

It should, however, be noted that condition 1.1.4 of the SCS embodies a new general provision to the effect that the SCS apply except as varied or excluded by the contract, so ensuring that, where there is a conflict, the individual negotiated terms will prevail over the SCS.

Condition 1.1.4 will also ensure that the general provisions of the SCS which determine the completion date (conditions 1.1.1(d) and 6.1.1), the contract rate (condition 1.1.1(e)) and the title guarantee to be given in the transfer (condition 4.6.2) will automatically take effect subject to any individual negotiated terms which deal with these matters. For that reason, these provisions no longer include words making them expressly subject to the particular terms of the agreement.

## Front and back pages: specified incumbrances

The back page no longer contains a special condition stating that the property is sold subject to the incumbrances set out on the front page. However, condition 3.1.2(a) provides that the property is sold subject to the incumbrances specified in the contract, and the front page includes space for specifying any incumbrances to which the sale is expressly made subject. The sale will, therefore, continue to take effect subject to any incumbrances there set out.

## Chattels

The SCS now make fuller provision for cases in which a separate price is agreed for any chattels included in the sale. In such a case, the 'purchase price' will refer to the price agreed for the property and the 'chattels price' (as defined in condition 1.1.1(b)) will refer to the price separately agreed for the chattels. The SCS provide for the deposit to be 10 per cent of the total of the purchase price and the chattels price (condition 2.2.1). They also provide for the chattels price to be taken into account in calculating any licence fee payable where the buyer goes into occupation before completion (condition 5.2.2(d)), in working out the amount payable on completion (condition 6.4) and in working out any compensation payable on late completion (condition 7.3.2).

It should, however, be noted that condition 10 will apply to any chattels included in the sale whether or not a separate price is payable for them.

## 'Conveyancer'

In this edition, 'conveyancer' has replaced 'solicitor' as the defined term used to refer to the various categories of persons who may lawfully carry out conveyancing work for reward (condition 1.1.1(f)). Note, however, that, in a case where the property is being sold otherwise than at auction and the deposit is paid by cheque, the cheque may be drawn only on a solicitor's or licensed conveyancer's client account (conditions 2.2.3 and 2.2.4). This requirement reflects the fact that solicitors and licensed conveyancers (in contrast, for example, to barristers) hold money on client account and can be expected to have taken steps to comply with their obligations under the general law and professional rules to ensure that their client accounts are not being used for money-laundering purposes.

## Payment by direct credit

In the light of developments in conveyancing practice, the present edition of the SCS no longer gives the buyer the option of paying the deposit by banker's draft, or of paying the money due on completion by banker's draft or legal tender. The current position is that, unless the property is being sold by auction, the deposit must be paid either by direct credit or (as noted above) by cheque drawn on a solicitor's or licensed conveyancer's client account (conditions 2.2.3 and 2.2.4). The money due on completion may now be paid only by direct credit, coupled where appropriate wth the release of any deposit held by a stakeholder (condition 6.7). For these purposes, 'direct credit' is defined in condition 1.1.1(g) as meaning a direct transfer of cleared funds to an account nominated by the seller's conveyancer and maintained by a 'clearing bank', that is to say, a bank which is a shareholder in CHAPS Clearing Co. Ltd (condition 1.1.1(c)).

*Ready, able and willing to complete*

Condition 1.1.3 contains a new general provision stating when a party is ready, able and willing to complete. The provision is relevant in applying conditions 6.1.3 and 6.8.1.

*Notices and documents*

Condition 1.3.6 now makes it clear that the presumed times of receipt set out in condition 1.3.7 may be displaced not only by proof of the actual time at which a notice or document was received, but also by proof that the notice or document was not received at all.

Condition 1.3.3(b) is a new provision, which enables a notice or document to be sent by e-mail where delivery of the original is not essential. It is important to appreciate that condition 1.3.3(b) permits notices or documents to be sent in this way if, but only if, an e-mail address for the intended recipient is given in the contract. Thus, a party's conveyancers should not include their e-mail address in the contract unless they are prepared to accept service by e-mail at that address.

Two further provisions relevant to the use of e-mail should be noted. First, condition 1.3.5(c) provides that, where a notice or document sent by e-mail prompts an automated response that the intended recipient is out of the office, the response (while in reality establishing that the message has reached its intended destination) is to be treated as proof that the notice or document has not been received. The sender may, therefore, need to consider other means for sending the notice or document to its intended recipient (eg, hand delivery or fax). Secondly, condition 1.3.7(e) provides that (in the absence of proof to the contrary under condition 1.3.6) a notice or document sent by e-mail is treated as having been received before 4.00 pm on the first working day after dispatch. It will be noted that this is later than the time of receipt presumed by condition 1.3.7(d) for a notice or document sent by fax (one hour after despatch). The reason for this is that the receipt of an e-mail may on occasion be delayed for several hours without the delay in transmission being readily apparent to the sender.

*Assignment*

Condition 1.5 now contains a general prohibition on the transfer by the buyer of the benefit of the contract. The specific prohibitions which formerly applied to the transfer of contracts for the grant or assignment of a lease or sub-lease have accordingly been deleted.

*Appendix 1*

*Auctions*

Condition 2.3.6 now follows the SCPC in providing that, on a sale by auction, the deposit is to be paid to the auctioneer as agent for the seller.

*Proof of title*

Condition 4.1.1 requires the seller to provide the buyer with proof of his title to the property and of his ability to transfer it or to procure its transfer (the latter alternative applying, for example, to a sub-sale).

Where the title is registered, the effect of condition 4.1.2 is that the proof must include official copies of the individual register and any title plan referred to in it, and of any document referred to in the register and kept by the registrar (unless the document is to be discharged or overidden at or before completion).

*Requisitions*

Previous editions of the SCS have allowed the buyer to raise requisitions after the making of the contract, whether or not title was deduced beforehand. The fourth edition recognises that where the seller deduces title before the contract is made (as he normally will, at least where the title is registered), the buyer should ensure that any concerns about the title so shown are raised before contract and, where necessary, appropriately provided for in the special condi-itons. Accordingly, condition 4.2.1(a) now bars the buyer from raising any requisitions on the title shown by the seller before the making of the contract. The buyer, however, retains the right to raise requisitions on matters coming to his attention for the first time after the contract is made (condition 4.2.2).

In cases where the seller deduces title (either in whole or in part) after the contract is made, condition 4.3.1 continues to allow the buyer to raise requisitions within six working days of the date of the contract or delivery of the seller's proof of title on which the requisitions are raised.

*Completion after 2.00 pm*

Conditions 6.1.2 and 6.1.3 clarify the position where the money due on completion is received after 2.00 pm. Condition 6.1.2 states the normal rule that, in such a case, apportionments are to be worked out as if completion had taken place on the next working day, and compensation is to be calculated as if completion had been deferred to that day as a result of the buyer's default. It would, however, be unfair to adopt that approach where completion has been delayed because the seller has failed to vacate the property by 2.00 pm. Condition 6.1.3 therefore disapplies condition 6.1.2 in a case where the sale is with vacant possession and the buyer is ready, able and willing to complete (as to which, see condition 1.1.3(a)) but does not pay the money due on completion because the seller has not vacated the property by 2.00 pm. In such a case, condition 6.1.3 provides that the seller is to be treated as in default, so that compensation will be calculated on that basis under condition 7.3.

*Consent*

Condition 8.3.1(a) ensures that condition 8.3 now applies not only in cases where the landlord's consent is required for the assignment of an existing lease or the creation of a sub-lease but also in cases where consent is required for the creation of a new lease of freehold land.

Two changes to condition 8.3 have been made in the light of the decision of the Court of Appeal in *Aubergine Enterprises Ltd.* v. *Lakewood International Ltd.* [2002] 1 WLR 2149. First, condition 8.3.1(b) confirms that any necessary consent must be in the form which satisfies the requirement to obtain it. Secondly, condition 8.8.3 now provides that, where the parties agree to complete the contract after the contractual completion date, the right to rescind will not arise unless the consent has not been obtained by three working days before the later date agreed for completion.

*Commonhold*

The new commonhold regime is made the subject of express provision in two ways. First, the seller is required to provide the buyer with current copies of the memorandum and articles of the commonhold association and the common-hold community statement. If the buyer then enters into the contract, he is treated as doing so knowing and accepting their terms (condition 9.3, and *cf.* condition 3.3.2(a), which makes similar provision with regard to the terms of leases affecting the property). Secondly, cases in which the consent of the commonhold association is required to the sale of part only of a commonhold unit are dealt with (in condition 9.4) in a way which parallels the provision made in conditions 8.3.2(a) and 8.3.3 for cases in which a consent to let, assign or sub-let is required to complete the contract.

# Appendix 2

# The Standard Commercial Property Conditions (2nd Edition)

© The Law Society. Reproduced with kind permission of The Law Society and Solicitors' Law Stationery Society.

## PART 1

1. GENERAL

1. *Definitions*

1.1.1 In these conditions:

(a) "accrued interest" means:

(i) if money has been placed on deposit or in a building society share account, the interest actually earned

(ii) otherwise, the interest which might reasonably have been earned by depositing the money at interest on seven days' notice of withdrawal with a clearing bank.

less, in either case, any proper charges for handling the money

(b) "apportionment day" has the meaning given in condition 8.3.2

(c) "clearing bank" means a bank which is a shareholder in CHAPS Clearing Co. Limited

(d) "completion date" has the meaning given in condition 8.1.1

(e) "contract rate" is the Law Society's interest rate from time to time in force

(f) "conveyancer" means a solicitor, barrister, duly certified notary public, licensed conveyancer or recognised body under sections 9 or 23 of the Administration of Justice Act 1985

(g) "direct credit" means a direct transfer of cleared funds to an account nominated by the seller's conveyancer and maintained at a clearing bank

(h) "election to waive exemption" means an election made under paragraph 2 of Schedule 10 to the Value Added Tax Act 1994

(i) "lease" includes sub-lease, tenancy and agreement for a lease or sublease

(j) "notice to complete" means a notice requiring completion of the contract in accordance with condition 8

(k) "post" includes a service provided by a person licensed under the Postal Services Act 2000

(l) "public requirement" means any notice, order or proposal given or made (whether before or after the date of the contract) by a body acting on statutory authority

(m) "requisition" includes objection

(n) "transfer" includes conveyance and assignment

(o) "working day" means any day from Monday to Friday (inclusive) which is not Christmas Day, Good Friday or a statutory Bank Holiday.

1.1.2   In these conditions the terms "absolute title" and "official copies" have the special meanings given to them by the Land Registration Act 2002.

1.1.3   A party is ready, able and willing to complete:

(a) if it could be, but for the default of the other party, and

(b) in the case of the seller, even though a mortgage remains secured on the property, if the amount to be paid on completion enables the property to be transferred freed of all mortgages (except those to which the sale is expressly subject).

1.1.4   (a) The conditions in Part 1 apply except as varied or excluded by the contract.

(b) A condition in Part 2 only applies if expressly incorporated into the contract.

1.2   *Joint parties*

If there is more than one seller or more than one buyer, the obligations which they undertake can be enforced against them all jointly or against each individually.

1.3   *Notices and documents*

1.3.1   A notice required or authorised by the contract must be in writing.

1.3.2   Giving a notice or delivering a document to a party's conveyancer has the same effect as giving or delivering it to that party.

1.3.3   Where delivery of the original document is not essential, a notice of document is validly given or sent if it is sent:

(a) by fax, or

(b) by e-mail to an e-mail address for the intended recipient given in the contract.

1.3.4   Subject to conditions 1.3.5 to 1.3.7, a notice is given and a document delivered when it is received.

1.3.5   (a) A notice or document sent through the document exchange is received when it is available for collection

(b) A notice or document which is received after 4.00 pm on a working day, or on a day which is not a working day, is to be treated as having been received on the next working day

(c) An automated response to a notice or document sent by e-mail that the intended recipient is out of the office is to be treated as proof that the notice or document was not received.

1.3.6 Condition 1.3.7 applies unless there is proof:

(a) that a notice or document has not been received, or

(b) of when it was received.

1.3.7 Unless the actual time of receipt is proved, a notice or document sent by the following means is treated as having been received as follows:

(a) by first class post: before 4.00 pm on the second working day after posting

(b) by second-class post: before 4.00 pm on the third working day after posting

(c) through a document exchange: before 4.00 pm on the first working day after the day on which it would normally be available for collection by the addressee

(d) by fax: one hour after despatch

(e) by e-mail: before 4.00 pm on the first working day after despatch.

1.3.8 In condition 1.3.7, "first class post" means a postal service which seeks to deliver posted items no later than the next working day in all or the majority of cases.

1.4 *VAT*

1.4.1 The seller:

(a) warrants that the sale of the property does not constitute a supply that is taxable for VAT purposes

(b) agrees that there will be no exercise of the election to waive exemption in respect of the property, and

(c) cannot require the buyer to pay any amount in respect of any liability to VAT arising in respect of the sale of the property, unless condition 1.4.2 applies.

1.4.2 If, solely as a result of a change in law made and coming into effect between the date of the contract and completion, the sale of the property will constitute a supply chargeable to VAT, the buyer is to pay to the seller on completion an additional amount equal to that VAT in exchange for a proper VAT invoice from the seller.

1.4.3 The amount payable for the chattels is exclusive of VAT and the buyer is to pay to the seller on completion an additional amount equal to any VAT charged on that supply in exchange for a proper VAT invoice from the seller.

1.5   *Assignment and sub-sales*

1.5.1   The buyer is not entitled to transfer the benefit of the contract.

1.5.2   The seller may not be required to transfer the property in parts or to any person other than the buyer.

2.   FORMATION

2.1   *Date*

2.1.1   If the parties intend to make a contract by exchanging duplicate copies by post or though a document exchange, the contract is made when the last copy is posted or deposited at the document exchange.

2.1.2   If the parties' conveyancers agree to treat exchange as taking place before duplicate copies are actually exchanged, the contract is made as so agreed.

2.2   *Deposit*

2.2.1   The buyer is to pay a deposit of 10 per cent of the purchase price no later than the date of the contract.

2.2.2   Except a sale by auction the deposit is to be paid by direct credit and is to be held by the seller's conveyancer as stakeholder on terms that on completion it is to be paid to the seller with accrued interest.

2.3   *Auctions*

2.3.1   On a sale by auction the following conditions apply to the property and, if it is sold in lots, to each lot.

2.3.2   The sale is subject to a reserve price.

2.3.3   The seller, or a person on its behalf, may bid up to the reserve price.

2.3.4   The auctioneer may refuse any bid.

2.3.5   If there is a dispute about a bid, the auctioneer may resolve the dispute or restart the auction at the last undisputed bid.

2.3.6   The auctioneer is to hold the deposit as agent for the seller.

2.3.7   If any cheque tendered in payment of all or part of the deposit is dishonoured when first presented, the seller may, within seven working days of being notified that the cheque has been dishonoured, give notice to the buyer that the contract is discharged by the buyer's breach.

3.   MATTERS AFFECTING THE PROPERTY

3.1   *Freedom from incumbrances*

3.1.1   The seller is selling the property free from incumbrances, other than those mentioned in condition 3.1.2.

3.1.2   The incumbrances subject to which the property is sold are:

(a) those specified in the contract

(b) those discoverable by inspection of the property before the contract

(c) those the seller does not and could not reasonably know about

(d) matters, other than monetary charges or incumbrances, disclosed or which would have been disclosed by the searches and enquiries which a prudent buyer would have made before entering into the contract

(e) public requirements.

3.1.3 After the contract is made, the seller is to give the buyer written details without delay of any new public requirement and of anything in writing which he learns about concerning a matter covered by condition 3.1.2.

3.1.4 The buyer is to bear the cost of complying with any outstanding public requirement and is to indemnify the seller against any liability resulting from a public requirement.

3.2 *Physical state*

3.2.1 The buyer accepts the property in the physical state it is in at the date of the contract unless the seller is building or converting it.

3.2.2 A leasehold property is sold subject to any subsisting breach of a condition or tenant's obligation relating to the physical state of the property which renders the lease liable to forfeiture.

3.2.3 A sub-lease is granted subject to any subsisting breach of a condition or tenant's obligation relating to the physical state of the property which renders the seller's own lease liable to forfeiture.

3.3 *Retained land*

Where after the transfer the seller will be retaining land near the property:

(a) the buyer will have no right of light or air over the retained land, but

(b) in other respects the seller and the buyer will each have the rights over the land of the other which they would have had if they were two separate buyers to whom the seller had made simultaneous transfers of the property and the retained land.

The transfer is to contain appropriate express terms.

4. LEASES AFFECTING THE PROPERTY

4.1 *General*

4.1.1 This condition applies if any part of the property is sold subject to a lease.

4.1.2 The seller having provided the buyer with full details of each lease or copies of documents embodying the lease terms, the buyer is treated as entering into the contract knowing and fully accepting those terms.

4.1.3 The seller is not to serve a notice to end the lease nor to accept a surrender.

4.1.4 The seller is to inform the buyer without delay if the lease ends.

4.1.5 The buyer is to indemnify the seller against all claims arising from the lease after actual completion; this includes claims which are unenforceable against a buyer for want of registration.

4.1.6 If the property does not include all the land let, the seller may apportion the rent and, if the lease is a new tenancy, the buyer may require the seller to apply under section 10 of the Landlord and Tenant (Covenants) Act 1995 for the apportionment to bind the tenant.

4.2　*Property management*

4.2.1　The seller is promptly to give the buyer full particulars of:

(a) any court or arbitration proceedings in connection with the lease, and

(b) any application for a licence, consent or approval under the lease.

4.2.2　Conditions 4.2.3 to 4.2.8 do not apply to a rent review process to which condition 5 applies.

4.2.3　Subject to condition 4.2.4, the seller is to conduct any court or arbitration proceedings in accordance with written directions given by the buyer from time to time (for which the seller is to apply), unless to do so might place the seller in breach of an obligation to the tenant or a statutory duty.

4.2.4　If the seller applies for directions from the buyer in relation to a proposed step in the proceedings and the buyer does not give such directions within 10 working days, the seller may take or refrain from taking that step as it thinks fit.

4.2.5　The buyer is to indemnify the seller against all loss and expense resulting from the seller's following the buyer's directions.

4.2.6　Unless the buyer give written consent, the seller is not to:

(a) grant of formally withhold any licence, consent or approval under the lease, or

(b) serve any notice or take any action (other than action in court or arbitration proceedings) as landlord under the lease.

4.2.7　When the seller applies for the buyer's consent under condition 4.2.6:

(a) the buyer is not to withhold its consent or attach conditions to the consent where to do so might place the seller in breach of an obligation to the tenant or a statutory duty

(b) the seller may proceed as if the buyer has consented when:

(i) in accordance with paragraph (a), the buyer is not entitled to withhold its consent, or

(ii) the buyer does not refuse its consent within 10 working days.

4.2.8　If the buyer withholds or attaches conditions to its consent, the buyer is to idemnify the seller against all loss and expense.

4.2.9　In all other respects, the seller is to manage the property in accordance with the principles of good estate management until completion.

4.3　*Continuing liability*

At the request and cost of the seller, the buyer is to support any application by the seller to be released from the landlord convenants in a lease to which the property is sold subject.

5.　RENT REVIEWS

5.1　*Subject to condition 5.2, this condition applies if:*

(a) the rent reserved by a lease of all or part of the property is to be reviewed,

(b) the seller is either the landlord or the tenant,

(c) the rent review process starts before actual completion, and

(d) no reviewed rent has been agreed or determined at the date of the contract.

5.2 The seller is to conduct the rent review process until actual completion, after which the buyer is to conduct it.

5.3 Conditions 5.4 and 5.5 cease to apply on actual completion if the reviewed rent will only be payable in respect of a period after that date.

5.4 In the course of the rent review process, the seller and the buyer are each to:

(a) act promptly with a view to achieving the best result obtainable,

(b) consult with and have regard to the views of the other,

(c) provide the other with copies of all material correspondence and papers relating to the process,

(d) ensure that its representations take account of matters put forward by the other, and

(e) keep the other informed of the progress of the process.

5.5 Neither the seller nor the buyer is to agree a rent figure unless it has been approved in writing by the other (such approval not to be unreasonably withheld).

5.6 The seller and the buyer are each to bear their own costs of the rent review process.

5.7 Unless the rent review date precedes the apportionment day, the buyer is to pay the costs of a third party appointed to determine the rent.

5.8 Where the rent review date precedes the apportionment day, those costs are to be divided as follows:

(a) the seller is to pay the proportion that the number of days from the rent review date to the apportionment day bears to the number of days from that rent review date until either the following rent review date or, if none, the expiry of the term, and

(b) the buyer is to pay the balance.

6. TITLE AND TRANSFER

6.1 *Proof of title*

6.1.1 Without cost to the buyer, the seller is to provide the buyer with proof of the title to the property and of his ability to transfer it, or to procure its transfer.

6.1.2 Where the property has a registered title the proof is to include official copies of the items referred to in rules 134(1)(a) and (b) and 135(1)(a) of the Land Registration Rules 2003, so far as they are not to be discharged or overridden at or before completion.

6.1.3 Where the property has an unregistered title, the proof is to include:

(a) an abstract of title or an epitome of title with photocopies of the documents, and

(b) production of every document or an abstract, epitome or copy of it with an original marking by a conveyancer either against the original or an examined abstract or an examined copy.

6.2    *Requisitions*

6.2.1  The buyer may not raise requisitions:

(a) on the title shown by the seller taking the steps described in condition 6.1.1 before the contract was made

(b) in relation to the matters covered by condition 3.1.2.

6.2.2  Notwithstanding condition 6.2.1, the buyer may, within six working days of a matter coming to his attention after the contract was made, raise written requisitions on that matter. In that event steps 3 and 4 in condition 6.3.1 apply.

6.2.3  On the expiry of the relevant time limit under condition 6.2.2 or condition 6.3.1, the buyer loses his right to raise requisitions or to make observations.

6.3    *Timetable*

6.3.1  Subject to condition 6.2 and to the extent that the seller did not take the steps described in condition 6.1.1 before the contract was made, the following are the steps for deducing and investigating the title to the property to be taken within the following time limits:

| Step | Time limit |
| --- | --- |
| 1. The seller is to comply with condition 6.1.1 | Immediately after making the contract |
| 2. The buyer may raise written requisitions | Six working days after either the date of the seller's evidence of title on which the contract or the date of delivery of the requisitions are raised whichever is the later |
| 3. The seller is to reply in writing to any requisitions raised | Four working days after receiving the requisitions |
| 4. The buyer may make written observations on the seller's replies | Three working days after receiving the replies |

The time limit on the buyer's right to raise requisitions applies even where the seller supplies incomplete evidence of its title, but the buyer may, within six working days from delivery of any further evidence, raise further requisitions resulting from that evidence.

6.3.2  The parties are to take the following steps to prepare and agree the transfer of the property within the following time limits:

| Step | Time limit |
| --- | --- |
| A. The buyer is to send the seller a draft transfer | At least twelve working days before completion date |
| B. The seller is to approve or revise that draft and either return it or retain it for use as the actual transfer | Four working days after delivery of the draft transfer |

C. If the draft is returned the    At least five working days before
    buyer is to send an engross-    completion date
    ment to the seller

6.3.3 Periods of time under condiitons 6.3.1 and 6.3.2 may run concurrently.

6.3.4 If the period between the date of the contract and completion date is less than 15 working days, the time limits in conditions 6.2.2, 6.3.1 and 6.3.2 are to be reduced by the same proportion as that period bears to the period of 15 working days. Fractions of a working day are to be rounded down except that the time limit to perform any step is not to be less than one working day.

6.4    *Defining the property*

6.4.1 The seller need not, further than it may be able to do from information in its possession:

(a) prove the exact boundaries of the property

(b) prove who owns fences, ditches, hedges or walls

(c) separately identify parts of the property with different titles.

6.4.2 The buyer may, if to do so is reasonable, require the seller to make or obtain, pay for and hand over a statutory declaration about facts relevant to the matters mentioned in condition 6.4.1. The form of the declaration is to be agreed by the buyer, who must not unreasonably withhold its agreement.

6.5    *Rents and rentcharges*

The fact that a rent or rentcharge, whether payable or receivable by the owner of the property, has been or will on completion be, informally apportioned is not to be regarded as a defect in title.

6.6    *Transfer*

6.6.1 The buyer does not prejudice its right to raise requisitions, or to require replies to any raised, by taking steps in relation to the preparation or agreement of the transfer.

6.6.2 Subject to condition 6.6.3, the seller is to transfer the property with full title guarantee.

6.6.3 The transfer is to have effect as if the disposition is expressly made subject to all matters covered by condition 3.1.2.

6.6.4 If after completion the seller will remain bound by any obligation affecting the property and disclosed to the buyer before the contract was made, but the law does not imply any covenant by the buyer to indemnify the seller against liability for future breaches of it:

(a) the buyer is to covenant in the transfer to indemnify the seller against liability for any future breach of the obligation and to perform it from then on, and

(b) if required by the seller, the buyer is to execute and deliver to the seller on completion a duplicate transfer prepared by the buyer.

6.6.5 The seller is to arrange at its expense that, in relation to every document of title which the buyer does not receive on completion, the buyer is to have the benefit of:

(a) a written acknowledgement of the buyer's right to its production, and

(b) a written undertaking for its safe custody (except while it is held by a mortgagee or by someone in a fiduciary capacity).

7. INSURANCE

7.1 *Responsibility for insuring*

7.1.1 Conditions 7.1.2 and 7.1.3 apply if:

(a) the contract provides that the policy effected by or for the seller and insuring the property or any part of it against loss or damage should continue in force after the exchange of contracts, or

(b) the property or any part of it is let on terms under which the seller (whether as landlord or as tenant) is obliged to insure against loss or damage.

7.1.2 The seller is to:

(a) do everything required to continue to maintain the policy, including the prompt payment of any premium which falls due

(b) increase the amount or extent of the cover as requested by the buyer, if the insurers agree and the buyer pays the additional premium

(c) permit the buyer to inspect the policy, or evidence of its terms, at any time

(d) obtain or consent to an endorsement on the policy of the buyer's interest, at the buyer's expense

(e) pay to the buyer immediately on receipt, any part of an additional premium which the buyer paid and which is returned by the insurers

(f) if before completion the property suffers loss or damage:

(i) pay to the buyer on completion the amount of policy moneys which the seller has received, so far as not applied in repairing or reinstating the property, and

(ii) if no final payment has then been received, assign to the buyer, at the buyer's expense, all rights to claim under the policy in such form as the buyer reasonably requires and pending execution of the assignment, hold any policy moneys received in trust for the buyer

(g) on completion:

(i) cancel the insurace policy

(ii) apply for a refund of the premium and pay the buyer, immediately on receipt, any amount received which relates to a part of the premium which was paid or reimbursed by a tenant or third party. The buyer is to hold the money paid subject to the rights of that tenant or third party.

7.1.3 The buyer is to pay the seller a proportionate part of the premium which the seller paid in respect of the period from the date when the contract is made to the date of actual completion, except so far as the seller is entitled to recover it from a tenant.

7.1.4 Unless condition 7.1.2 applies:

    (a) the seller is under no obligation to the buyer to insure the property

    (b) if payment under a policy effected by or for the buyer is reduced, because the property is covered against loss or damage by an insurance policy effected by or for the seller, the purchase price is to be abated by the amount of that reduction.

7.1.5 Section 47 of the Law of Property Act 1925 does not apply.

8.      COMPLETION

8.1    *Date*

8.1.1 Completion date is twenty working days after the date of the contract but time is not of the essence of the contract unless a notice to complete has been served.

8.1.2 If the money due on completion is received after 2.00 pm, completion is to be treated, for the purposes only of conditions 8.3 and 9.3, as taking place on the next working day as a result of the buyer's default.

8.1.3 Condition 8.1.2 does not apply if:

    (a) the sale is with vacant possession of the property or a part of it, and

    (b) the buyer is ready, willing and able to complete but does not pay the money due on completion until after 2.00 pm because the seller has not vacated the property or that part by that time.

8.2    *Place*

Completion is to take place in England and Wales, either at the seller's conveyancer's office or at some other place which the seller reasonably specifies.

8.3    *Apportionments*

8.3.1 Subject to condition 8.3.6 income and outgoings of the property are to

be apportioned between the parties so far as the change of ownership on completion will effect entitlement to receive or liability to pay them.

8.3.2 The day from which apportionment is to be made ("apportionment day') is:

    (a) if the whole property is sold with vacant possession or the seller exercises its option in condition 9.3.4, the date of actual completion, or

    (b) otherwise, completion date.

8.3.3 In apportioning any sum, it is to be assumed that the buyer owns the property from the beginning of the day on which the apportionment is to be made.

8.3.4 A sum to be apportioned is to be treated as:

    (a) payable for the period which it covers, except that if it is an instalment of an annual sum the buyer is to be attributed with an amount equal to 1/365th of the annual sum for each day from and including the apportionment day to the end of the instalment period

(b) accruing–

    (i) from day to day, and

    (ii) at the rate applicable from time to time.

8.3.5 When a sum to be apportioned, or the rate at which it is to be treated as accruing, is not known or easily ascertainable at completion, a provisional apportionment is to be made according to the best estimate available. As soon as the amount is known, a final apportionment is to be made and notified to the other party. Subject to condition 8.8.3, any resulting balance is to be paid no more than ten working days later, and if not then paid the balance is to bear interest at the contract rate from then until payment.

8.3.6 Where a lease of the property requires the tenant to reimburse the landlord for expenditure on goods or services, on completion:

(a) the buyer is to pay the seller the amount of any expenditure already incurred by the seller but not yet due from the tenant and in respect of which the seller provides the buyer with the information and vouchers required for its recovery from the tenant, and

(b) the seller is to credit the buyer with payments already recovered from the tenant but not yet incurred by the seller.

8.3.7 Condition 8.3.8 applies if any part of the property is sold subject to a lease and either:

(a) (i)   on completion any rent or other sum payable under the lease is due but not paid

    (ii) the contract does not provide that the buyer is to assign to the seller the right to collect any arrears due to the seller under the terms of the contract, and

    (iii) the seller is not entitled to recover any arrears from the tenant, or

(b) (i)   as a result of a rent review to which condition 5 applies a reviewed rent is agreed or determined after actual completion, and

    (ii) an additional sum then becomes payable in respect of a period before the apportionment day.

8.3.8 (a) The buyer is to seek to collect all sums due in the circumstances referred to in condition 8.3.7 in the ordinary course of management, but need not take legal proceedings or distrain.

(b) A payment made on account of those sums is to be apportioned between the parties in the ratio of the amounts owed to each, notwithstanding that the tenant exercises its right to appropriate the payment in some other manner.

(c) Any part of a payment on account received by one party but due to the other is to be paid no more than ten working days after the receipt of cash or cleared funds and, if not then paid, the sum is to bear interest at the contract rate until payment.

8.4    *Amount payable*

The amount payable by the buyer on completion is the purchase price (less any deposit already paid to the seller or its agent) adjusted to take account of:

(a) apportionments made under condition 8.3

(b) any compensation to be paid under condition 9.3

(c) any sum payable under condition 7.1.2 or 7.1.3.

8.5    *Title deeds*

8.5.1  As soon as the buyer has complied with all its obligations on completion the seller must hand over the documents of title.

8.5.2  Condition 8.5.1 does not apply to any documents of title relating to land being retained by the seller after completion.

8.6    *Rent receipts*

The buyer is to assume that whoever gave any receipt for a payment of rent which the seller produces was the person or the agent of the person then entitled to that rent.

8.7    *Means of payment*

The buyer is to pay the money due on completion by direct credit and, if appropriate, by an unconditional release of a deposit held by a stake-holder.

8.8    *Notice to complete*

8.8.1  At any time on or after completion date, a party who is ready, able and willing to complete may give the other a notice to complete.

8.8.2  The parties are to complete the contract within ten working days of giving a notice to complete, excluding the day on which the notice is given. For this purpose, time is of the essence of the contract.

9     REMEDIES

9.1    *Errors and omissions*

9.1.1  If any plan or statement in the contract, or in the negotiations leading to it, is or was misleading or inaccurate due to an error or omission, the remedies available are as follows.

9.1.2  When there is a material difference between the description or value of the property as represented and as it is, the buyer is entitled to damages.

9.1.3  An error or omission only entitles the buyer to rescind the contract:

(a) where the error or omission results from fraud or recklessness, or

(b) where the buyer would be obliged, to its prejudice, to accept property differing substantially (in quantity, quality or tenure) from that which the error or omission had led it to expect.

9.2    *Rescission*

If either party rescinds the contract:

(a) unless the rescission is a result of the buyer's breach of contract the deposit is to be repaid to the buyer with accrued interest

(b) the buyer is to return any documents received from the seller and is to cancel any registration of the contract

(c) the seller's duty to pay any returned premium under condition 7.1.2(e) (whenever received) is not affected.

9.3 *Late completion*

9.3.1 If the buyer defaults in performing its obligations under the contract and completion is delayed, the buyer is to pay compensation to the seller.

9.3.2 Compensation is calculated at the contract rate on the purchase price (less any deposit paid) for the period between completion date and actual completion, but ignoring any period during which the seller was in default.

9.3.3 Any claim by the seller for loss resulting from delayed completion is to be reduced by any compensation paid under this contract.

9.3.4 Where the sale is not with vacant possession of the whole property and completion is delayed, the seller may give notice to the buyer, before the date of actual completion, that it will take the net income from the property until completion as well as compensation under condition 9.3.1.

9.4 *After completion*

Completion does not cancel liability to perform any outstanding obligation under the contract.

9.5 *Buyer's failure to comply with notice to complete*

9.5.1 If the buyer fails to complete in accordance with a notice to complete, the following terms apply.

9.5.2 The seller may rescind the contract, and if it does so:

(a) it may

(i) forfeit any deposit and accrued interest

(ii) resell the property

(iii) claim damages

(b) the buyer is to return any documents received from the seller and is to cancel any registration of the contract.

9.5.3 The seller retains its other rights and remedies.

9.6 *Seller's failure to comply with notice to complete*

9.6.1 If the seller fails to complete in accordance with a notice to complete, the following terms apply:

9.6.2 The buyer may rescind the contract, and if it does so:

(a) the deposit is to be repaid to the buyer with accrued interest

(b) the buyer is to return any documents it received from the seller and is, at the seller's expense, to cancel any registration of the contract.

9.6.3 The buyer retains its other rights and remedies.

10. LEASEHOLD PROPERTY

10.1 *Existing leases*

10.1.1 The following provisions apply to a sale of leasehold land.

10.1.2 The seller having provided the buyer with copies of the documents embodying the lease terms, the buyer is treated as entering into the contract knowing and fully accepting those terms.

10.1.3 The seller is to comply with any lease obligations requiring the tenant to insure the property.

10.2 *New leases*

10.2.1 The following provisions apply to a contract to grant a new lease.

10.2.2 The conditions apply so that:

"seller" means the proposed landlord

"buyer" means the proposed tenant

"purchase price" means the premium to be paid on the grant of a lease.

10.2.3 The lease is to be in the form of the draft attached to the contract.

10.2.4 If the term of the new lease will exceed seven years, the seller is to deduce a title which will enable the buyer to register the lease at the Land Registry with an absolute title.

10.2.5 The seller is to engross the lease and a counterpart of it and is to send the counterpart to the buyer at least five working days before completion date.

10.2.6 The buyer is to execute the counterpart and deliver it to the seller on completion.

10.3 *Consents*

10.3.1 (a) The following provisions apply if a consent to let, assign or sub-let is required to complete the contract

(b) In this condition "consent" means consent in a form which satisfied the requirement to obtain it.

10.3.2 (a) The seller it to:

(i) apply for the consent at its expense, and to use all reasonable efforts to obtain it

(ii) give the buyer notice forthwhith on obtaining the consent

(b) The buyer is to comply with all reasonable requirements, including requirements for the provision of information and references.

10.3.3 Where the consent of a reversioner (whether or not immediate) is required to an assignment or sub-letting, then so far as the reversioner lawfully imposes such a condition:

(a) the buyer is to:

(i) covenant directly with the reversioner to observe the tenant's covenants and the conditions in the seller's lease

(ii) use reasonable endeavours to provide guarantees of the performance and observance of the tenant's covenants and the conditions in the seller's lease

(iii) execute or procure the execution of the licence

(b) the seller, in the case of an assignment, is to enter into an authorised guarantee agreement.

10.3.4 Neither party may object to a reversioner's consent given subject to a condition:

(a) which under section 19(1A) of the Landlord and Tenant Act 1927 is not regarded as unreasonable, and

(b) which is lawfully imposed under an express term of the lease.

10.3.5 If any required consent has not been obtained by the original completion date:

(a) the time for completion is to be postponed until five working days after the seller gives written notice to the buyer that the consent has been obtained or four months from the original completion date whichever is the earlier

(b) the postponed date is to be treated as the completion date.

10.3.6 At any time after four months from the original completion date, either party may rescind the contract by notice to the other, if:

(a) consent has still not been given, and

(b) no declaration has been obtained from the court that consent has been unreasonably withheld.

10.3.7 If the contract is rescinded under condition 10.3.6 the seller is to remain liable for any breach of condition 10.3.2(a) or 10.3.3(b) and the buyer is to remain liable for any breach of condition 10.3.2(b) or 10.3.3(a). In all other respects neither party is to be treated as in breach of contract and condition 9.2 applies.

10.3.8 A party in breach of its obligations under condition 10.3.2 or 10.3.3 cannot rescind under condition 10.3.6 for so long as its breach is a cause of the consent's being withheld.

11.   COMMONHOLD

11.1   Terms used in this condition have the special meanings given to them in Part 1 of the Commonhold and Leasehold Reform Act 2002.

11.2   This condition applies to a disposition of commonhold land.

11.3   The seller having provided the buyer with copies of the current versions of the memorandum and articles of the commonhold association and of the commonhold community statement, the buyer is treated as entering into the contract knowing and fully accepting their terms.

11.4   If the contract is for the sale of property which is or includes part only of a commonhold unit:

(a) the seller is, at its expense, to apply for the written consent of the commonhold association and is to use all reasonable efforts to obtain it.

(b) either the seller, unless it is in breach of its obligation under paragraph (a), or the buyer may rescind the contract by notice to the other party if three working days before completion date (or before a later date on which the parties have agreed to complete the contract) the consent has not been given. In that case, neither party is to be treated as in breach of contract and condition 9.2 applies.

12.  CHATTELS

12.1  The following provisions apply to any chattels which are included in the contract.

12.2  The contract takes effect as a contract for the sale of goods.

12.3  The buyer takes the chattels in the physical state they are in at the date of the contract.

12.4  Ownership of the chattels passes to the buyer on actual completion but they are at the buyer's risk from the contract date.

**PART 2***

*The conditions in Part 2 do not apply unless expressly incorporated. See condition 1.1.4(b).

A.    VAT

A1    *Standard rated supply*

A1.1   Conditions 1.4.1 and 1.4.2 do not apply.

A1.2   The seller warrants that the sale of the property will constitute a supply chargeable to VAT at the standard rate.

A1.3   The buyer is to pay to the seller on completion an additional amount equal to the VAT in exchange for a proper VAT invoice from the seller.

A2    *Transfer of a going concern*

A2.1   Condition 1.4 does not apply.

A2.2   In this condition "TOGC" means a transfer of a business as a going concern treated as neither a supply of goods nor a supply of services by virtue of article 5 of the Value Added Tax (Special Provisions) Order 1995.

A2.3   The seller warrants that it is using the property for the business of letting to produce rental income.

A2.4   The buyer is to make effort to comply with the conditions to be met by a transferee under article 5(1) and 5(2) for the sale to constitute a TOGC.

A2.5   The buyer will, on or before the earlier of:

(a) completion date, and

(b) the earliest date on which a supply of the property could be treated as made by the seller under this contract if the sale does not constitute a TOGC,

notify the seller that paragraph (2B) of article 5 of the VAT (Special Provisions) Order 1995 does not apply to the buyer.

A2.6   The parties are to treat the sale as a TOGC at completion if the buyer provides written evidence to the seller before completion that it is a taxable person and that it has made an election to waive exemption in respect of the property and has given a written notification of the making of such election in conformity with article 5(2) and has given the notification referred to in condition A2.5.

A2.7 The buyer is not to revoke its election to waive exemption in respect of the property at any time.

A2.8 If the parties treat the sale at completion as a TOGC but it is later determined that the sale was not a TOGC, then within five working days of that determination the buyer shall pay to the seller:

(a) an amount equal to the VAT chargeable in respect of the supply of the property, in exchange for a proper VAT invoice from the seller; and

(b) except where the sale is not a TOGC because of an act or omission of the seller, an amount equal to any interest or penalty for which the seller is liable to account to HM Customs and Excise in respect of or by reference to that VAT.

A2.9 If the seller obtains the consent of HM Customs and Excise to retain its VAT records relating to the property, it shall make them available to the buyer for inspection and copying at reasonable times on reasonable request during the six years following completion.

B.    CAPITAL ALLOWANCES

B1    To enable the buyer to make and substantiate claims under the Capital Allowances Act 2001 in respect of the property, the seller is to use its reasonable endeavours to provide, or to procure that its agents provide:

(a) copies of all relevant information in its possession or that of its agents, and

(b) such co-operation and assistance as the buyer may reasonably require.

B2.1 The buyer is only to use information provided under condition B1 for the stated purpose.

B2.2 The buyer is not to disclose, without the consent of the seller, any such information which the seller expressly provides on a confidential basis.

B3.1 On completion, the seller and the buyer are jointly to make an election under section 198 of the Capital Allowances Act 2001 which is consistent with the apportionment in the Special Conditions.

B3.2 The seller and the buyer are each to submit the amount fixed by that election to the Inland Revenue for the purposes of their respective capital allowances computations.

C.    REVERSIONARY INTERESTS IN FLATS

C1    *No tenants' rights*

C1.1 In this condition, sections refer to sections of the Landlord and Tenant Act 1987 and expressions have the special meaning given to them in that Act.

257

C1.2 The seller warrants that:

(a) it gave the notice required by section 5,

(b) no acceptance notice was served on the landlord or no person was nominated for the purposes of section 6 during the protected period, and

(c) that period ended less than 12 months before the date of the contract.

C2 *Tenants' right of first refusal*

C2.1 In this condition, sections refer to sections of the Landlord and Tenant Act 1987 and expressions have the special meanings given to them in that Act.

C2.2 The seller warrants that:

(a) it gave the notice required by section 5, and

(b) it has given the buyer a copy of:

(i) any acceptance notice served on the landlord and

(ii) any nomination of a person duly nominated for the purposes of section 6.

C2.3 If the is sale by auction:

(a) the seller warrants that it has given the buyer a copy of any notice served on the landlord electing that section 8B shall apply,

(b) condition 8.1.1 applies as if "thirty working days" were substituted for "twenty working days",

(c) the seller is to send a copy of the contract to the nominated person as required by section 8B(3), and

(d) if the nominated person serves notice under section 8B(4):

(i) the seller is to give the buyer a copy of the notice, and

(ii) condition 9.2 is to apply as if the contract had been rescinded.

## SPECIAL CONDITIONS

1. This contract incorporates the Standard Commercial Property Conditions (Second Edition).

2. The property is sold with vacant possession.

(or)

2. The property is sold subject to the leases or tenancies set out on the attached list but otherwise with vacant possession on completion.

3. The chattels at the Property and set out on the attached list are included in the sale. [The amount of the purchase price apportioned to those chattels is £   ]

4. The conditions in Part 2 shown against the boxes ticked below are included in the contract:

- ☐ Condition A1 (VAT: standard rate)

[or]

- ☐ Condition A2 (VAT: transfer of a going concern)

- ☐ Condition B (capital allowances). The amount of the purchase price apportioned to plant and machinery at the property for the purposes of the Capital Allowances Act 2001 is £

- ☐ Condition C1 (flats: no tenants' rights of first refusal)

[or]

- ☐ Condition C2 (flats: with tenants' rights of first refusal).

*Seller's Conveyancers\*:*

*Buyer's Conveyancers\*:*

\*Adding an e-mail address authorises service e-mail: see condition 1.3.3(b).

## Explanatory notes on the Standard Commercial Property Conditions of Sale (second edition)

*General*

The second edition of the Standard Commercial Property Conditions (the SCPC) takes effect on 1 June 2004. It takes account of the Land Registration Act 2002 and also anticipates the coming into force in the summer of 2004 of the provisions relating to commonhold in Part I of the Commonhold and Leasehold Reform Act 2002. In addition, it covers a number of other developments.

The SCPC are intended primarily for use in more complex commercial transactions. Conveyancers are likely to find that, for residential sales and the sale of small business premises, the Standard Conditions of Sale (the SCS) are better suited to their needs.

The fourth edition of the SCS came into effect on 13 October 2003 and represents the 24th Edition of the National Conditions of Sale and the 2003 revision of the Law Society's Conditions of Sale. It should be noted that the second edition of the SCPC does not represent a further edition or revision of either of those sets of conditions. References in existing legal documents to 'the current' edition of the National Conditions of Sale or the Law Society Conditions of Sale accordintly continue to have effect as reference to the fourth edition of the SCS.

*Front page and special conditions*

In contract to the first edition of the SCPC (which provided for any amount payable for chattels to be stated separately from the purchase price for the property), the purchase price to be entered on the front page is now the total sum payable both for the property and for any chattels which are included in the sale. Special condition 3 makes provision for chattels included in the sale to be set out on an attached list, and, if part of the purchase price has been apportioned to the chattels, for that amount to be stated.

The special conditions no longer provide that the property is sold subject to the incumbrances set out on the front page. Instead, condition 3.1.2(a) provides that the property is sold subject to the incumbrances specified in the contract, and the front page includes space for specifying any incumbrances to which the sale is expressly made subject. The sale will, therefore, continue to take effect subject to any incumbrances there set out.

'Conveyancer'

In this edition, 'conveyancer' has replaced 'solicitor' as the defined term used to refer to the various categories of persons who may lawfully carry out conveyancing work for reward (condition 1.1.1(f)).

*Ready, able and willing to complete*

Condition 1.1.3 contains a new general provision stating when a party is ready, able and willing to complete. The provision is relevant in applying conditions 6.1.3 and 6.8.1.

*Part 1 and Part 2*

The new edition is in two parts. Part 1 is an updated and expanded version of the first edition. Part 2 is new, and contains a number of optional further conditions which the parties may wish to incorporate in particular cases.

As is apparent from condition 1.1.4, the conditions in Part 1 apply except as varied or excluded by the contract, whereas a condition in Part 2 will not apply unless expressly incorporated into the contract by a special condition.

A particular effect of condition 1.1.4(a) is that the general provisions in Part 1 which determine the completion date (conditions 1.1.1(d) and 8.1.1), the contract rate (Condition 1.1.1(e)) and the title guarantee to be given in the transfer (condition 6.6.2) will automatically take effect subject to any individually negotiated terms which deal with these matters. For that reason, these provisions no longer include words making them expressly subject to the particular terms of the agreement.

*Notices and documents*

Condition 1.3.6 now makes it clear that the presumed times of receipt set out in condition 1.3.7 may be displaced not only by proof of the actual time at which a notice or document was received, but also by proof that the notice or document was not received at all.

Condition 1.3.3(b) is a new provision, which enables a notice or document to be sent by e-mail where delivery of the original is not essential. It is important to appreciate that condition 1.3.3(b) permits notices or documents to be sent in this way if, but only if, an e-mail address for the intended recipient is given in the contract. Thus, a party's conveyancers should not include their e-mail address in the contract unless they are prepared to accept service by e-mail at that address.

Two further provisions relevant to the use of e-mail should be noted. First, condition 1.3.5(c) provides that, where a notice or document sent by e-mail prompts an automated response that the intended recipient is out of the office, the response (while in reality establishing that the message has reached its intended destination) is to be treated as proof that the notice or document has not been received. The sender may, therefore, need to consider other means for sending the notice or document to its intended recipient (eg, hand delivery or fax). Secondly, condition 1.3.7(e) provides that (in the absence of proof to the contrary under condition 1.3.6) a notice or document sent by e-mail is treated as having been received before 4.00 pm on the first working day after dispatch. This is later than the time of receipt presumed by condition 1.3.7(d) for a notice or document sent by fax (one hour after despatch), because the receipt of an e-mail may on occasion be delayed for several hours without the delay in transmission being readily apparent to the sender.

*VAT*

Condition 1.4 now includes a warranty by the seller that the sale of the property (as distinct from any chattels) is exempt from VAT and an agreement by the seller not to elect to waive that exemption before completion. In a case where it is intended either that the sale is to be standard rated for VAT, or that it is to be treated as the transfer of a going concern, condition 1.4 should be excluded, either partly or completely, by special condition. In such cases, users may wish to adopt condition A1 or A2 in Part 2 (see below), which have the effect of partly or wholly excluding condition 1.4, as appropriate.

*Leases affecting the property*

Condition 4 corresponds to condition 3.3 in the first edition, but has been expanded and rationalised. Condition 4.1, preserves the former condition 3.3.1 and 3.3.2, which specified the circumstances in which the condition applied and provided that the seller should provide the buyer with details of leases affecting the property before exchange and the buyer should then be treated as knowing and accepting the terms of each lease. It expands the terms previously found in condition 3.3.6 by providing not only that the seller is debarred from serving a notice to end the lease but also that it must not accept a surrender (condition 4.1.3). It is then provided that the seller is to inform the buyer if the lease ends (condition 4.1.4). Conditions 4.1.5 and 4.1.6 adopt the previous conditions 3.3.7 and 3.3.8 relating to the indemnity to be given by the buyer to the seller and the apportionment of the rent.

Provisions relating to the management of the property are then gathered together in condition 4.2. The information which the seller must give the buyer now extends to court or arbitration proceedings as well as to applications, and relevant applications are identifed as applications for a licence, consent or approval (condition 4.2.1). Conditions 4.2.3 to 4.2.8 (which do not, however, apply to a rent review process governed by condition 5) distinguish between the conduct of court or arbitration proceedings and the taking of other steps in connection with the lease.

As regards court or arbitration proceedings, condition 4.2.3 requires the seller to conduct the proceedings in accordance with the buyer's directions (for which the seller must apply), unless the seller might thereby be placed in breach of an obligation to the tenant or a statutory duty. If the buyer fails to give directions with regard to a proposed step in the proceedings within 10 working days, the seller can decide for itself whether or not to take that step (condition 4.2.4). Where directions are given, the buyer must indemnify the seller against all loss or expense which it incurs by following those directions (condition 4.2.5).

As regards other steps in connection with the lease, condition 4.2.6 provides that the written consent of the buyer is required before the seller may grant or formally withhold any licence, consent or approval under the lease or take any other action as landlord under the lease. The previous provision prohibiting a buyer from refusing consent or attaching conditions where to do so might place the seller in breach of an obligation or statutory duty is now in condition 4.2.7(a), and additionally the seller is entitled to proceed as if the buyer has consented when the buyer is not entitled to refuse consent or, if so entitled, has not in fact refused consent within 10 working days. The buyer must indemnify the seller against loss and expense resulting from the refusal of consent or the attaching of conditions to consent (condition 4.2.8).

The general obligation to manage the property in accordance with the principles of good estate management is retained and now appears in condition 4.2.9.

A new condition (condition 4.3) has been included obliging the buyer, at the request and cost of the seller, to support any application by the seller to be released from the landlord covenants in the lease (see sections 6 to 8 of the Landlord and Tenant (Covenants) Act 1995).

*Rent reviews*

Condition 5 is new, and makes specific provision for cases in which a rent review is in progress during some or all of the period between the date of the contract and actual completion. As will be apparent from condition 5.1(a), the condition applies whether the seller's position is that of landlord or tenant: condition 5.4(a) will normally oblige the parties to press for the highest rent in the former case and the lowest rent in the latter.

The general rule is that condition 5 will continue to apply after actual completion if the rent review process has not been concluded by then. If the reviewed rent will be payable only in respect of a period which will begin after actual completion (so that the seller has no interest in the amount of the reviewed rent), the obligation to conduct the review in accordance with conditions 5.4 and 5.5 will cease to apply on actual completion (condition 5.2). Accordingly, the buyer will be a free agent in conducting the review process from then on.

The seller and buyer will each bear their own costs of the rent review process (condition 5.6). Where a third party is appointed to determine the rent, the buyer is to pay the third party's costs, except that, if the rent review date precedes the apportionment date, those costs are to be divided between the buyer and seller in accordance with condition 5.8.

Where the seller is the landlord and a new rent is not agreed or determined until after actual completion, conditions 8.3.7(b) and 8.3.8 make provision for any additional rent which becomes due in respect of the period before the completion date to be collected by the buyer and paid to the seller.

### Proof of title

Condition 6.1.1 requires the seller to provide the buyer with proof of its title to the property and of its ability to transfer it or to procure its transfer (the latter alternative applying, for example, to a sub-sale).

Where the title is registered, the effect of condition 6.1.2 is that the proof must include official copies of the individual register and any title plan referred to in it, and of any document referred to in the register and kept by the registrar (unless the document is to be discharged or overridden at or before completion).

### Requisitions

The first edition of the SCPC allowed the buyer to raise requisitions after the making of the contract, whether or not title was deduced beforehand. The present edition recognises that where the seller deduces title before the contract is made (as it normally will, at least where the title is registered), the buyer should ensure that any concerns about the title so shown are raised before contract and, where necessary, appropriately provided for in the special conditions. Accordingly, condition 6.2.1(a) now bars the buyer from raising any requisitions on the title shown by the seller before the making of the contract. The buyer, however, retains the right to raise requsitions on matters coming to its attention for the first time after the contract is made (condition 6.6.2). The prohibition in condition 6.2.1(a) will not prevent the buyer from making enquiries about the seller's arrangements for discharging any mortgages because these enquiries relate to matters of conveyance rather than matters of title and are not, strictly speaking, requisitions.

In cases where the seller deduces title (either in whole or in part) after the contract is made, condition 6.3.1 continues to allow the buyer to raise requisitions within six working days of the date of the contract or delivery of the seller's proof of title on which the requisitions are raised.

### Insurance

The old condition 5, which was entitled 'Pending completion' has been radically amended by the removal of the provisions relating to the occupation of the property by the buyer. The view was taken that in the commercial context such occupation would be upon terms specifically negotiated and the general provisions of condition 5.2 were unlikely to be used to a significant extent. The material then remaining in the condition related to the insurance of the property, and so condition 7 (as it is now) has been re-titled 'Insurance'. The provisions themselves have also been considerably revised.

Condition 7.1.4 maintains the general principle that the seller is under no obligation to the buyer to insure the property. However, in the circumstances specified in condition 7.1.1 (namely, where the contract provides for the seller's policy to continue after exchange or where the seller is obliged by the terms of a lease to continue to insure), the general rule is displaced and the position is governed by conditions 7.1.2 and 7.1.3. The obligations in relation to insurance which the seller then comes under are generally similar to those which previously applied, but it is now expressly provided that to the extent that the policy proceeds are applied in repairing or reinstating insured property which has been damaged, the seller is not obliged to pay the proceeds to the buyer (condition 7.1.2(f)). The provisions for the situation on completion which were formerly contained separately in condition 5.1.3 are now incorporated in condition 7.1.2 as paragraph (g). The buyer is still obliged to pay the seller a proportionate part of the premium paid by the seller for the period between contract and completion, but an exception has been introduced for the case in which the seller is entitled to recover the premium from a tenant (condition 7.1.3).

Section 47 of the Law of Property Act 1925 continues to be excluded, now by condition 7.1.5.

### Completion after 2.00 pm

Conditions 8.1.2 and 8.1.3 clarify the position where the money due on completion is received after 2.00 pm. Condition 8.1.2 states the normal rule that, in such a case, apportionments and compensation are to be worked out as if completion had taken place on the next working day as a result of the buyer's default. It would, however, be unfair to adopt that approach where completion has been delayed because the seller has failed to vacate the property by 2.00 pm. Condition 8.1.3 therefore disapplies condition 8.1.2 in a case where the sale is with vacant possession and the buyer is ready, able and willing to complete (as to which, see condition 1.1.3(a)) but does not pay the money due on completion because the seller has not vacated the property by 2.00 pm.

### Apportionments

Condition 8.3.2 identifies the day (called the 'apportionment day') from which income and outgoings are to be apportioned. That day will be the date of actual completion where the whole property is being sold with vacant possession or where (in a case where completion of tenanted property is delayed through the buyer's default) the seller opts to take the net income from the property until completion as well as compensation from the buyer. In any other case, the apportionment day will be the completion date.

Condition 8.3.4 explains how the apportionment is to be carried out. For these purposes, condition 8.3.4(a) provides that a sum to be apportioned is to be treated as payable for the period which it covers (so that, for example, a monthly rent will be treated as paid for the relevant month, however many days it may contain, and not as an equal twelfth part of the rent that would be payable over a complete year). Where, however, the sum is an instalment of an annual sum (*eg* a yearly rent payable by twelve monthly instalments), condition 8.3.4(a) will require the buyer to be credited or debited with 1/365th of the annual sum for each day from and including the apportionment day to the end of the instalment period. Thus, where, for example, the seller receives a quarterly instalment of rent and the apportionment day falls 10 days before the end of the relevant quarter, the buyer will be treated as entitled to so much of the instalment as corresponds to 10/365ths of the annual rent. It is thought that this accords with normal commercial practice. Condition 8.3.4(b) provides that sums are to be treated as accruing from day to day and at the rate applicable from time to time. Accordingly, changes in the daily rate occurring at any time during the period covered by the payment will need to be taken into account.

Condition 8.3.6 is no longer limited to service charge payments, but covers any expenditure on goods or services incurred, or to be incurred, by the seller in its capacity as landlord under a lease of the property. Under condition 8.3.6(a), the buyer's obligation to reimburse the seller for expenditure already incurred but not yet due from the tenant is dependent on the provision by the seller of the information and vouchers which the buyer will need to recover the expenditure form the tenant.

*Seller's right to net income and compensation*

Condition 9.3.4 (formerly condition 7.3.4) provides for cases in which the property is tenanted. It allows the seller to recover the income from the property in addition to any compensation to which it may be entitled under condition 9.3.1. While a provision to this effect is commonly encountered in contracts for the sale of commercial property, there is thought to be a risk that, if challenged, it would be struck down as a penalty. A particular source of difficulty is that the object of the compensation is to place the seller in the position it would have been in if the contract had been completed on time: if, however, the contract had been completed on time, the seller would not have received any income from the property following the completion date. The seller may, therefore, need to satisfy the court that the inclusion of the provision is justified by the particular circumstances of the sale.

*Consent*

The consent provision of condition 10.3 (formerly condition 8.3) have undergone some significant amendment. Condition 10.3.1(a) ensures that condition 10.3 now applies not only in cases where the landlord's consent is required for the assignment of an existing lease or the creation of a sub-lease but also in cases where consent is required for the creation of a new lease of freehold land (eg from a mortgagee). In the light of the decision of the Court of Appeal in *Aubergine Entgerprises Ltd.* v. *Lakewood Internatonal Ltd.* [2002] 1 W.L.R. 2149, condition 10.3.1(b) confirms that any necessary consent must be in a form which satisfies the requirement to obtain it.

Condition 10.3.2(b) now obliges the buyer to comply with all reasonable requirements, including requirements for the provision of information and references (thereby slightly rephrasing the obligation under the old condition 8.3.3(a) to use reasonable endeavours to provide promptly all information and references). This obligation applies whether the consent is required for a new lease or for an assignment or for a sub-letting. The further obligations which applied to the buyer in the case of an assignment or sub-letting under the previous edition are now included in condition 10.3.3. As regards the seller's obligations, these remain unchanged in content, but the seller's obligations in connection with applying for consent and giving notice to the buyer apply in all cases (condition 10.3.2(a)), whereas condition 10.3.3(b) now expressly provides that an authorised guarantee agreement may be required only in cases of assignment.

The remaining provisions of the old condition 8.3 appear in the new condiiton 10.3, subject to minor drafting amendments and a change in the order of the provisions.

*Commonhold*

The new commonhold regime is made the subject of express provision in two ways. First, the seller is required to provide the buyer with current copies of the memorandum and articles of the commonhold association and the common-hold community statement. If the buyer then enters into the contract, it is treated as doing so knowing and accepting their terms (condition 11.3, and *cf.* condition 4.1.2, which makes similar provision with regard to the terms of leases affecting the property). Secondly, in cases in which the consent of the commonhold association is required to the sale of part only of a commonhold unit, condition 11.4 places the onus on the seller to apply for the association's consent and to use all reasonable efforts to obtain it; a right of rescission will normally be available to either party if the association's consent has not been given three working days before completion date.

*Part 2*

As already noted, Part 2 consists of optional provisions which the parties may wish to incorporate by special condition in particular cases.

Conditions A1 and A2 offer two alternatives to the provision for VAT made in condition 1.4 of Part 1 (which assumes that the sale will be exempt from VAT). Condition A1 is designed for cases where the purchase price will attract VAT at the standard rate (either because exemption is not available or because it has been waived). Condition A2 is designed for cases where (i) the seller is using the property for the business of letting to produce a rental income (ii) the seller has waived the exemption from VAT or for some other reason the sale attracts VAT (*eg* where the property consists of a newly constructed building) and (iii) it is intended that the sale should be treated as the transfer of a going concern (so that it will not be treated as the supply of either goods or services for VAT purposes).

Condition B is offered for use in cases where the seller has claimed capital allowances in respect of plant and machinery at the property and it is intended that, on completion, the parties will make an election under section 198 of the Capital Allowances Act 2001 which will determine the amount of the sale price which is to be treated as expenditure incurred by the buyer on the provision of the plant and machinery. It should be noted that condition B3.1 assumes that the special conditions will include an apportionment of part of the total price to plant and machinery.

Condition C contains two alternative provisions which may be relevant if the seller is selling a reversionary interest in a building which contains flats held by tenants who qualify for the right of first refusal conferred by the Landlord and Tenant Act 1987. Condition C1 is intended for use in cases where the seller, having served an offer notice on the tenants under section 6 of the Act, is free to proceed with the sale to the buyer (*ie* because the tenants did not accept the offer, or failed to nominate a person to take a transfer of the property, within the relevant time limits). Condition C2 is intended for use in cases where, at the date of the contract, the qualifying tenants have exercised, or may yet exercise, the right of first refusal conferred by the 1987 Act. Condition C2.3 makes provision for cases in which the sale is by auction. Among other things, it caters for the possibility that, following the auction, a person nominated by the tenants exercises the right under section 8B(4) to take over the contract: should that happen, the consequences as between the seller and the buyer will be the same as if the contract had been rescinded.

*Error on first print of SCPC 2nd edition*

Condition 10.3.4 should refer to section 19(1A), not section 19A, of the Landlord and Tenant 1927.

# Appendix 3

# The Common Auction Conditions

Copyright Royal Institute of Chartered Surveyors and reproduced with their consent.

RICS (The Royal Institution of Chartered Surveyors) in the largest organisation for professionals in property, land, construction and related environmental issues worldwide. We promote **best practice**, regulation and **consumer protection** to business and the public. With 110 000 members, RICS is the leading source of property related knowledge, providing independent, **impartial advice** to governments and global organisations.

## Important note

You may use these conditions freely, but if you do:

- You must rely on your own legal advice as to their suitability for your use
- You agree that the Royal Institution of Chartered Surveyors and those who advised it have no liability to you or anyone who relies on the conditions
- You must either reproduce the conditions in full or show clearly where you have made changes to them
- You must use the title Common Auction Conditions and acknowledge that they are reproduced with the consent of RICS

The conditions have been produced for real estate auctions in England and Wales in the hope that they will be adopted by most auction houses and set a common standard across the industry.

The introduction explains what the common auction conditions are and how they apply. The introduction does not itself form part of the conditions and auctioneers who use the conditions may adapt the introduction as part of their own notes if they prefer.

# Chairman's foreword

**Since the launch of the first edition in May 2002, the members of the RICS Real Estate Auction Group have been greatly encouraged by the support for the RICS common auction conditions shown by auctioneers. The take up has been faster and more widespread than was originally anticipated. Equally pleasing, and critically important, has been the support the conditions have received from the legal profession. Many vendors' solicitors are using the template, which is either available from the auctioneers themselves or downloads free of charge from the RICS website, www.rics.org/cac**

This edition has been written in response to the feedback and suggestions we have received since 2002. We have tried to incorporate all the suggestions made where we believe they reflect the original aims of the conditions. It may be worth reminding ourselves of the original reasons for the launch of the conditions.

1. To strike a balance between the contractual needs of the seller and the buyer while recognising that the seller will wish to determine the principal terms under which they wish to sell

2. To make it easier to see all the contract terms by having one document that embodies all the terms within it rather than by reference to other documents such as the 'Standard conditions of sale'

3. To ensure the contract is as user-friendly as possible by adopting simple headings and by using plain English

4. To increase the convenience of going to auction for the benefit of sellers and buyers, by providing a common set of conditions for all auctioneers in England and Wales

5. To reduce the legal costs to buyers and sellers by using a contract that is in common use, that is easy to read and understand and that comes with a simple to complete legal form for the property-specific special conditions of sale

6. To highlight differences in general conditions used by individual auctioneers, through the need to indicate separately any extra general conditions of sale.

To ensure that the conditions evolve to meet the current needs of the market place, a steering group has been set up under the auspices of RICS. The group, which comprises auctioneers and solicitors, will meet regularly to consider feedback and make recommendations for future editions.

If you have reason to use these conditions, please give us your feedback. You have a valuable part to play in ensuring that we continue to achieve our aims.

Finally, I would like to acknowledge and thank Paul Clark for his immense contribution to the creation of these conditions.

Richard H Auterac
Chairman of RICS Real Estate Auction Group
October 2005

# Introduction

The common auction conditions have three main sections:

1. Glossary

This gives special meanings to some words used in the rest of the conditions

2. The conduct of the auction

   These conditions regulate the conduct of the auction. If you read our catalogue or attend the auction you do so on the basis that you accept them

3. Conditions of sale

   If you buy a lot you will sign a **sale memorandum** under which you agree to be bound by the conditions of sale that apply to that lot. These conditions are:

- General conditions that apply to all lots
- Any extra general conditions in the catalogue or an addendum
- Special conditions that only apply to the lot you are buying (and which may vary the general conditions)

   The conditions are legally binding.

# Important notice

A prudent buyer will, before bidding for a lot at an auction:

- Take professional advice from a conveyancer and, in appropriate cases, a chartered surveyor and an accountant
- Read the conditions
- Inspect the lot
- Carry out usual searches and make usual enquiries
- Check the content of all available leases and other documents relating to the lot
- Check that what is said about the lot in the catalogue is accurate
- Have finance available for the deposit and purchase price
- Check whether **VAT** registration and election is advisable.

The conditions assume that the buyer has acted like a prudent buyer.

If you choose to buy a lot without taking these normal precautions you do so at your own risk.

In the **conditions** wherever it makes sense:

- singular words can be read as plurals, and plurals as singular words
- a 'person' includes a corporate body
- words of one gender include the other genders

and where the following words appear in blue* they have the specified meanings:

*In bold in the text that follows.

# Actual completion date

The date when **completion** takes place or is treated as taking place for the purposes of apportionment and calculating interest

# Addendum

An amendment or addition to the **conditions** whether contained in a supplement to the **catalogue**, a written notice from the **auctioneers** or an oral announcement at the **auction**

### Agreed completion date

(a) the date specified in the **special conditions**, or

(b) if no date is specified, **20 business days** after the **contract date**

but if that date is not a **business day** the first subsequent **business day**

# Arrears

**Arrears** of rent and other sums due under the **tenancies** but unpaid on the **actual completion date**

# Auction

The auction advertised in the **catalogue**

# Auctioneers

The auctioneers at the **auction**

# Business day

Any day except (a) a Saturday or a Sunday (b) a bank holiday in England and Wales or (c) Good Friday or Christmas Day

# Buyer

The person who agrees to buy the **lot** or, if applicable, that person's personal representatives: if two or more are jointly the **buyer** all obligations can be enforced against them jointly or against each of them separately

## Catalogue

The catalogue to which the **conditions** refer including any supplement to it

## Completion

Completion of the sale of the **lot**

## Conditions

This glossary, the conditions for the conduct of the **auction**, the **general conditions,** any **extra conditions** and the **special conditions**

## Contract

The contract by which the **seller** agrees to sell and the **buyer** agrees to buy the **lot**

## Contract date

The date of the **auction** or, if the **lot** is not sold at the **auction**:

(a) the date of the **sale memorandum** signed by both the **seller** and **buyer** or

(b) if contracts are exchanged, the date of exchange. If exchange is not effected in person or by an irrevocable agreement to exchange made by telephone, fax or electronic mail the date of exchange is the date on which both parts have been signed and posted or otherwise placed beyond normal retrieval.

## Documents

Documents of title (including, if title is registered, the entries on the register and the title plan) and other documents listed or referred to in the **special conditions** relating to the **lot**

## Extra conditions

Any additions to or variations of the **conditions** that are of general application to all **lots**

# General conditions

The conditions so headed

# Interest rate

If not specified in the **special conditions**, 4% above the base rate from time to time of Barclays Bank plc

# Lot

Each separate property described in the **catalogue** or (as the case may be) the property that the **seller** has agreed to sell and the **buyer** to buy

# Old arrears

**Arrears** due under any of the **tenancies** that are not 'new tenancies' as defined by the Landlord and Tenant (Covenants) Act 1995

# Particulars

The section of the **catalogue** that contains descriptions of each **lot**

# Practitioner

A receiver, administrative receiver or liquidator or a trustee in bankruptcy

# Price

The price that the **buyer** agrees to pay for the **lot**

# Ready to complete

Ready, willing and able to complete: if **completion** would enable the **seller** to discharge all financial charges secured on the **lot** that have to be discharged by **completion**, then those outstanding financial charges do not prevent the **seller** from being **ready to complete**

## Sale memorandum

The form so headed set out in the **catalogue** in which the terms of the **contract** for the sale of the **lot** are recorded

## Seller

The person selling the **lot**

## Special conditions

The conditions so headed that relate to the **lot**

## Tenancies

Tenancies, leases, licences to occupy and agreements for lease and any documents varying or supplemental to them

## Transfer

Includes a conveyance or assignment (and to transfer includes to convey or to assign)

## TUPE

The Transfer of Undertakings (Protection of Employment) Regulations 1981 as modified or re-enacted from time to time

## VAT

Value Added Tax or other tax of a similar nature

## VAT election

an election to waive exemption from **VAT** in respect of the **lot**

## We (and us and our)

The **auctioneers**

**You** (and **your**)

Someone who has a copy of the **catalogue** or who attends or bids at the **auction**, whether or not a **buyer**

The **catalogue** is issued only on the basis that **you** accept these conditions relating to the conduct of the **auction**. They override all other **conditions** and can only be varied if **we** agree.

## Our role

As agents for each **seller** we have authority to:

- prepare the **catalogue** from information supplied by or on behalf of each **seller**

- offer each **lot** for sale

- sell each **lot**

- receive and hold deposits

- sign each **sale memorandum**

- treat a **contract** as repudiated if the **buyer** fails to sign a **sale memorandum** or pay a deposit as required by the **conditions**.

**Our** decision on the conduct of the **auction** is final.

**We** may cancel the **auction**, withdraw **lots** from sale, or alter the order in which **lots** are offered for sale. **We** may also combine or divide **lots**.

**You** acknowledge that to the extent permitted by law **we** owe **you** no duty of care and **you** have no claim against **us** for any loss.

## Bidding and reserve prices

**We** may refuse to accept a bid. **We** do not have to explain why.

If there is a dispute over bidding **we** are entitled to resolve it, and **our** decision is final.

Unless stated otherwise each **lot** is subject to a reserve price. If no bid equals or exceeds that reserve price the **lot** will be withdrawn from the **auction**. The **seller** may bid (or ask **us** or another agent to bid on the **seller's** behalf) up to the reserve price but may not make a bid equal to or exceeding the reserve price.

Where a guide price is given that price is not to be taken as an indication of the value of the **lot** or of the reserve price.

# The particulars and other information

**We** have taken reasonable care to prepare **particulars** that correctly describe each **lot**. However the **particulars** are based on information supplied by or on behalf of the **seller** and **we** are not responsible for errors.

The **particulars** are for **your** information but **you** must not rely on them. They do not form part of any **contract** between the **seller** and the **buyer**.

If **we** provide any information or a copy of any document **we** do so only on the basis that **we** are not responsible for its accuracy.

# The contract

A successful bid is one **we** accept as such.

If **you** make a successful bid for a **lot you** are obliged to buy that **lot** on the terms of the **sale memorandum**. The **price** will be the amount **you** bid plus **VAT** (if applicable). **You** must before leaving the **auction**:

* provide all information **we** reasonably need from **you** to enable us to complete the **sale memorandum** (including proof of your identity that complies with money laundering regulations)

* sign the completed **sale memorandum** and

* pay the deposit

and if **you** do not **we** may either:

* as agent for the **seller** treat that failure as **your** repudiation of the **contract** and offer the **lot** for sale again: the **seller** may then have a claim against **you** for breach of contract; or

* sign the **sale memorandum** on **your** behalf.

Deposits must be paid by cheque or by bankers' draft drawn in **our** favour on a UK clearing bank or building society. The **catalogue** states whether **we** also accept debit or credit cards.

**We** may retain the **sale memorandum** signed by or on behalf of the **seller** until **we** receive the deposit in cleared funds.

If **you** make a successful bid for a **lot**:

* **You** are personally liable to buy it even if **you** are acting as an agent. It is **your** responsibility to obtain an indemnity from the person for whom **you** are the agent

* Where the **buyer** is a company **you** warrant that the **buyer** is properly constituted and able to buy the **lot**

* If the **buyer** does not comply with its obligations under the **contract you** are personally liable to buy the **lot** and must indemnify the **seller** in respect of any loss the **seller** incurs as a result of the **buyer's** default.

The **general conditions** apply except to the extent that they are varied by **extra conditions**, the **special conditions** or by an **addendum**.

1. **The lot**

1.1 The **lot**, including any rights granted and reserved, is described in the **special conditions**.

1.2 The **lot** is sold subject to all subsisting **tenancies**, but otherwise with vacant possession on **completion**.

1.3 The **lot** is sold subject to all matters contained or referred to in the **documents** (except financial charges: these the **seller** must discharge on or before **completion**) and to such of the following as may affect it, whether they arise before or after the **contract date** and whether or not they are disclosed by the **seller** or are apparent from inspection of the **lot** or from the **documents**:

   (a) matters registered or capable of registration as local land charges

   (b) matters registered or capable of registration by any competent authority or under the provisions of any statute

   (c) notices, orders, demands, proposals and requirements of any competent authority

   (d) charges, notices, orders, restrictions, agreements and other matters relating to town and country planning, highways or public health

   (e) rights, easements, quasi-easements, and wayleaves

   (f) outgoings and other liabilities

   (g) any interest which overrides, within the meaning of the Land Registration Act 2002

   (h) matters that ought to be disclosed by the searches and enquiries a prudent buyer would make, whether or not the **buyer** has made them

   (i) anything the **seller** does not and could not reasonably know about

   and where any such matter would expose the **seller** to liability the **buyer** is to comply with it and indemnify the **seller** against liability.

1.4 The **seller** must notify the **buyer** of any notices, orders, demands, proposals and requirements of any competent authority of which it learns after the **contract date** but the **buyer** must comply with them and keep the **seller** indemnified.

1.5 The **lot** does not include any tenant's or trade fixtures or fittings.

1.6 Where chattels are included in the **lot** the **buyer** takes them as they are at **completion** and the **seller** is not liable if they are not fit for use.

1.7 The **buyer** buys with full knowledge of:

   (a) the **documents** whether or not the **buyer** has read them

    (b)  the physical condition of the **lot** and what could reasonably be discovered on inspection of it, whether or not the **buyer** has inspected it.

1.8  The **buyer** is not relying on the information contained in the **particulars** or in any replies to preliminary enquiries but on the **buyer's** own verification of that information. If any information is not correct any liability of the **seller** and any remedy of the **buyer** are excluded to the extent permitted by law.

## 2. Deposit

2.1  The amount of the deposit is the greater of:

    (a)  any minimum deposit stated in the **catalogue** (or the total **price**, if this is less than that minimum), and

    (b)  10% of the **price** exclusive of **VAT**.

2.2  The deposit:

    (a)  must be paid to the **auctioneers** by cheque or banker's draft drawn on a UK clearing bank or building society (or by such other means of payment as they accept)

    (b)  is to be held as stakeholder unless the **special conditions** provide that it is to be held as agent for the **seller**.

2.3  Where the **auctioneers** hold the deposit as stakeholder they are authorised to release it and any interest on it to the **seller** on **completion** or, if **completion** does not take place, to the person entitled to it under the **conditions**.

2.4  If a cheque for the deposit is not cleared on first presentation the **seller** is entitled to treat the **contract** as at an end and bring a claim against the **buyer** for breach of contract.

2.5  Interest earned on the deposit belongs to the **seller** unless the **conditions** provide otherwise.

## 3. Transfer of risk and insurance

3.1  From the **contract date** the **seller** is under no obligation to insure the **lot** and the **buyer** bears all risk of loss or damage unless:

    (a)  the **lot** is sold subject to a **tenancy** that requires the **seller** to insure the **lot** or

    (b)  the **special conditions** require the **seller** to insure the **lot**.

3.2  If the **seller** is to insure the **lot** then the **seller**:

    (a)  must produce to the **buyer** on request relevant insurance details

    (b)  must use reasonable endeavours to maintain that or equivalent insurance and pay the premiums when due

(c)  gives no warranty as to the adequacy of insurance

(d)  must, at the request of the **buyer**, use reasonable endeavours to have the **buyer's** interest noted on any insurance policy that does not cover a contracting purchaser

(e)  must, unless otherwise agreed, cancel the insurance at **completion**

(f)  is to hold in trust for the **buyer** any insurance payments that the **seller** receives in respect of loss or damage arising after the **contract date**

and the **buyer** must on **completion** reimburse to the **seller** the cost of insurance (to the extent it is not paid by a tenant or other third party) from and including the **contract date**

3.3  If under a **tenancy** the **seller** insures the **lot** then unless otherwise agreed with the **buyer** the **seller** is to pay any refund of premium.

(a)  to the **buyer** or

(b)  if the **special conditions** so state, to each tenant in the proportion that the tenant pays premiums under its **tenancy**, first deducting any arrears of premium due from that tenant.

3.4  Section 47 of the Law of Property Act 1925 does not apply.

3.5  Unless the **buyer** is already lawfully in occupation of the **lot** the **buyer** has no right to enter into occupation prior to **completion**.

## 4.  Title

4.1  Unless **general condition** 4.2 applies, the **buyer** accepts the title of the **seller** to the lot as at the **contract date** and may raise no requisition or objection except in relation to any matter following the **contract date**.

4.2  The **buyer** may raise no requisition or objection to any **documents** made available before the **auction** but in relation to any of the **documents** that is not available before the **auction** the following provisions apply:

(a)  if the **lot** is registered land the **seller** is to give to the **buyer** within five **business days** of the **contract date** an official copy of the entries on the register and title plan and of all documents noted on the register that affect the **lot**

(b)  if the **lot** is not registered land the **seller** is to give to the **buyer** within five **business days** an abstract or epitome of title starting from the root of title mentioned in the **special conditions** (or, if none is mentioned, a good root of title more than 15 years old) and must produce to the **buyer** the original or an examined copy of every relevant **document**

(c)  the **buyer** has no right to object to or make requisitions on any title information more than seven **business days** after that information has been given to the **buyer**.

4.3 Unless otherwise stated in the **special conditions** the **seller** sells with full title guarantee except that:

(a) all matters recorded in registers open to public inspection are to be treated as within the actual knowledge of the **buyer** and

(b) any implied covenant as to compliance with tenant's obligations under leases does not extend to the state or condition of the **lot** where the **lot** is leasehold property.

4.4 If title is in the course of registration title is to consist of certified copies of:

(a) the **documents** sent to the Land Registry

(b) the application to the Land Registry

and a letter under which the **seller** or its conveyancer agrees to use all reasonable endeavours to answer any requisitions raised by the Land Registry and to instruct the Land Registry to send the completed registration documents to the **buyer**.

4.5 The **transfer** is to have effect as if expressly subject to all matters subject to which the **lot** is sold under the **contract**.

4.6 The **seller** does not have to produce, nor may the **buyer** object to or make a requisition in relation to, any prior or superior title even if it is referred to in the **documents**.

**5 Transfer**

5.1 Unless a form of **transfer** is set out in the **special conditions**:

(a) the **buyer** must supply a draft **transfer** to the **seller** at least ten **business days** before the **agreed completion date** and the engrossment (signed as a deed by the **buyer** if condition 5.2 applies) five **business days** before that date or (if later) two **business days** after the draft has been approved by the **seller** and

(b) the **seller** must approve or revise the draft **transfer** within five **business days** of receiving it from the **buyer**.

5.2 If the **seller** remains liable in any respect in relation to the **lot** (or a **tenancy**) following **completion** the **buyer** is specifically to covenant in the **transfer** to indemnify the **seller** against that liability.

5.3 The **seller** cannot be required to transfer the **lot** to anyone other than the **buyer**, or by more than one **transfer**.

**6. Completion**

6.1 **Completion** is to take place at the offices of the **seller's** conveyancer, or where the **seller** may reasonably require, on the **agreed completion date**. The **seller** can only be required to complete on a **business day** and between the hours of 0930 and 1700.

6.2 The amount payable on **completion** is the balance of the **price** adjusted to take account of apportionments plus (if applicable) **VAT** and interest.

6.3 Payment is to be made in pounds sterling and only by:

    (a) direct transfer to the **seller's** conveyancer's client account and

    (b) the release of any deposit held by a stakeholder.

6.4 Unless the **seller** and the **buyer** otherwise agree **completion** takes place when both have complied with their obligations under the **contract** and the total payment is unconditionally received in the **seller's** conveyancer's client account.

6.5 If **completion** takes place after 1400 hours for a reason other than the **seller's** default it is to be treated, for the purposes of apportionment and calculating interest, as if it had taken place on the next **business day**.

6.6 Where applicable the **contract** remains in force following **completion**.

## 7 Notice to complete

7.1 The **seller** or the **buyer** may on or after the **agreed completion date** but before **completion** give the other notice to complete within 10 **business days** (excluding the date on which the notice is given) making time of the essence.

7.2 The person giving the notice must be **ready to complete**.

7.3 If the **buyer** fails to comply with a notice to complete the **seller** may, without affecting any other remedy the **seller** has:

    (a) rescind the **contract**

    (b) claim the deposit and any interest on it if held by a stakeholder

    (c) forfeit the deposit and any interest on it

    (d) resell the **lot** and

    (e) claim damages from the **buyer**.

7.4 If the **seller** fails to comply with a notice to complete the **buyer** may, without affecting any other remedy the **buyer** has:

    (a) rescind the **contract** and

    (b) recover the deposit and any interest on it from the **seller** or, if applicable, a stakeholder.

## 8. If the contract is brought to an end

If the **contract** is rescinded or otherwise brought to an end:

    (a) the **buyer** must return all papers to the **seller** and appoints the **seller** its agent to cancel any registration of the **contract**

    (b) the **seller** must return the deposit and any interest on it to the **buyer** (and the **buyer** may claim it from the stakeholder, if applicable) unless the **seller** is entitled to forfeit the deposit under general condition 7.3.

**9. Landlord's licence**

9.1 Where the **lot** is leasehold land and licence to assign is required this condition applies.

9.2 The **contract** is conditional on that licence being obtained, by way of formal licence if that is what the landlord can lawfully require.

9.3 The **agreed completion date** is to be not earlier than the date five **business days** after the **seller** has given notice to the **buyer** that the licence has been obtained.

9.4 The **seller** must:

(a) use all reasonable endeavours to obtain the licence at the **seller's** expense and

(b) enter into any authorised guarantee agreement properly required.

9.5 The **buyer** must:

(a) promptly provide references and other relevant information, and

(b) comply with the landlord's lawful requirements.

9.6 If within three months of the **contract date** (or such longer period as the **seller** and **buyer** agree) the licence has not been obtained the **seller** or the **buyer** may (if not then in breach of any obligation under this condition) by notice to the other rescind the **contract** at any time before licence is obtained. Rescission is without prejudice to the claims of either **seller** or **buyer** for breach of this condition 9.

**10. Interest and apportionments**

10.1 If the **actual completion date** is after the **agreed completion date** for any reason other than the **seller's** default the **buyer** must pay interest at the **interest rate** on the **price** (less any **deposit** paid) from the **agreed completion date** up to and including the **actual completion date**.

10.2 The **seller** is not obliged to apportion or account for any sum at **completion** unless the **seller** has received that sum in cleared funds. The **seller** must pay to the **buyer** after **completion** any sum to which the buyer is entitled that the **seller** subsequently receives in cleared funds.

10.3 Income and outgoings are to be apportioned at **actual completion date** unless:

(a) the **buyer** is liable to pay interest and

(b) the **seller** has given notice to the **buyer** at any time up to **completion** requiring apportionment on the date from which interest becomes payable.

10.4 Apportionments are to be calculated on the basis that:

(a) the **seller** receives income and is liable for outgoings for the whole of the day on which apportionment is to be made

(b)    annual income and expenditure accrues at an equal daily rate assuming 365 days in a year and income and expenditure relating to a period of less than a year accrues at an equal daily rate during the period to which it relates

(c)    where the amount to be apportioned is not known at **completion** apportionment is to be made by reference to the best estimate then available and further payment is to be made by **seller** or **buyer** as appropriate within five **business days** of the date when the amount is known

(d)    rent payable in arrear for a period that includes the day of apportionment is to be apportioned for that period as if paid in advance.

## 11. Arrears

11.1 The **seller** retains the right to receive and recover **old arrears**.

11.2 While any **arrears** due to the **seller** remain unpaid the **buyer** must:

(a)    try to collect them in the ordinary course of management but need not take legal proceedings, distrain or forfeit the **tenancy**

(b)    pay them to the **seller** within five **business days** of receipt in cleared funds (plus interest at the **interest rate** calculated on a daily basis for each subsequent day's delay in payment)

(c)    on request, at the cost of the **seller**, assign to the **seller** or as the **seller** may direct the right to demand and sue for **old arrears**, such assignment to be in such form as the **seller's** conveyancer may reasonably require

(d)    if reasonably required, allow the **seller's** conveyancer to have on loan the counterpart of any **tenancy** against an undertaking to hold it to the **buyer's** order

(e)    not release any tenant or surety from liability to pay **arrears** or accept a surrender of or forfeit any **tenancy** under which **arrears** are due; and

(f)    if the **buyer** disposes of the **lot** prior to recovery of all **arrears** obtain from the **buyer's** successor in title a covenant in favour of the **seller** in similar form to this condition 11.

11.3 Where the **seller** has the right to recover **arrears** it must not without the **buyer's** written consent bring insolvency proceedings against a tenant or seek the removal of goods from the **lot**.

## 12  Management

12.1 This condition applies where the **lot** is sold subject to **tenancies**.

12.2 The **seller** is to manage the **lot** in accordance with its standard management policies pending **completion**.

12.3 Unless set out in the **special conditions** the **seller** must consult the **buyer** on all management issues that would affect the **buyer** after **completion**, such as an application for licence or a rent review under a **tenancy**, a variation, surrender, agreement to surrender or proposed forfeiture of a **tenancy**, or a new tenancy or agreement to grant a new tenancy and:

(a) the **seller** must comply with the **buyer's** reasonable requirements unless to do so would (but for the indemnity in paragraph (c)) expose the **seller** to a liability that the **seller** would not otherwise have, in which case the **seller** may act reasonably in such a way as to avoid that liability

(b) if the **seller** gives the **buyer** notice of the **seller's** intended act and the **buyer** does not object within five **business days** giving reasons for the objection the **seller** may act as the **seller** intends, and

(c) the **buyer** is to indemnify the **seller** against all loss or liability the **seller** incurs through acting as the **buyer** requires, or by reason of delay caused by the **buyer**.

## 13. Rent deposits

13.1 This condition applies where the **seller** is holding or otherwise entitled to money by way of rent deposit in respect of a **tenancy**. In this condition 'rent deposit deed' means the deed or other document under which the rent deposit is held.

13.2 If the rent deposit is not assignable the **seller** must on **completion** hold the rent deposit on trust for the **buyer** and, subject to the terms of the rent deposit deed, comply at the cost of the **buyer** with the **buyer's** lawful instructions.

13.3 Otherwise the **seller** must on **completion** pay and assign its interest in the rent deposit to the **buyer** under an assignment in which the **buyer** covenants with the **seller** to:

(a) observe and perform the **seller's** covenants and conditions in the rent deposit deed and indemnify the **seller** in respect of any breach

(b) give notice of assignment to the tenant and

(c) give such direct covenant to the tenant as may be required by the rent deposit deed.

## 14. VAT

14.1 Where the **conditions** require money to be paid the payer must also pay any **VAT** that is chargeable on that money, but only if given a valid **VAT** invoice.

14.2 Where the **special conditions** state that no **VAT election** has been made the **seller** confirms that none has been made by it or by any company in the same **VAT** group nor will be prior to **completion**.

## 15. Transfer as a going concern

15.1 Where the **special conditions** so state the **seller** and the **buyer** intend the sale to be treated as a transfer of a going concern and this condition applies.

15.2 The **seller** confirms that the **seller** or a company in the same **VAT** group:

(a)  is registered for **VAT** and

(b)  has, where necessary, made in relation to the **lot** a **VAT election** that remains valid.

15.3 The **buyer**:

(a)  is registered for **VAT**, either in the **buyer's** name or as a member of a **VAT** group

(b)  has made, or will make before **completion**, a **VAT election** in relation to the **lot**

(c)  is to give to the **seller** as early as possible before the **agreed completion date** evidence of the **VAT** registration and that a **VAT election** has been made and notified in writing to HM Revenue and Customs

(d)  must not revoke the **VAT election**.

and if it does not produce the relevant evidence at least two **business days** before the **agreed completion date**, general condition 14.1 applies at **completion**.

15.4 The **buyer** confirms that after **completion** the **buyer** intends to:

(a)  retain and manage the **lot** for the **buyer's** own benefit as a continuing business as a going concern subject to and with the benefit of the **tenancies**, and

(b)  collect the rents payable under the **tenancies** and charge **VAT** on them.

15.5 Unless the **seller** obtains agreement to the contrary from HM Revenue and Customs

(a)  the **seller** must on or as soon as reasonably practicable after **completion** transfer to the **buyer** all **VAT** records for the **lot** and

(b)  the **buyer** must keep those records available for inspection by the **seller** at all reasonable times.

15.6 If, after **completion**, it is found that the sale of the **lot** is not a transfer of a going concern then:

(a)  the **seller's** conveyancer is to notify the **buyer's** conveyancer of that finding and provide a **VAT** invoice in respect of the sale of the **lot** and

(b)  the **buyer** must within five **business days** of receipt of the **VAT** invoice pay to the **seller** the **VAT** due and

(c) if **VAT** is payable because the **buyer** has not complied with this condition 15, the **buyer** must pay and indemnify the **seller** against all costs, interest, penalties or surcharges that the **seller** incurs as a result.

## 16.  Capital allowances

16.1 This condition applies where the **special conditions** state that there are capital allowances available in respect of the **lot**.

16.2 The **seller** is promptly to supply to the **buyer** all information reasonably required by the **buyer** in connection with the **buyer's** claim for capital allowances.

16.3 The value to be attributed to those items on which capital allowances may be claimed is set out in the **special conditions**.

16.4 The **seller** and **buyer** agree:

(a)  to make an election on **completion** under Section 198 of the Capital Allowances Act 2001 to give effect to this condition, and

(b) to submit the value specified in the **special conditions** to HM Revenue and Customs for the purposes of their respective capital allowance computations.

## 17  Maintenance agreements

17.1 The **seller** agrees to use reasonable endeavours to transfer to the **buyer**, at the **buyer's** cost, the benefit of the maintenance agreements specified in the **special conditions**.

17.2 The **buyer** must assume, and indemnify the **seller** in respect of, all liability under such contracts from the **actual completion date**.

## 18.  Landlord and Tenant Act 1987

18.1 This condition applies where the sale is a relevant disposal for the purposes of Part I of the Landlord and Tenant Act 1987.

18.2 Unless the **special conditions** state otherwise the **seller** warrants that the **seller** has complied with sections 5B and 7 of that Act and that the requisite majority of qualifying tenants has not accepted the offer.

## 19.  Sale by practitioner

19.1 This condition applies where the sale is by a **practitioner** as agent of the **seller**.

19.2 The **practitioner** has been duly appointed and is empowered to sell the **lot**.

19.3 The **practitioner** and the **practitioner's** partners and staff have no personal liability in connection with the sale or the performance of the **seller's** obligations. The **transfer** is to include a declaration excluding the personal liability of the **practitioner** and of the **practitioner's** partners and staff.

19.4 The **lot** is sold:

(a)   in its condition at **completion**

(b)   whether or not vacant possession is provided

(c)   for such title as the **seller** may have and

(d)   with no title guarantee.

and the **buyer** has no right to rescind the contract or any other remedy if information provided about the **lot** is inaccurate, incomplete or missing.

19.5 Where relevant:

(a)   the **documents** must include certified copies of the charge under which the **practitioner** is appointed, the document of appointment by the lender and the **practitioner's** acceptance of appointment, and

(b)   the **seller** may require the **transfer** to be by the lender exercising its power of sale under the Law of Property Act 1925.

19.6 The **buyer** understands this condition 19 and agrees that it is fair in the circumstances of a sale by a **practitioner**.

## 20. TUPE

20.1 Unless the **special conditions** state that **TUPE** applies then the **seller** warrants that there are no employees whose contracts of employment will transfer to the **buyer** on **completion**.

20.2 If the **special conditions** state that **TUPE** applies then:

(a)   the **seller** has informed the **buyer** of those employees whose contracts of employment will transfer to the **buyer** on **completion**

(b)   not less than five **business days** before the **agreed completion date** the **buyer** must confirm to the **seller** that the **buyer** has offered to employ those employees on the same terms as, or better terms than, their existing contracts of employment

(c)   the **buyer** is to keep the **seller** indemnified against all liability for those employees after **completion**.

## 21. Environmental

21.1 This condition only applies where the **special conditions** so provide.

21.2 The **seller** has made available such reports as the **seller** has as to the environmental condition of the **lot** and has given the **buyer** the opportunity to carry out investigations (whether or not the **buyer** has read those reports or carried out any investigation) and the **buyer** admits that the **price** takes into account the environmental condition of the **lot**.

21.3 The **buyer** agrees to indemnify the **seller** in respect of all liability for or resulting from the environmental condition of the **lot**.

## 22. Service charge

22.1 This condition applies where the **lot** is sold subject to **tenancies** that include service charge provisions.

22.2 No apportionment is to be made at **completion** in respect of service charges.

22.3 Within two months after **completion** the **seller** must provide to the **buyer** a detailed service charge account for the service charge year current on **completion** showing:

(a)   service charge expenditure attributable to each **tenancy**

(b)   payments on account of service charge received from each tenant

(c)   any amounts due from a tenant that have not been received

(d)   any service charge expenditure that is not attributable to any **tenancy** and is for that reason irrecoverable.

22.4 In respect of each **tenancy**, if the service charge account shows that:

(a)   payments on account (whether received or still then due from a tenant) exceed attributable service charge expenditure, the **seller** must pay to the **buyer** an amount equal to the excess when it provides the service charge account

(b)   attributable service charge expenditure exceeds payments on account (whether those payments have been received or are still then due), the **buyer** must use all reasonable endeavours to recover the shortfall from the tenant at the next service charge reconciliation date and pay the amount so recovered to the **seller** within five **business days** of receipt in cleared funds

and in respect of payments on account that are still due from a tenant **condition** 11 (**arrears**) applies.

22.5 In respect of service charge expenditure that is not attributable to any **tenancy** the **seller** must pay any incurred in respect of the period before **actual completion date** and the **buyer** must pay any incurred in respect of the period after **actual completion date**. Any necessary monetary adjustment is to be made within five **business days** of the **seller** providing the service charge account to the **buyer**.

22.6 If the **seller** holds any reserve or sinking fund on account of future service charge expenditure:

(a)   the **seller** must assign it (including any interest earned on it) to the **buyer** on **completion** and

(b)   the **buyer** must covenant with the **seller** to hold it in accordance with the terms of the **tenancies** and to indemnify the **seller** if it does not do so.

**23. Rent reviews**

23.1 This condition applies where the **lot** is sold subject to a **tenancy** under which a rent review due on or before the **actual completion date** has not been agreed or determined.

23.2 The **seller** may continue negotiations or rent review proceedings up to the **actual completion date** but may not agree the level of the revised rent or commence rent review proceedings without the written consent of the **buyer**, such consent not to be unreasonably withheld or delayed.

23.3 Following **completion** the **buyer** must complete rent review negotiations or proceedings as soon as reasonably practicable but may not agree the level of the revised rent without the written consent of the **seller**, such consent not to be unreasonably withheld or delayed.

23.4 The **seller** must:

(a) give to the **buyer** full details of all rent review negotiations and proceedings, including copies of all correspondence and other papers, and

(b) use all reasonable endeavours to substitute the **buyer** for the **seller** in any rent review proceedings.

23.5 The **seller** and the **buyer** are to keep each other informed of the progress of the rent review and have regard to any proposals the other makes in relation to it.

23.6 When the rent review has been agreed or determined the **buyer** must account to the **seller** for any increased rent and interest recovered from the tenant that relates to the **seller's** period of ownership within five **business days** of receipt of cleared funds.

23.7 If a rent review is agreed or determined before **completion** but the increased rent and any interest recoverable from the tenant has not been received by **completion** the increased rent and any interest recoverable is to be treated as **arrears**.

23.8 The **seller** and the **buyer** are to bear their own costs in relation to rent review negotiations and proceedings.

**24. Tenancy renewals**

24.1 This condition applies where the tenant under a **tenancy** has the right to remain in occupation under Part II of the Landlord and Tenant Act 1954 (as amended) and references to notices and proceedings are to notices and proceedings under that Act.

24.2 Where practicable, without exposing the **seller** to liability or penalty, the **seller** must not without the written consent of the **buyer** (which the **buyer** must not unreasonably withhold or delay) serve or respond to any notice or begin or continue any proceedings.

24.3 If the **seller** receives a notice the **seller** must send a copy to the **buyer** within five **business days** and act as the **buyer** reasonably directs in relation to it.

24.4 Following **completion** the **buyer** must:

(a)   with the co-operation of the **seller** take immediate steps to substitute itself as a party to any proceedings

(b)   use all reasonable endeavours to conclude any proceedings or negotiations for the renewal of the **tenancy** and the determination of any interim rent as soon as reasonably practicable at the best rent or rents reasonably obtainable

(c)   if any increased rent is recovered from the tenant (whether as interim rent or under the renewed **tenancy**) account to the **seller** for the part of that increase that relates to the **seller's** period of ownership of the **lot** within five **business days** of receipt of cleared funds.

24.5 The **seller** and the **buyer** are to bear their own costs in relation to the renewal of the **tenancy** and any proceedings relating to this.

## 25.   Warranties

25.1 Available warranties are listed in the **special conditions**.

25.2 Where a warranty is assignable the **seller** must:

(a)   on **completion** assign it to the **buyer** and give notice of assignment to the person who gave the warranty

(b)   apply for, and the **seller** and the **buyer** must use all reasonable endeavours to obtain, any consent to assign that is required. If consent has not been obtained by **completion** the warranty must be assigned within five **business days** after the consent has been obtained.

25.3 If a warranty is not assignable the **seller** must on **completion**:

(a)   hold the warranty on trust for the **buyer**

(b)   at the **buyer's** cost comply with such of the lawful instructions of the **buyer** in relation to the warranty as do not place the **seller** in breach of its terms or expose the **seller** to any liability or penalty.

## 26.   No assignment

The **buyer** must not assign, mortgage or otherwise transfer or part with the whole or any part of the **buyer's** interest under this **contract**.

## 27.   Notices and other communications

27.1 All communications, including notices, must be in writing. Communication to or by the **seller** or the **buyer** may be given to or by their conveyancers.

27.2 If a communication is delivered by hand or is otherwise proved to have been received then it is given when delivered or received. If delivered or received after 1700 hours on a **business day** it is to be treated as received on the next **business day**.

27.3 If a communication is to be relied on that is not delivered by hand or otherwise proved to have been received it must be sent by first-class registered or recorded delivery post to the address of the person to whom it is to be given as specified in the **sale memorandum**. Such a communication will be treated as received on the second **business day** after it has been posted.

## 28 Contracts (Rights of Third Parties) Act 1999

The **contract** is enforceable only by the **seller** and the **buyer** and (if applicable) their successors in title and, to the extent permitted by the **conditions**, by the **auctioneers**.

LOT number —————————————————————————————————

**Brief description of the lot**

*Postal address*

**Name and address of the seller**

*[Name and address]*

[Undisclosed. To be identified in the **sale memorandum**.]

**Name, address and reference of the seller's conveyancer**

*Name, address and reference*

## Title

[Freehold]

[Leasehold *brief description of terms of lease*]

## Registered or unregistered?

[Registered *at name of land registry with quality of title*
title number *number*]
[Unregistered commencing with *describe root of title*]

## Title guarantee

[Full title guarantee]

[Limited title guarantee]

[No title guarantee, for such right and title as the **seller** may have]

## Deposit

[10%] of the **price** [[plus **VAT**] to be held as [stakeholder][agent for the **seller**]]

## Interest rate

[ ]% over [                              ] base rate from time to time

## Agreed completion date

*Date*

## VAT

[**VAT** is payable]

[The sale is a transfer of a going concern]

[The **seller** has not made a **VAT election**]

## Insurance

[The **seller** is to insure] [and any refund of insurance payments is to be made to the tenants]

[The **buyer** is to insure]

## Vacant or let?

[The sale is with vacant possession]

[The sale is subject to the **tenancies** listed in the tenancy schedule]

## Rights sold with the lot

[None]

*[details]*

## Exclusions from the sale

[None]

*[details]*

## Reservations to the seller

[None]

*[details]*

**What the sale is subject to**

The matters set out in the **general conditions** [and]

*[list existing covenants and encumbrances and any new ones to be created on sale]*

**Amendments to the general conditions**

[None]

[The following conditions replace the **general conditions** of the same number: *details*]

**Extra special conditions**

[None]

*[details]*

**Transfer**

[The prescribed form of **transfer** is annexed]

[The **transfer** is to contain the following provisions:                    ]

**Capital allowances**

[There are none]

[Capital allowances are available in respect of the following items, to which the value attributed is                    ]

## Maintenance agreements

[There are no maintenance agreements]

[Details of maintenance agreements are:

*details*]

## TUPE

[There are no employees to which TUPE applies]

[Details of the contracts of employment for those employees to whom TUPE applies are:
*details*]

## Environmental

General condition 21 (Environmental) applies.

The following reports have been supplied by the **seller**:

*details*

## Warranties

The following warranties are to be assigned to or held in trust for the **buyer**:

# Tenancy schedule

The **lot** is sold subject to and with the benefit of the **tenancies** listed below:

| Property | Date | Original landlord and tenant | Current tenant | Term current rent |
|---|---|---|---|---|
|  |  |  |  |  |

# Sale memorandum

Date

Name and address of **seller**

Name and address of **buyer**

The **lot**

The **price** (excluding any **VAT**)

**Deposit paid**

The **seller** agrees to sell and the **buyer** agrees to buy the **lot** for the **price**. This agreement is subject to the **conditions** so far as they apply to the **lot**.

We acknowledge receipt of the deposit. _____

Signed by the **buyer**

Signed by us as agent for the **seller**

The **buyer's** conveyancer is

Name

Address

Contact

# Index